The Secret Search for Peace in Vietnam

The Secret Search for Peace in Vietnam

by DAVID KRASLOW

and STUART H. LOORY

RANDOM HOUSE
New York

For Bernice and Marjorie

Contents

PART III Channels and Phases

Preface

Somehow a great power found itself where it did not expect to be—fighting a ground war in Asia, spilling American blood, rending the American spirit, spending American wealth—in a seemingly bottomless morass.

The Johnson Administration has said its public record as a peace-seeker in Vietnam meshes with the secret record. Until the President announced a unilateral de-escalation of the war on March 31, critics charged that in its private dealings the Administration had not been as eager to negotiate as it professed to be publicly. They charged that the United States was at least as responsible as North Vietnam for the delay in getting to the bargaining table.

This report is an effort to test the public record of Vietnam diplomacy against the private record.

It is the product of more than 150,000 words of notes taken in interviews with scores of officials and other sources (in Washington, Princeton, New York, the United Nations, Cambridge, Boston, Ottawa, London, Paris, Rome, Florence, Vatican City, Prague and Warsaw) and a study of the voluminous but fragmented public record on Vietnam.

Almost all those interviewed still hold office and thus requested an assurance of anonymity. They talked about events that are still highly classified. Many revealed their true feelings, even when these feelings were contrary to the official views of their government. The desire for anonymity is particularly understandable in Washington. As one important source observed: "This Administration is so leak-conscious that God help anyone to whom a leak can be traced."

We were careful to check and double-check information, considering that our sources most often spoke from memory. Nevertheless, it would be surprising if occasional errors in detail did not find their way into the narrative.

This book is a *Los Angeles Times* project. When we first proposed it to Robert J. Donovan, the *Times'* Washington Bureau chief, it received his immediate and wholehearted endorsement. His encouragement and forbearance never flagged.

Editor Nick B. Williams and Managing Editor Frank Haven had faith in and unstintingly supported this costly undertaking although, for many months, there was no assurance that anything worth publishing would result.

Among the many who helped, we also acknowledge:

—The important information contributed by Tom Lambert, Don Cook and Ted Sell of the *Times* staff.

—The special assistance of Louis B. Fleming, Robert C. Toth, William Tuohy and John J. Goldman of the *Times* staff.

—The perceptive and indispensable research work of Katherine McNett, who also did the index.

—The many chores at the typewriter and in the library by Joann Wilson, Lucy Lazarou and Patricia Fahey of the *Times* staff.

—The typing of the manuscript by Bernice and Ellen Anne Kraslow.

—The improvement in the manuscript resulting from the sound judgment and sensitive blue pencil of Robert D. Loomis, our editor at Random House.

While acknowledging gratefully these contributions, we, of course, assume sole responsibility for what this book says.

David Kraslow and Stuart H. Loory

WASHINGTON, D.C.

MAY 5, 1968

part I

Marigold

Here's flowers for you;
Hot lavender, mints, savory, marjoram;
The marigold, that goes to bed wi' the sun,
And with him rises weeping . . .

—William Shakespeare
The Winter's Tale

CHAPTER ONE

The Meetings in Durong Pasteur

For anyone involved in the making of decisions regarding national security affairs, Saturday, December 3, 1966, was to be a quiet day. There would be no decisions to make.

Lyndon Baines Johnson was at his Texas ranch. He was recuperating from recent surgery, preparing the 1967 legislative program and making ready for a joyous tour later in the day of the Mexican-American border area.

At the Department of State, important and most secret but nonetheless technical preparations were going forward to brief Ambassador John A. Gronouski in Warsaw for what could be the opening three days hence of a peace negotiation to end the Vietnam war. Would anything come of it? No one knew.

Saturday was to be a quiet interlude between five months of secret negotiations that had just culminated the day before in Saigon and the new phase ahead in Warsaw. A policy-maker could do nothing useful to advance the cause of peace this weekend.

That morning a senior official in the national security apparatus awoke, dressed and went downstairs to the breakfast table. He picked up his Washington *Post*, unfolded it and scanned the top of the front page. His eyes stopped and focused on the one-column headline at the top of the extreme left-hand column—the article newsmen call the "off-lead" or second most important story of the day.

U. S. Bombs
Site 5 Miles
From Hanoi

Raids Are Closest
To Reds' Capital
Since Last June

"Oh my God!" the official said. He read on with growing alarm:

From News Dispatches

SAIGON, Dec. 2—U.S. fighter-bombers attacked a truck park and an oil depot near Hanoi today in the closest raids to the North Vietnamese capital since June.

About 20 Navy planes from carriers in the Tonkin Gulf hit the Vandien vehicle park between four and five miles south of the capital. At the same time, from 50 to 70 Air Force Phantoms struck the Hagia oil depot 14 miles north of Hanoi.

(In Washington terms, four to five miles is the distance between the Washington Monument and the Carter Barron Amphitheater.)

U.S. spokesmen said there were no immediate reports on the bomb damage.

The North Vietnamese news agency claimed 11 American planes were shot down during the day, two near Hanoi. It charged the U.S. jets had attacked a populated area in Hanoi's southern outskirts and two populated areas inside the city. There was no confirmation from any American source of the plane loss claim . . .

The rest of the story concerned reports of ground action in South Vietnam the day before. The official put the paper aside. He knew of a file in the State Department, entitled "Marigold," which contained:

A cable on the forthcoming meeting in Warsaw . . . others

on the five months of secret negotiations in Saigon . . . Henry Cabot Lodge's long presentation on American aspirations for Southeast Asia to Polish and Italian diplomats . . . reports on trips to Hanoi . . . a memorandum on an elegant luncheon in Rome . . . the names of Giovanni D'Orlandi and Janusz Lewandowski . . .

The official remembered, now, the approval granted some two weeks before by the President and his principal advisers for the first bombing of Hanoi in five months. These raids, reported in the morning newspaper, could, he realized, damage the frail Marigold.

"Oh my God," he muttered. "We lost control."

The official's shock grew from the fact that a foreign capital had been bombed and the President and his top civilian lieutenants had forgotten that they had authorized it.

Saturday, December 3, 1966, turned suddenly sour, and it had just begun.

It is unlikely that American intelligence officials updating their dossier on Janusz Lewandowski as he flew into Saigon one day in April, 1966, realized the extent of his ambition: to try his hand at making peace in Vietnam.

At thirty-five, the conservatively dressed, self-assured Polish diplomat had come to take charge of his country's mission to the International Commission for Supervision and Control in Vietnam (the ICC). He carried the rank of ambassador. Yet, with his slim and short figure, with his light beard and oversized thick glasses, he more closely resembled a college undergraduate than a carefully trained diplomat.

The American intelligence people were to have persistent trouble distinguishing between Janusz Lewandowski and Bogdan Lewandowski, then the young head of the Polish Foreign Ministry's department controlling relations between the Warsaw government and international organizations. For example, the Americans matched Janusz to Bogdan's wife, an American from Pittsburgh, and otherwise listed Bogdan's career credits in Janusz's *curriculum vitae*. It was only after Bogdan became deputy director of the foreign affairs department of the Polish

Communist Party Secretariat that things began to straighten themselves out.

In the spring of 1966 the commission Lewandowski was joining stood—as it had for years and still does—as a symbol of the 1954 Geneva Conference's failure to settle the problems of Indochina once and for all. The Geneva agreements had provided for the temporary partition of Vietnam, after the French defeat at Dien Bien Phu, into two "regrouping zones"— one north of the 17th parallel under the control of Ho Chi Minh's Viet Minh, and the other south of the parallel under the control of the old French Union or any government that succeeded the French. The ICC, composed of Canada (friendly to the Western powers), Poland (friendly to the Communist powers) and India (scrupulously nonaligned), had been formed to police Vietnam, Laos and Cambodia to make sure the accords were being honored. Until the proposed reunification under the Geneva accords was accomplished by free elections in July, 1956, the ICC had been empowered to supervise all military activities in the two zones, guard against the introduction of foreign troops into them and settle, unanimously, any military disputes that might arise. As the years passed and as the violations of the Geneva accords piled one on top of the other, practically smothering the commission, the ICC was shunted further into the background. First its troop complement was reduced from 400 to about 250. Then the number of inspection teams was reduced from seven in each part of Vietnam to five. Next the North Vietnamese, after the United States began bombing their country in February, 1965, ordered the shutdown of the northern inspection posts. Later the South Vietnamese refused to allow the five southern posts to function freely.

So by the time Lewandowski arrived, the ICC was as moribund as the Geneva agreements that had given it life.

The representatives of the three commission powers had all but retired to their headquarters camp outside Saigon as their authority waned over the years. They spent their time in meaningless meetings, plotting ways to reassert their authority gradually, and thus bring peace to Vietnam.

In fact, the commissioners had become little more than the board of trustees for a ramshackle airline and perhaps its most frequent passengers. The ICC operated an antique Boeing 307 Stratoliner—a 1938 vintage airplane that had been a wonder in its day as the first fully pressurized passenger liner—which made regular runs between Saigon and Hanoi, with stops along the way in Phnom Penh, Cambodia, and Vientiane, Laos.

These flights were microcosmic examples of everything that was wrong with the Geneva accords, the ICC and the failure of all concerned to bring a settlement to Vietnam. Because the French were not living up to their pledge to support the commission financially, the plane was in sad shape (some felt it was downright unsafe) and could make only three flights every two weeks. It took off from Saigon every Tuesday and every other Friday. On alternate Fridays it rested at Saigon's Tansonnhut Airport while mechanics gave it a once-over that was just enough to keep the plane airworthy and its French crew from rebelling.

The plane flew a flight plan worked out at the sufferance of the United States government to avoid the bombing raids on the North. It never, for example, flew into Hanoi during the daytime, when American air activity was at its height. Even at night it flew a carefully controlled corridor from Vientiane. With that precaution, it was often turned back at the Hanoi approach by North Vietnamese ground controllers on the pretext that there might be American attacks. However, its Hanoi base—Gialam Airport—was never hit by American attackers.

Added to the safety hazards created by the lack of French interest and the potential military hazards from the Americans, there was the native hazard of nervous Laotians and North Vietnamese country people who, armed with rifles, took pot shots at anything with wings, regardless of markings.

Despite all the emptiness of the ICC's functions, both sides in the war made sure to keep its structure alive. It served as a valuable channel of communication, should either side wish to use it, and it also served as a framework around which, at some future time, a possible settlement could be built.

From the time of his arrival, Lewandowski attended the ICC meetings and deprecated the efforts of his colleagues to reassert their control through such schemes as really demilitarizing the six-mile-wide demilitarized zone between North and South

Vietnam or by policing effectively the frontiers of South Vietnam.

"What to do here, what to do there, gentlemen, is not the right approach," the callow Lewandowski would tell his senior colleagues.

In the meantime, Lewandowski busied himself with making acquaintances in the diplomatic community. Because his country is Communist and friendly to the North, his first get-acquainted duties were in Hanoi. Almost immediately after his April arrival, he took the first of what were to be monthly flights to Hanoi.

Once in the North Vietnamese capital, the young Pole followed strict diplomatic form, presenting his credentials to the army officer who was North Vietnam's liaison with the ICC and then calling on the heads of each of the diplomatic missions from foreign countries in Hanoi.

Though the occasions called for small talk, Lewandowski constantly listened for any indications of changes in position that might lead to negotiations. He did not discuss his own ideas or those of his government on the manner in which a settlement should be pursued. It is possible that he talked with North Vietnamese government leaders at a higher level than the ICC liaison during that first trip, but if he did, it was as an extracurricular activity.

His introductions among the Communists completed, Lewandowski flew back to Saigon on the old Stratoliner and began the diplomatic rounds all over again. The first man on whom he called was the dean of the diplomatic corps, Giovanni D'Orlandi, the fifty-year-old ambassador from Italy. D'Orlandi was a soft-speaking, suave man of delicate style for whom the niceties of protocol were tools to be used with all the skill a great surgeon uses in performing an operation.

His training ground was the same as that which produced the great Florentine intriguers of the Renaissance or the diplomats of the Vatican who have walked with sure footing through the corridors of history for centuries. Diplomacy to D'Orlandi was not work for the dilettante. Missions overseas were not places where out-of-favor generals or big political contributors should be sent either to keep them quiet or as a reward for services rendered. Diplomacy to D'Orlandi was a profession, with rules of conduct and methods of operations strictly defined to keep international relations on an even keel. These were beliefs D'Orlandi learned and treasured all the time he was working his way up through the bureaucracy of the Italian Foreign Ministry, from the time he joined it in 1940 as a young lawyer until he arrived in Saigon as an ambassador on July 17, 1962. They were beliefs D'Orlandi taught passionately to several classes of American graduate students at Johns Hopkins University's Center for European Studies at the University of Bologna. His associates have described D'Orlandi as a "very sedate" and "clever" man whose inner hardness never really became known until he won the Saigon post, his first overseas assignment. For most of his career he handled the bread and butter of European diplomacy—continental economic relations.

Within a year after he arrived in Saigon, he had, by virtue of seniority, become the dean of the diplomatic corps. He first showed his strength in August, 1963, when the Diem regime, during the infamous raids on the Buddhist pagodas, tried to extend its censorship of news leaving the country to include any diplomatic cables. The messages, the South Vietnamese Foreign Office said, would have to be sent uncoded over commercial cable and wireless channels. D'Orlandi immediately presented himself at the Foreign Office in Saigon and said that if the new regulation were enforced he would leave the country in thirty-six hours. It was a classic diplomatic ploy. He used it without any authority from Rome, and before his superiors there could decide whether he acted properly in presenting the ultimatum, the Diem regime rescinded its ruling. From that time forward, D'Orlandi was established as a man to be reckoned with in Saigon. His colleagues, the South Vietnamese government, the powerful American mission and all the anti-Diem dissidents in Saigon's fragmented body politic paid him respect.

A few months after that show of diplomatic force, just as D'Orlandi was sitting down to lunch in his apartment on November 1, 1963, the Diem regime fell in a bloody palace coup. Within ten minutes of the first reports of trouble, a handful of deposed Diem officials were knocking on D'Orlandi's door and asking for asylum in the Italian Embassy.

D'Orlandi reacted instantly. He could not grant asylum, he said. That would involve complicated cables back and forth to Rome, and the bloody circumstances of the moment did not allow time for that. But, please, he told the frightened former ministers, be the Italian ambassador's guests for lunch. That established a precedent which served the rest of his career in Saigon. At each one of the nine successive coups, D'Orlandi answered knocks on the door by generals, cabinet ministers, police chiefs and assorted other functionaries on the run who sought a safe Italian meal. There was even one case in which the wife of a general planning a coup made a luncheon reservation in advance.

She knocked on D'Orlandi's door one night, told him of the coup her husband was plotting for the next morning, and related that she had forbidden her spouse to take part unless he had a guarantee that in case of failure he could safely end up in the Italian Embassy rather than in military prison or some ad hoc execution chamber. With all due regard for the proper forms of diplomacy, there is no available record of what D'Orlandi told the hen-pecked general's distraught wife.

All of this has some relevance to the relationship D'Orlandi and Lewandowski began to establish after the Pole's courtesy call in the late spring of 1966. The two became part of a complicated, behind-the-scenes effort to bring peace to Vietnam. There was a third man in the effort—Ambassador Henry Cabot Lodge of the United States—and the secret meeting place of the three men was D'Orlandi's apartment at 135 Durong Pasteur, one of the two streets in Saigon to retain its old French name.

The apartment was considered secure from all the prying eyes and ears of Saigon because it was not watched or bugged. This was so, D'Orlandi felt, because each short-lived generation of security agents in Saigon knew that someday they, too, might have need of a free lunch and a safe haven.

The apartment of Giovanni D'Orlandi had become a truly inviolate piece of extraterritoriality.

But this skips ahead. Lewandowski and D'Orlandi completed their first meeting, and then, in the following days, the Pole continued down the list of ambassadors. Finally, as protocol demanded, he arrived in Lodge's office on June 6, 1966.

Professionally the two men had come to their meeting in Saigon by opposite routes. The American had learned the art of conducting international relations from the top down—as a United States senator, as an ambassador to the United Nations, as a vice-presidential candidate.

Lewandowski, by contrast, was a technician learning his craft carefully. In 1957, while Lodge held center stage on television as a Cold War debater at the United Nations, Lewandowski, then twenty-six, was a back-bench apprentice diplomat in the little-noticed Polish delegation at the UN. (The two men had met casually during the UN years.) In the early 1960s, while Lodge was nursing the political wounds he suffered while running for vice-president on Richard M. Nixon's Republican ticket, Lewandowski was sharpening his skills in African posts, including service as chargé d'affaires of the Polish mission in Tanganyika.

Lewandowski's courtesy call was the first of several meetings in which Lodge would grow to like this quiet—even shy—cultured, undoctrinaire Pole. Lodge thought him realistic and unencumbered by the blinders often worn by those who embrace Marxist doctrine without question, but realized, of course, that Lewandowski must be deeply committed to communism. He came from a military family, grew up during the post-World War II years when the Polish army was virtually under the complete command of the Soviet Union, and was educated at the University of Kiev.

Despite the wide divergencies in background, the sixty-four-year-old Lodge, a tall, silver-haired, distinguished New England patrician, would on occasion find himself reflecting that Lewandowski was the same age and had many of the same attributes as his own son, George.

Lodge saw the value of maintaining close contact with his new colleague. The late spring of 1966 had been a period of intense probing by the United States to see if the other side was ready for peace talks. All efforts were being made to gather intelligence from Hanoi. The Americans were looking for word that the large build-up of American forces was beginning to hurt the enemy, that the war of attrition General William C. Westmoreland had mounted under the strategy planned in Washington was beginning to turn the tide, that the big bombing raids on North Vietnam—the Rolling Thunder, as they were called—were bringing Ho Chi Minh's government to its knees.

By late June, Lodge, listening to the reports of recent travelers to Hanoi,[1] thought he detected signs that Hanoi was weakening. The bombing raids were hurting, he reported to Washington. Roads were tied up. The Soviet-donated SAM antiaircraft missiles were not working properly. The North Vietnamese were having trouble supplying their troops and the Viet Cong forces of the National Liberation Front in the South. Three different visitors to Hanoi had given Lodge this kind of assessment and told him they found there was a real desire in the North Vietnamese capital to open talks.

The Johnson Administration viewed its bombing of North Vietnam as one method of forcing the Hanoi government to the negotiating table under conditions favorable to the United States and the South Vietnamese. Lodge's reports about the situation in Hanoi, then, could have been taken in Washington as an indication that more bombing could bring about favorable negotiations even more quickly. On June 29 the United States escalated the bombing severely.

That day American dive bombers from the United States Navy's aircraft carriers on Yankee Station in the Gulf of Tonkin and from the Air Force bases in Thailand struck the so-called POL dumps—the petroleum storage depots in the Hanoi-Haiphong area—for the first time. With the half-day time difference, it was night in Washington as the bombers left on their mission. It became known in the White House as "the night of the little monks." For months afterward President Johnson would tell occasional visitors how he worried that night that the raids

---

[1] In addition to the Poles, the Canadian and Indian members of the ICC made regular trips to Hanoi. Other travelers included occasional Englishmen, bound for the British consulate in Hanoi, and various Frenchmen—doctors, journalists, diplomats—many of whom had maintained contacts from the colonial era. By this time the North Vietnamese had already permitted three American pacifists—Herbert Aptheker, the American Communist theoretician; Thomas Hayden, the New Leftist, and Staughton Lynd, then assistant professor of history at Yale—to visit Hanoi as well.

would somehow go wrong and an errant bomb would strike a Soviet ship in Haiphong harbor and start World War III.

He worried so much that his daughter Luci, returning home from a date with her fiancé, Pat Nugent, urged the President to pray. She had converted to Catholicism some months before and now she urged her father to seek solace in the church. Nugent made the arrangements for their visit to St. Dominic's in southwest Washington. At 10:30 P.M. a waiting Dominican monk saw two black limousines drive up to the entrance of the neo-Gothic building. The President, Mrs. Johnson, Luci and Nugent stepped out of one car; a detail of Secret Service men, from the other.

The entire group entered the dim, empty church. The presidential party dropped to its knees and prayed silently.

Back in the White House, the President remained awake most of the night, awaiting the final reports on the raids. At 4:30 A.M., satisfied that no great mishap had occurred, he went to sleep. He awoke, refreshed, late in the morning. And when Luci went to her father's bedroom to inquire about the raids, she learned of their success.

"You see," she told the President, "that's what my little monks can do for you."

While American intelligence reports were reflecting deterioration in the North Vietnamese position and plans were in the works for escalation, Lewandowski and D'Orlandi were busy making themselves better acquainted and talking of what they could do to create the atmosphere for a settlement. With the encouragement of their governments, the two formulated a scheme for conducting "a diplomatic exercise in style." Basically, their idea was intended to bring representatives of both the United States and North Vietnam together in a place where they could exchange ideas on just what kind of permanent settlement they envisioned for South Vietnam.

Until then, all the ideas—like those discussed in the ICC meetings—had been schemes for a gradual, mutual de-escalation of the war which would lead eventually to a cease-fire.

The North Vietnamese were demanding a halt—"unconditionally and for good," according to Ho Chi Minh the previous January—to the bombing of their country before talks could begin.

The United States said it was bombing North Vietnam to punish it for the war, to increase the cost of the war to the North, to shore up South Vietnamese morale and to reduce the infiltration from the North. The North Vietnamese admitted no such infiltration.

In this situation, men like D'Orlandi saw little hope of a settlement. In fact, they pictured a ludicrous negotiation that went like this:

American representative: "Okay, we will stop the bombing of your country. Now what will you do in return?"

North Vietnamese representative: "We will continue not bombing the United States."

It was not long before D'Orlandi and Lewandowski thought they had a good enough approach, however, to begin talking with the adversaries in the war. D'Orlandi arranged an appointment with his friend "Cabot."

Ironically, their meeting took place on June 29, the day of the "little monk" raids.

D'Orlandi's approach to Lodge was that the United States and North Vietnam set down what each considered to be the "least unacceptable" settlement of the situation. The underlying philosophy of this approach, the Italian told Lodge, was that a comparison of these "least unacceptable" views would yield some basis for a compromise settlement that would be at least minimally acceptable to both sides.

In short, D'Orlandi was thinking of a textbook approach to the situation—the kind of approach he would develop with his graduate students at the Bologna seminars—during which the professional diplomats would step in and finally act as the brokers in attempting to strike a good bargain for both sides.

As D'Orlandi and Lewandowski had formulated the idea, there would be no need for any de-escalation of the war to get the talks started, since this was to be a stylistic exercise relating to the ultimate outcome. That approach effectively skirted the stop-the-bombing demand of the North Vietnamese. It was obviously a feature that had great appeal for the United States, offering, as it did, the opportunity for the Johnson Administration to keep up its pressure on the North while undertaking talks. This was to be the uniquely attractive aspect of the initiative. In return, the United States would reveal how far it would go in meeting the Communist demands for a permanent settlement. Ever since the air war in North Vietnam had begun more than a year before, the United States had been probing North Vietnamese attitudes toward negotiations.

Diplomats and mediators, amateur and otherwise, who had lent a hand in trying to effect a settlement suffered confusion over the American position.

"Frankly, I did not know and I still do not know what the American position is on a settlement," one Eastern European commented as late as December, 1967, "unless it is the unconditional surrender of the North Vietnamese and the NLF and establishment of permanent American bases in Southeast Asia against the Chinese." Non-Communists have expressed this assessment as well.

Confusion among outsiders over the long-range American position was not without justification. A friend of Chester L. Cooper—the former CIA official and White House aide who worked many months as deputy to W. Averell Harriman, U.S. ambassador-for-peace—quoted Cooper as once saying: "The position papers for a peace conference will be written on the plane to the conference . . . to write them any earlier would blow Washington sky-high."

The friend said Cooper was referring to all the conflicting parties in Congress and in the Executive Branch who had their own ideas on what kind of peace to obtain and who would do their utmost to scuttle any contrary proposal as soon as it became known. A number of American officials, from the earliest days of the war, had written such papers but had locked them in their own desks. They were afraid to pass their ideas forward to superiors and be labeled pessimistic, defeatist or unduly idealistic.

Particularly during the latter half of 1964 and early 1965, those running the war equated negotiations with surrender. The South Vietnamese regime, and thus the American bargaining position, was that weak.

If the United States really was interested in negotiating in mid-1966, Lewandowski wanted to take a solid indication of that fact to Hanoi. The Polish diplomat knew how much the North Vietnamese leaders distrusted the United States—or any Western power, for that matter—when it came to bargaining. He knew that Ho Chi Minh and his followers felt they had been outmaneuvered and cheated at each peace negotiation they had tried since World War II. He knew the Vietnamese had won their revolutions against French power on the battlefield only to lose their gains in talks at Paris and Geneva. Against that background, Lewandowski recognized the extreme importance of presenting to the North Vietnamese the long-range aspirations of the United States in Southeast Asia.

Lodge learned of Lewandowski's desires during his June 29 meeting with D'Orlandi, and reported the Pole's ideas to Washington. His cable made the rounds of a select group of officials, ranging from the President down through the bureaucracy to the Vietnam Working Group—a special task force that had been organized to handle the day-to-day chores of the diplomatic, political and economic questions of the war.

The approach D'Orlandi had suggested required a reorientation in American thinking. But as the cable circulated, some officials pointed out that the idea was worth exploration, that indeed such a long-range approach had been previously considered in the State Department.

In a week's time Lodge received word from Washington that he could guardedly pursue the matter with D'Orlandi and Lewandowski. Now the stage was set for the lengthy negotiation that was to begin with hope and end six months later with new recriminations about just how sincere the United States really was in seeking peace. It was to end with diplomats and others around the world wondering just how much control the Johnson Administration had over its part of the war. And in Washington it was to leave a legacy of bitterness against the Polish government that would threaten much of the good resulting from the years of effort by this country to draw Poland as far out of the Soviet sphere of influence as possible.

None of this could be foreseen as Lodge, in July, 1966, let D'Orlandi know he would be agreeable to a meeting with Lewandowski. The D'Orlandi apartment—that refuge of runaway governments on the top floor of a five-story building—was chosen as the site. The ground floor of 135 Durong Pasteur and the one above it housed the Italian chancery. The green, white and red striped flag of Italy almost always flew above the entrance to the ocher-colored stucco-and-glass building constructed during the French period.

Lodge could enter the building without attracting attention. Various officials in the American Embassy whom he visited socially lived there. Also, it was situated next door to a twin structure that was then the headquarters of General Westmoreland and the rest of the United States Military Assistance Command—MACV. Located in a former upper-class French residential area, the two buildings were separated by a garden that was partially given over to automobile parking. Thus, Lodge could park in the lot and then disappear into either the Italian Embassy's building or MACV without being noticed from the street. The ambassador could even take his choice of several entrances in the apartment house to help confound any followers.

Henry Cabot Lodge, like any American ambassador, was always followed wherever he went in Saigon. He was followed not only by the Viet Cong but also by the Saigon government, which, apparently, could never be quite certain that the United States had what Saigon considered to be Vietnam's best interests at heart. In addition, he was usually trailed by at least one member of the ICC. To guard against a mishap, he always took a U.S. Marine with him.

There were times when Lodge wanted to be alone. On those occasions he would shun his official limousine and would scrunch his six-foot-three frame down onto the floor in the back seat of an old Toyota compact car. His Marine guard, in mufti, would drive through the gates of the embassy—seemingly alone. Safely away from the would-be followers, Lodge would sit up and go his way without recognition through the teeming city.

On July 9 Lodge, accompanied by the Marine guard and followed by the South Vietnamese police (who were nominally protecting him and not tracing his comings and goings) and assorted other tails, drove out of the old American Embassy compound in downtown Saigon. The procession moved along the crowded Durong Pasteur in the direction of MACV. Lodge's car pulled into the parking lot, and the ambassador, instead of visiting General Westmoreland, entered the apartment house next door. Lewandowski arrived separately.

Now the three men met together for business in D'Orlandi's apartment for the first time. They exchanged pleasantries, then sat down to establish the ground rules for their talks. The basic rule was that in success or failure the details of the discussions would remain forever secret and that none of them would discuss even the fact of the meetings with others. It was understood, of course, that they would have to make reports to their respective governments. Thus, a three-sided record does exist.

The D'Orlandi-Lewandowski-Lodge meetings developed into a series of what one American described as "drink-in-hand, feet-up bull sessions." The talks were in English, which D'Orlandi and Lewandowski spoke with ease.

At first Lodge explained to the other two the American aims for Vietnam. D'Orlandi and Lewandowski said it would help their understanding if they could get clarification from the United States on two important points:

1. Did the Johnson Administration view the war as part of a wider conflict or as one limited to Vietnam?

2. Would the Americans dismantle their bases and leave Vietnam after a settlement?

Lodge apparently decided that rather than answer these questions casually, he would consult the State Department. The meeting adjourned, Lodge cabled Washington, an answer was received—and a second session was held on July 24. At that time Lodge told the Pole and the Italian he could report that the United States truly saw the war as limited and that American military forces would certainly be withdrawn when the war was over.

After that, for reasons that are unclear, United States involvement in the Polish-Italian initiative faded. State Department officials said nothing resulted from the July meetings because Hanoi wasn't interested. But D'Orlandi and Lewandowski continued to meet and D'Orlandi kept Lodge informed on these discussions. Between the talks, Lewandowski continued his monthly trips on the Stratoliner to Hanoi. On none of his trips during the summer did he detect any interest by Hanoi in immediate talks.

By summer's end, however, the initiative in Saigon had achieved something of a life of its own. For D'Orlandi, it was diplomacy in action at its finest. It was the justification for twenty-five years of training in the art of negotiating. It was the opportunity to add meaning and substance to all the carefully learned form and style.

For the young, ambitious Lewandowski, it was a chance to probe the American mind and expand his own horizons while helping to mediate a possible settlement.

For the veteran Lodge, it was an enjoyable interlude, offering some hope in an otherwise frustrating assignment. The initiative had attracted only a skeptical interest in Washington even though Lodge's cables gave the impression that something serious was in progress which could conceivably lead to a negotiation.

The State Department, in order not to compromise the secrecy of the venture, gave it a code name so that access to the material could be better controlled. They called it Marigold— not Operation Marigold, not Project Marigold, but simply Marigold.

All during the early months of the Marigold initiative the war grew hotter. Perhaps this is why no progress was made on the initiative in that period. The June 29 raids were the opening of a big air offensive in the North, though the POL dumps in the Hanoi and Haiphong areas were not hit again. In Saigon, in early July, Premier Nguyen Cao Ky urged an invasion of North Vietnam during a speech to a graduating class at the South Vietnamese military academy. The United States dissociated itself from Ky's proposal two weeks later, when State Department spokesman Robert J. McCloskey said: "I would say our position of not seeking any wider war has been made repeatedly clear and remains our position. We do not threaten any regime."

Four days later fifteen eight-engined B-52 Stratofortresses flew 2,500 miles from Guam to bomb, for the first time, targets in the southern half of the demilitarized zone straddling the 17th parallel. The high-flying bombers came back for repeat performances July 31 and August 4 and 5 as officials in Washington denied speculation that the big planes were softening up the territory for a ground assault. The officials said the raids were intended to keep the zone from becoming a sanctuary for the North Vietnamese main force units that were infiltrating into the South.

The North Vietnamese protested to the ICC, and the commission's Indian chairman issued a statement "viewing with concern" the newest developments in the DMZ. That was the extent of the ICC's power to control the situation.

Then President Johnson, in October, 1966, brought all of South Vietnam's allies together for a conference in Manila. The two-day meeting of the leaders of South Vietnam, the United States, South Korea, Thailand, the Philippines, Australia and New Zealand produced a communiqué and a four-point "Declaration of Peace." The communiqué promised that the allies would withdraw their forces from South Vietnam "after close consultation" within six months after "the other side withdraws its forces to the North, ceases infiltration and the level of violence thus subsides." The Declaration stressed the need for a peaceful settlement, saying 1) aggression must not succeed; 2) the bonds of poverty, illiteracy and disease must be broken; 3) economic, social and cultural cooperation with the Asian and Pacific region must be strengthened, and 4) the allies must seek peace in Asia.

The somewhat ambiguous promise of the United States to withdraw within six months pre-empted the headlines for the last few days of October, along with President Johnson's post-conference tour of Vietnam and the countries of the Asian allies. The Declaration was attacked as "shameless humbug" and "out and out blackmail" by North Vietnam's allies—the Soviet Union and Red China—but D'Orlandi saw in it the opportunity to nourish his peace initiative.

His chance came when, unnoticed in the post-summit hubbub, Averell Harriman left Manila to make a long trip through Asia, Africa and Europe as an interpreter of the American position on Vietnam. Accompanied by Chester Cooper and Robert J. McCloskey, the State Department spokesman, Harriman stopped in Singapore, Ceylon, Indonesia, India, Pakistan, Iran, Italy, France, West Germany, Britain and Morocco. He spoke to government leaders about the Manila decisions and of how the United States appraised the situation in Southeast Asia.

Harriman's party arrived in Rome on November 2, and the governor, with characteristic energy, began a busy round of conferences with Italian leaders. In addition to the formal meetings, the Italian Foreign Ministry arranged an elegant, exclusive luncheon in the Renaissance-style Villa Madama—designed by the artist Raphael—on Monte Mario overlooking the Tiber River west of Rome. Giovanni D'Orlandi just happened to be present. (While in Vietnam, D'Orlandi had picked up a persistent parasitic infection that would progressively debilitate him. He underwent continual treatment for it by American army doctors; but periodically he returned to Rome for further treatment by Italian hematologists as well as to brief Foreign Minister Amintore Fanfani on developments in Saigon.)

Usually, there were twenty-four guests at ceremonial luncheons in the Villa Madama dining room. For this occasion, the guest list was held to ten, testifying to the secret atmosphere everyone felt was required for the delicate subject to be discussed. For the Americans there were Harriman, Cooper, McCloskey, G. Frederick Reinhardt, the American ambassador in Rome, and his deputy, Francis E. Meloy, Jr. On the Italian side, beside Fanfani and D'Orlandi, there was Egidio Ortona, the secretary general of the Foreign Ministry who was soon to become ambassador to Washington, and two other officials.

The Italians arranged the seating plan so that D'Orlandi and Cooper sat side by side. During the meal the Italian gave Cooper a detailed, first-hand account of the conversations at 135 Durong Pasteur. D'Orlandi told Cooper that peace possibilities in Vietnam were more alive than anyone in the Johnson Administration realized.

He informed Cooper he was planning to leave for Saigon the next day, and that soon after he arrived at his post Lewandowski would be making another journey to Hanoi. If only there were something concrete for the Pole to take with him, some clear expression of the American attitude, D'Orlandi said, the North Vietnamese might talk.

Cooper explained that he and Harriman still had many miles to travel before they returned to Washington and could present the problem to the proper people. He urged D'Orlandi to convince Lewandowski to delay his trip. The State Department,

Cooper said, might be able to give Lodge some instructions on dealing with Lewandowski that would prove useful. D'Orlandi told Cooper that in any event he planned to spend some time in Cairo en route back to Saigon. (He found that with his medical problem it helped to break up the eastbound journey to Saigon so that his metabolism could adjust slowly to the seven-hour time change on the trip from Rome.)

After lunch D'Orlandi and Harriman went off to a corner of the dining room for several minutes of private conversation. Taking note of the two men huddled so intently, Fanfani turned to a colleague, smiled and said: "I don't know what they're talking about and I don't want to know. But I hope it works out."

Until this luncheon Marigold had been treated in Washington as little more than one of the routine "peace feelers" the United States had received from time to time through various third parties. But now the prospects excited Harriman and Cooper.

When the Marigold record is made public, it will show a cable from Harriman and Cooper in Rome to Secretary of State Dean Rusk, reporting the substance of their luncheon conversations and urging that the Department supply Lodge with a talking position for the next meeting with Lewandowski.

Leaving Rome, Harriman and Cooper continued their journey to Paris, Bonn, London and Rabat before flying back to Washington on November 9.

From the time their plane landed in Washington and they went to work in their offices, Marigold, which had started out as a vague "exercise" on the part of D'Orlandi and Lewandowski, two little-known diplomats, became a powerful peace initiative of the United States. Most of the diplomatic resources of the government were marshaled behind it.

Those that were not may have unwittingly done it in.

CHAPTER TWO

A Toast to Something Worthwhile

At first glance, there is not much in the educational background of Chester Lawrence Cooper to recommend him as a Vietnam peace-seeker. He was born in Boston on January 13, 1917. He studied public administration and engineering at the Massachusetts Institute of Technology from 1935 to 1937 before moving on to New York University, where he earned a B.S. degree in 1939 and then a master's degree in business administration the following year. He received a doctorate in economics from American University in 1959. His scholarly writings include *Case Studies in Public Finance,* the *War Agency Handbook* and *Trends in Important New York State Industries.*

During World War II he entered the Office of Strategic Services—the U.S. wartime intelligence agency—and served for an extended period in China. In 1947 he became a charter employe of the Central Intelligence Agency as a "bright young man" in the growing intelligence community. In seventeen years with the CIA, Cooper's principal assignment was with the Office of National Estimates, a high-level unit that does long-range studies on the strengths and weaknesses of foreign countries and contributes to the daily intelligence estimate of world conditions prepared for the President. Cooper became an Asian specialist.

In 1954, while still a CIA official, he was a member of the United States delegation to the Geneva Conference which settled the war between the French and the Viet Minh. His analyses of the conference went to Secretary of State John Foster Dulles.

In 1955 Cooper was sent to London as a special representative of the Office of National Estimates. He returned to Washington two years later.

When the 1962 Geneva Conference to settle the Laotian problem by establishing a coalition government began, Cooper was there as a member of the American delegation led by Averell Harriman. He impressed Harriman greatly. In 1964 Cooper left the CIA to join the White House staff of McGeorge Bundy, President Johnson's special assistant for national security affairs, as a Vietnam expert.[1]

On the National Security Council staff, during the early days of the Vietnam war escalation, Cooper established himself more as a gadfly than a dove—challenging the basic assumptions of the evolving Vietnam policy. He became known throughout the Administration for his efforts to coax superiors into reacting meaningfully to any peace possibility that came along—however remote it might appear. When some in the Administration were thinking of ways to increase military pressure on the enemy, Cooper was thinking of ways to negotiate a settlement which would be satisfactory to all combatants—the United States, North Vietnam, the National Liberation Front, the Saigon government and the countries that contributed troops on the American side.

In April, 1966, Cooper resigned from the NSC staff, then

---

[1] When Cooper moved to the National Security Council, two other bright young men of the CIA's early days were already intimately involved in managing the Vietnam problem for the Johnson Administration. They were McGeorge Bundy's older brother, William P., who by then had become Assistant Secretary of State for East Asian and Pacific Affairs, and Robert Komer, who was then also on McGeorge Bundy's NSC staff. Komer later went to Saigon with the rank of ambassador to direct the pacification program to win the allegiance of Vietnamese to the Saigon government. The program was brought to a virtual standstill by the 1968 Tet offensive of the Viet Cong. William Bundy became the target of criticism from within and outside the Administration as the debate over Vietnam policy grew more intense.

headed by Walt W. Rostow, to do writing and independent research at the Institute for Defense Analysis, a nonprofit research corporation that works mostly for the Pentagon. He rejoined government on Ambassador Harriman's staff in August, 1966, when the President gave Harriman a special mandate for peace-seeking.

Almost immediately after his arrival in Washington from the post-Manila tour with Harriman, Cooper began lobbying for support of the Marigold talks in Saigon. Ambassador Lodge, he argued, should be given a detailed paper on the American position to expound to D'Orlandi and Lewandowski. As in all his peace campaigns, Cooper argued his point with anyone who would listen in Foggy Bottom.

While Cooper was making his rounds at the State Department, Lodge, on November 14, attended another meeting in the D'Orlandi apartment in Saigon. He learned that Lewandowski was planning to leave the next day on a trip to Hanoi. Once again the Pole asked for some word to take with him on the American position. Lodge said he had not yet heard from Washington.

He returned to the American Embassy and dispatched a new cable. The thirteen-hour time difference between Saigon and Washington makes for a good working relationship between the State Department and its front-line outpost. Lodge could file cables at the end of a working day and have them arrive in Washington well before the working day was beginning there. Similarly, Washington could take all day to prepare an answer, knowing that in Saigon the officials were asleep. By the time Saigon came awake, instructions from the State Department could be awaiting them.

In this manner Lodge found Marigold instructions for a talk with Lewandowski on his desk when he came to work the morning of November 15. In guarded telephone conversations, a new meeting was quickly arranged. In talking with each of the other two men, D'Orlandi would never invite them to a meeting. He would simply inform them of a time for their lunch or dinner or drinks. In Saigon, as in many other world capitals these days, even when one is sure privacy is inviolate he takes no chances —especially on a telephone.

The meeting of November 15 was, up to that time, by far the most important of those "feet-up" sessions. Lodge had his cable with him, and now he finally began to detail the American position on Vietnam. His talk was long and rambling. It was interrupted from time to time by questions from D'Orlandi and Lewandowski. The Pole, both as the junior member of the group and as the one who would represent these views in Hanoi, took careful notes. Lodge covered a broad range of questions dealing with the American attitudes toward the Geneva accords, Hanoi's "four points," the Manila Declaration, timetables for postwar elections in South Vietnam, withdrawal of troops, the policing of any peace arrangements, and how the actual cessation of fighting could be arranged.

From the American point of view, the part of Lodge's presentation that dealt with the manner in which the fighting could be quickly stopped—through mutual de-escalation leading to a cease-fire—was most important. Lewandowski and D'Orlandi, on the other hand, were more interested in the sections dealing with the long-range American ideas for a complete settlement in South Vietnam. In fact, they were prepared to reject another plan for a simple reciprocal de-escalation if Lodge had presented it.

As the meeting broke up, neither Lodge nor the State Department still had any clear idea of just how much Lewandowski was speaking for himself, how much for his government and how much as a representative of the North Vietnamese. But Lodge was nonetheless convinced that this undoctrinaire, urbane young Communist was, whatever the role he was playing, sincere in trying to bring about peace.

With Lewandowski in the air, once again heading toward Hanoi, the United States stake in Marigold grew even more serious. And so, to protect that stake, the national security bureaucracy reacted according to a well-tested rule of thumb: The more serious any undertaking, the fewer the number of people who should know about it.

And this is where the code name Marigold and the keeper of the codes, Ben Read, become important.

Before the mid-November meetings in Saigon there were perhaps forty officials in Washington—most of them in the State Department—who knew of Marigold. Several months later one of them described the reaction in Washington to Marigold's new promise this way: "The President woke up one morning, picked up the telephone and put the Lodge-Lewandowski business on a Nodis/Marigold basis with an order to cut the squad. He said he wanted to know the names of everyone who knew about it."

In an era when secret-keeping has become an important tool of government and a science on which millions of dollars are spent each year, the President's order meant work for Benjamin Huger Read, the forty-two-year-old chief secret-keeper of the State Department.

Read's primary tool in dealing with the presidential order was a book of code names in which Marigold appeared as one of the flower series. Flowers were used to name some important secret Vietnam peace initiatives. The names in themselves have absolutely no significance. The initiatives could as easily have been named after species of dogs, cities, states or stars in the sky.

But William P. Bundy, the Assistant Secretary of State for East Asian and Pacific Affairs, perhaps with an exquisite sense of irony, chose flowers, with all their symbolic meaning, for the dissident peace movement.[2]

Government officials are cleared by virtue of their personal

---

[2] That irony was not lost on some officials in the State Department. Ben Read once reportedly said to Bundy: "For Christ's sake, let's get off the flower kick and use something else." Several months later, after the authors began making inquiries about the flower series, the Department did change—except for one more "flower" code that did not relate to any specific peace initiative. Internal government reports on the authors' activities were code-named with the last in the flower series—Poppycock. Information on the secret Poppycock file, which included cables from American officials in foreign capitals visited by the authors, also leaked out of Read's office.

histories—particularly their loyalty and trustworthiness—to read
the standard confidential, secret or top-secret material that daily
jams the "in" and "out" baskets of official Washington. They are
cleared by virtue of their positions—cabinet members, under-
secretaries, assistant secretaries and so on down the line—to
read a hierarchy of material labeled "nodis" (no distribution),
"exdis" (exclusive distribution) or "limdis" (limited distribution) depending on their rank in the bureaucracy and their "need
to know." Nodis and exdis messages are all channeled through
Read's office. Limdis messages are distributed by the Department's Operations Center.

There is no blanket clearance for code-named operations.
For each of these, there is a separate list of officials who are
cleared to receive the information. These lists are prepared and
kept in Ben Read's office and also in the Operations Center.
When messages arrive from outside the Department with a
particular code name—or "slug," as they are called—the communications clerks simply consult their books to see who is
entitled to get copies.

Any nodis message, with or without a code name, goes to
Read's office, where some are summoned to read it and others
receive it hand-carried by either Read or his first deputy, John
Walsh.

Virtually unknown to the public, Read is more than a
common paper-shuffler. His title in the State Department's
Biographic Register is "special assistant to the secretary and
executive secretary of the Department." In a rare interview, he
described himself as a "bottleneck."

He is one of two or three paper-shufflers nonpareil in Washington. That difference in degree of importance as a technician
gives him a measure of power in the State Department similar
to that exercised in the White House by the supreme paper-
shuffler of them all—Walt W. Rostow, President Johnson's
special assistant for national security affairs.

Often Read contributes ideas as well as technical expertise.
As Walt Rostow sometimes writes drafts of presidential speeches,
Ben Read was for a long while one of only three men (with
Chester Cooper and William Bundy) called upon to draft the

most sensitive papers on Vietnam diplomacy for Dean Rusk.

Ben Read differs from Rostow, though, in his ability to remain truly behind the scenes. Rostow became one of the Administration's chief exponents—salesmen may be a better word —of Vietnam war policy. His detractors labeled him "superhawk" and noticed he was almost as accessible to some sympathetic Washington newsmen, to whom he kept a steady stream of favorable war news flowing, as he was to the President.

None of this can be said about Read. To understand his importance fully, picture him as the engineer in charge of a huge power grid. He sits at a control point in room 7224 of the State Department—between Dean Rusk's cavernous suite 7226 and Undersecretary Nicholas deB. Katzenbach's slightly less cavernous 7222—and directs the flow of information within the departmental headquarters and between it and all the embassies, missions, consulates and special offices abroad.

His touch must be as deft as any power engineer's if he is to keep the diplomatic sector of the national security information grid in balance. And he must keep his sector closely in tune with those run by the Department of Defense, the Central Intelligence Agency and the White House. One mistake on Read's part—one errant slash of his pen through a key name on a distribution list, for example—can cause the information grid to collapse with the same finality and the same disastrous results as happened in November, 1965, when electric power surged the wrong way in the Northeast Power Grid and forty million Americans were plunged into darkness. Seldom has information been a more jealously guarded commodity than it has been in Lyndon Johnson's Washington. He who has information has power. He who controls its flow keeps his power harnessed and working harmoniously for him.

High State Department officials are inclined to take all the precaution with a grain of salt, chuckling to themselves about the impossibility of maintaining a leak-tight system. "Limdis means read by less than five hundred people," one official said in pointing up what he believed to be the absurd aspects of secret-keeping in Washington. "Nodis means read by less than a hundred."

He went on to explain how officials, for additional security, write "for eyes only" on sensitive documents. This can cut the total number of readers down to seventy-five,[3] he said.

As a result of such situations, some officials have resorted to another classification of their own: "Literally for ————'s eyes only."

But with all the messengers carrying the papers, all the secretaries who type and receive them, and all of the aides ripping open envelopes to make themselves useful to their bosses, even this plaintive classification is no guarantee of confidentiality.

Despite all this, the system can work—if the overriding concern is secrecy, not efficiency. Marigold remained a deep secret in its lifetime. Not a word of it leaked to the public or, indeed, to most members of the State Department who were intimately involved in the management of the Vietnam war effort. This was a tribute to Ben Read.

In mid-November, 1966, Read examined the flow of Marigold information in keeping with the President's "cut-the-squad" order and began pulling the circuit breakers throughout the State Department information grid. Part of the desire was to please Ho Chi Minh. He had time and again led the United States to believe that the beginning of the end to the fighting could not come publicly. Because of his own domestic political problems and his fear of displeasing the Chinese colossus immediately to the north, he could not reveal his moves.

When Read finished going over the Marigold distribution list, he could report he had cut the squad to six in the State Department: Rusk, Katzenbach, Harriman, Cooper, Bundy and Leonard Unger, Bundy's principal deputy at the time.

Among those cut from the list were members of the Vietnam Working Group in Bundy's bureau—the functionaries who exercise day-to-day control over the political side of the war and set up coordination with the Defense Department on military actions. As Read, for reasons of national security, trimmed those

---

[3] An aide to a former undersecretary of state said he regularly opened messages addressed for his boss's "eyes only." He explained: "He expected me to do it. I wouldn't have been doing my job right if I didn't."

Another official said: "Every morning there are dozens of people in Washington reading papers marked "For the President's eyes only."

eligible to see Marigold cables, he set the stage for a bitter irony:

In the weeks ahead, Marigold was to be damaged severely, perhaps fatally, by those who were acting in ignorance. It was to suffer because no one on the Marigold list had specific, full-time responsibility for coordinating diplomatic and military moves; and those who could have performed such coordination were kept ignorant of Marigold.[4]

One of the important decisions confronting Lyndon Johnson as he returned from his Asian tour on November 2 and went to his Texas ranch for a rest was how to answer a request from the military to bomb targets near Hanoi again. The request was pending all during the first two weeks of November—during the same period that Harriman and Cooper, after they returned from their trip, were trying to drum up support for Marigold in the State Department.

After the emphasis that had been put on peace at Manila, the decision to renew the bombing of Hanoi could not have been easy to make. Defense Secretary Robert S. McNamara and General Earle G. Wheeler, chairman of the Joint Chiefs of Staff, probably discussed the question with the President when they visited him at the ranch November 5 to review the Manila Conference, reports from General Westmoreland and requests for the coming year's defense budget. It could have been discussed again five days later when McNamara and Wheeler returned to the ranch, this time with Walt Rostow, to go over the

---

[4] The limits to which the Department went to preserve secrecy were evident in Unger's office on the sixth floor of the State Department. Workers there reported that more than once the deputy assistant secretary received phone calls and as a result went padding furtively out of his office and up to 7224 to look at the latest Marigold report. Another young staff member recalls sitting in on a small conference where Marigold, which he had never heard of, was mentioned in an offhand manner. There was an embarrassed pause in the conversation. The subject was changed and the meeting continued. It was not until he read limited newspaper accounts months later that the staff member realized the Polish-Italian initiative had ever taken place, and it was not until he talked to the authors a year later that he realized that this peace initiative was the Marigold to which the others at that little meeting had referred.

budget. (At that time McNamara announced that the Soviet Union was building an antiballistic missile defense system.) A decision on the Hanoi bombing apparently was deferred.

The day following McNamara's second visit, Harriman appeared at the ranch to discuss with the President the results of his post-conference tour. Harriman later told reporters there were "no specific discussions going on" about peace nor any "signals" that the North Vietnamese were willing to talk. He went on to give a clue about Marigold's potentialities, however, when he said: "[There] are third-hand conversations which appear to indicate that Hanoi is willing to talk provided we do certain things. It is encouraging that all of the Eastern European countries indicate they are talking to Hanoi."

This was a clear public indication that Harriman had just finished giving Lyndon Johnson a full account of the Villa Madama lunch. But at that time the Marigold initiative had not yet reached that stage where direct United States–North Vietnamese discussions could be considered imminent.

On the evening of Monday, November 14, the President returned to Washington to undergo surgery to repair a hernia in his old gall bladder incision and to remove a nonmalignant polyp from his vocal cords. He entered Bethesda Naval Hospital on Tuesday evening. But before he went he had a regular Tuesday lunch with his national security advisers—Rusk, McNamara, Rostow and Bill D. Moyers, his press secretary and, perhaps, closest confidant at the time. At the lunch a new batch of North Vietnam bombing targets was "signed off"—that is, approved by the President.

For the first time since the "little monks" night of June 29, Hanoi area targets were among those authorized.

The White House decision came on the same day Lodge made the long presentation to D'Orlandi and Lewandowski of American aims in Southeast Asia, and on the same day that Lewandowski left for Hanoi.

Word of the approval went out from the White House to the Pentagon, and thence down the chain of command to Honolulu and Saigon and finally to the carriers on Yankee Station in the Gulf of Tonkin and to remote air bases in the jungles of north-eastern Thailand. On a line of supply and command stretching halfway around the world, thousands of American military men began preparations for the new operation.

In Hanoi, where Janusz Lewandowski had gone to present the American position, neither the Pole nor his hosts had any idea of what was coming. Lewandowski remained two weeks in the North Vietnamese capital. Part of that time was taken up with ICC business. Another part was spent discussing the Lodge talks with underlings in the government and Communist Party apparatus.

And still another part was spent doing that which anyone who has ever tried to do business in a Communist capital experiences —waiting, waiting by the telephone for a ring and for a voice to summon him to an important interview.

Finally Janusz Lewandowski heard that voice and he went off to the Presidential Palace to meet North Vietnamese Premier Pham Van Dong.

Some American analysts say that Hanoi, like Washington, has its hawks and doves, and that Ho Chi Minh, like Lyndon Johnson, has been trapped in the position of trying to balance each off against the other. The more prevalent view, however, is that official Hanoi is not populated by hawks and doves but by those who are "hawkish" or "dovish" about the methods to be used in achieving their goals—the defeat of the United States and the Saigon government, if not the communization of South Vietnam and its reunification with the North. Those who are hawkish say this must be done militarily. Those who are dovish say it could be done by political means, starting at the negotiating table. Most Communist and Western analysts agree that Pham Van Dong and Foreign Minister Nguyen Duy Trinh are dovish. Opposing them—at least in 1966 and 1967—it was believed, were Le Duan, the first secretary of the Communist Party and thus almost certainly the second most powerful man in Hanoi after Ho, and General Vo Nguyen Giap, the defense minister and hero of Dien Bien Phu.

By the time Lewandowski arrived in the North Vietnamese

premier's office, he had reduced Lodge's presentation of the American position to ten items, which later became known as the "ten points." The detail of the young Polish diplomat's talks with Pham Van Dong are still not known. It is believed, however, that Dong expressed great skepticism about the Americans' sincerity. Lewandowski argued that this time the Americans really meant to negotiate. Dong is believed to have retorted that the Americans would use this initiative, like the thirty-seven-day bombing pause of the previous winter, for propaganda purposes. They would try to portray Lyndon Johnson as a man of peace and Ho Chi Minh as the continuing instigator of the war.

Lewandowski could have countered with the agreement which he, Lodge and D'Orlandi had made on the secrecy of the talks (an agreement that was to be first broken by the Poles a few months hence).

Pham Van Dong ultimately agreed, according to versions of the story authorized later by Polish sources, to a meeting between American and North Vietnamese representatives to explore possibilities of negotiations. His stipulation was secrecy. No more must be done in Hanoi, he said, and if any talks were to be held, they must remain absolutely confidential. It is believed that he worried not only about sabotage of the initiative by the Chinese and the hawkish element in Hanoi but also about the effect talks would have on the cadre of the National Liberation Front in South Vietnam and the army fighting there. The fear was that the fighters in the South, thinking that peace was coming, would lay down their arms and return to private life to await a settlement.

Lewandowski received, then, a "yes" in Hanoi to his proposition, but the Polish government did not, it was said, really take it that way.

An Eastern European diplomat, discussing the matter a year later in Washington, said: "You must understand the Asian mind. When they say 'yes' they sometimes mean 'maybe.' When they say 'maybe' they sometimes mean 'no.' When they say 'no' they sometimes mean 'yes.' In this case, Lewandowski got a 'yes.' The Poles really took it as a 'maybe.' "

Armed with this brokerage license, Lewandowski flew back to Saigon on November 29. The following day he called

D'Orlandi to suggest another three-sided meeting. It was arranged for Thursday, December 1.

On that Thursday, assuming normal routine was observed,
four cablegrams went forward from the operational commands
of the Air Force and Navy in Southeast Asia to Honolulu and
Washington. Two of the cables—one from the Air Force and one
from the Navy—routinely reported the air actions over North
Vietnam during the previous twenty-four-hour period along with
a preliminary assessment of the damage. The other two—one
from the Air Force and one from the Navy—reported the targets
on the list to be struck during the next twenty-four hours, including December 2. The Hanoi area targets would have been
mentioned in those cables.

Meanwhile, Lodge, Lewandowski and D'Orlandi were together again for the first time in over two weeks. This time
Lewandowski did most of the talking as he reported on his trip
to Hanoi. He showed the other men the list of the ten points and
explained that these points represented a summation of the
position Lodge had described at the last meeting. He said he
had presented this position in Hanoi and that the North Vietnamese had agreed it could be used as a basis for talks. Since,
to Lewandowski's way of thinking, the ten points represented
the American position, he assumed he had produced agreement
from both sides for talks on the American terms. Further, he
was not even indicating any demands for preconditions to talks
from North Vietnam. Previously Hanoi had insisted that the
bombing of the North must stop unconditionally before talks
could occur.

Up to this juncture, the preliminary talks among the United
States, Poland and Italy (with, presumably, North Vietnam a
watchful monitor in the background) had gone on for five months
without any halt in the American bombing. The prospect of
having the talks continue, intensify and develop into secret face-
to-face meetings with the enemy—still without any change in
the bombing pattern—was one of great attraction to the Johnson

Administration. The American officials understood perfectly well how difficult it would be to convince public opinion—at home and abroad—of the need to resume the bombing, once stopped, if peace talks failed. It was this apparent lack of insistence by North Vietnam on a halt in the bombing that made the Marigold possibilities so appealing to the Administration.

The package looked good. But the wording of the ten points, Lodge knew, was not his own or the State Department's but Lewandowski's. Lodge had too much experience as a diplomat to pass judgment without consulting Washington.

He listened passively as Lewandowski discussed the points, perhaps with some instinct telling him they would subsequently become a matter of quiet dispute between the governments of Poland and the United States. What follows are not the points as Lewandowski presented them but the subjects apparently covered by them. The subjects may be instructive in indicating just how far the United States and North Vietnam, despite all their public utterances, were really willing to go in making peace in Vietnam:

1. The April 8, 1965, "four points" of Pham Van Dong as the basis for a settlement but not preconditions the United States had to accept before talks could begin.[5]

---

[5] For well over a year after they were published, the four points were interpreted by the United States as conditions the Administration had to accept before negotiations could begin even though the North Vietnamese never specifically said that. The four points are:

1. Recognition of the basic national rights of the Vietnamese people—peace, independence, sovereignty, unity and territorial integrity. According to the Geneva agreements, the U.S. government must withdraw from South Vietnam U.S. troops, military personnel and weapons of all kinds, dismantle all U.S. military bases there and cancel its military alliance with South Vietnam. It must end its policy of intervention and aggression in South Vietnam. According to the Geneva agreements, the U.S. government must stop its acts of war against North Vietnam and completely cease all encroachments on the territory and sovereignty of the DRV [the Democratic Republic of Vietnam].

2. Pending the peaceful reunification of Vietnam, while Vietnam is still temporarily divided into two zones the military provisions of the 1954 Geneva agreements on Vietnam must be strictly respected. The two zones must refrain from entering into any military alliance

2. The Geneva accords interpreted to bring them up to date.

3. The Manila Conference Declaration of October, 1966.

4. The unilateral cessation of the bombing of North Vietnam.

5. The withdrawal of North Vietnamese troops from South Vietnam.

6. A general cease-fire.

7. The problem of re-supplying troops of both sides in the South after the cease-fire and before the completion of withdrawal.

8. Principles on the organization of a new government.

9. Free elections to install a new government after agreement is reached.

10. An expanded role for the ICC in policing the settlement.

The fact that the topics, as presented here, are not in Lewandowski's wording cannot be overstressed. The wording was to become controversial. Communist sources have said the points were an accurate summary of Lodge's November presentation and that Lewandowski even used some of Lodge's exact language.

---

with foreign countries and there must be no foreign military bases, troops or military personnel in their respective territory.

3. The internal affairs of South Vietnam must be settled by the South Vietnamese people themselves in accordance with the program of the NFLSV (the National Liberation Front of South Vietnam) without any foreign interference.

4. The peaceful reunification of Vietnam is to be settled by the Vietnamese people in both zones without any foreign interference.

It was the third point which, in implying recognition of the NLF program, the United States could not accept. In their book *The United States in Vietnam,* Professors George McT. Kahin and John W. Lewis argue that the third point was originally published in Hanoi with commas enclosing the phrase "in accordance with the program of the NFLSV." This punctuation, while still ambiguous, could make the point relatively innocuous and possibly acceptable to the United States. Kahin and Lewis say the Chinese published the point in *People's Daily* in a manner which translates this way: "According to the program of the Southern National Liberation Front, the affairs of the South must be settled by the southern people themselves without foreign interference."

This formulation seems even more innocuous.

American officials, while declining to disclose Lewandowski's version, have ridiculed it as a hopeless "mishmash" of language. "It will never win the Metternich Award for distinguished diplomatic prose," one American official said.

But Americans acknowledge that the points were based on Lodge's presentation and that the ideas expressed in them were indeed American ideas.

On the night of December 1, the ten points, encoded in a Nodis/Marigold cable, were sent back to Washington. Dean Rusk was then preparing for a tour of the Far East on his way to an annual NATO Council meeting in Paris.

As Lodge had anticipated, the State Department raised questions from the start about the Lewandowski points, particularly the point about withdrawal of North Vietnamese troops. The Department instructed Lodge to accept the ten points as a basis for further discussion; he was told, however, to explain that clarifications—particularly of the troop question—would be necessary.

Once again matters were beginning to hinge more and more on just what Lewandowski's authority as a broker was. If he was a legitimate representative of North Vietnam, he now had authorization from responsible officials in both Washington and Hanoi to carry the initiative further.

When Lodge received his instructions on December 2, he signaled D'Orlandi for another meeting.

Over the Hanoi area on December 2 there was a break in the northeasterly monsoon for the first time in several weeks. For a brief time the thunderstorms, mist, fog and low-hanging clouds characteristic of monsoon weather disappeared. Air Force weathermen certified Friday, December 2, as a good day for precision bombing.

In D'Orlandi's apartment that day, Henry Cabot Lodge, Jr., had the pleasure to inform the Polish and Italian diplomats that the ten points, with some reservations, would be acceptable to the United States as a basis for discussions. He pointed up the problem of recognizing the existence of North Vietnamese troops in the South so that their eventual evacuation could be accomplished. According to one report, it was suggested that one way the recognition problem could be avoided would be to remove all the North Vietnamese troops beforehand. But if this was said, it was never understood by the Poles, at least, as an ultimatum or as a precondition to talks.

Seizing on that acceptance, Lewandowski proposed that the United States have a representative in Warsaw ready to talk directly to the North Vietnamese as early as the following Tuesday, December 6.

Once again Lodge said he would have to ask Washington if that was agreeable, and with the exciting prospect of a direct North Vietnamese–American talk taking place in only four days, the meeting ended.

The monsoon break meant activity at a half-dozen United States air bases in Thailand—bases with names like Khorat, Ubon and Nakhon Phanon—and on the aircraft carriers at Yankee Station. Powerful fighter-bombers were worked over, loaded and warmed up for a day's work.

Their target—for the first time in six months—Hanoi.

Thus, the same day that Lewandowski proposed a meeting date for the United States and North Vietnam, fifty to sixty F-105 Thunderchiefs and F-4C Phantoms of the U.S. Air Force and fifteen to twenty carrier-based Navy jets blazed into the Hanoi area, out of those clear skies, and dropped tons of 500-pound and 750-pound bombs. The Phantoms attacked a fuel dump fourteen and one half miles north of the capital. The Thunderchiefs, flying cover, took out four radar sites and an antiaircraft missile emplacement. The Navy planes hit a truck depot at Vandien described as five miles south of the capital. Other Navy planes hit a fuel dump forty miles northeast of Hanoi.

It was an intense attack but not, by any means, the heaviest thus far in the war. The losses to the United States were great, however. Eight planes—a record number for a single raid over North Vietnam—were shot down.

In Saigon, an American spokesman said the raids near Hanoi were consistent with United States policy and that improved weather was responsible for their being carried out on that day. He indicated the targets might have been hit earlier if pilots had not been thwarted by the weather.

The following day, Saturday, December 3, the North Vietnamese charged that American bombs had fallen in the southern suburbs of Hanoi. The North Vietnamese lodged a protest with the ICC, charging the Americans had again escalated the war. The charge, broadcast by Hanoi Radio and monitored in Tokyo, received little attention around the world.

While North Vietnam was airing this charge, Lodge, who had received word from Washington, met once again with D'Orlandi and Lewandowski. The session was the climax of their long association in D'Orlandi's "diplomatic exercise in style."

It should have been a joyous meeting in the Durong Pasteur apartment. But the bombing attacks of the day before changed that. When the three men got down to business, Lewandowski told Lodge that such attacks could do great damage to the initiative. Lewandowski was obviously delivering a warning, but it was not stern.

Lodge, in reply, said the raids had long been planned. They could not have been canceled, he continued, without compromising the secrecy of the initiative they had nursed for so long. A stand-down, he explained, involved changing orders for thousands of men. Some of them would talk of the change in plans and inevitably that talk would get to reporters. The newsmen, he said, would probably assume that the reason for a stand-down was a possible peace move. This would get into print and, as a result, the secrecy of their talks might be endangered.

There had been no conscious coordination between the raids and the diplomatic initiative, Lodge told Lewandowski and D'Orlandi. He tried to make it clear that the raids were certainly not intended to destroy the initiative, and he asked Lewandowski, in turn, to make that clear to Hanoi.

The Polish diplomat seemed to understand.

Then Lodge turned to his good news. He reported that overnight he had received word from Washington that an American representative would be prepared to meet a North Vietnamese representative in Warsaw on December 6. Lodge seemed to think that a meeting would take place on that day. D'Orlandi, though he had understood Lewandowski to say "as early as December 6" the day before, could see how Lodge might make the assumption.

Now the work of these three diplomats finally was done. The initiative would be moving on to a new venue. New people would take over what they had started. Hopefully, at the newer, higher level, something would come of it all.

D'Orlandi, proposing a toast, poured a ceremonial glass of Scotch whiskey for each man. Concern about the bombing dissolved as the three men hoisted their glasses.

"I thought I had done something worthwhile in my life," Lodge told an associate several months later in explaining how high his hopes were that Saturday in Saigon.

That same Saturday in Washington, officials learned for the first time from their newspapers of the Hanoi bombings of the day before.

The instant reaction among those familiar with the delicate status of Marigold was surprise—such as that registered by the official who read of the raids at breakfast and muttered, "Oh my God."

He was not alone. Another official said: "The bombing on the second took everyone by surprise."

Later, the surprise was to dissolve into consternation. How could this be allowed to happen? they asked.

And then during the succeeding days, as Administration officials reviewed the targets they had approved for bombing in the Hanoi area during any break in the monsoon, the consternation would become what one described as "grumblings and murmurings" of dissent on the seventh floor of the State Department.

At the LBJ Ranch in the remote Texas hill country, Lyndon Johnson, recovered now from his surgery, had more than the Vietnam war on his mind that Saturday morning. Although the President is never out of touch with his government thanks to an incredibly complex communications network, there is nothing in the communications system that demands he maintain a continuous interest. He was preparing that morning to do the thing he likes most—meet the people of the Rio Grande River valley. There would be cheering crowds as he met with Gustavo Diaz Ordaz to inspect the $78 million Amistad (Friendship) Dam across the Rio Grande River.

With the President was Secretary of State Rusk, who was to leave the next day for two weeks abroad, including a tour of the Far East. If the two men reviewed the Marigold initiative before they parted, that fact has not yet been disclosed.

As the day wore on in Washington, Ben Read's office carried out a little reorganization of the State Department's communications grid to prepare the circuit from Foggy Bottom to Warsaw for its part in Marigold.

CHAPTER THREE

Picking Targets at Tuesday Lunch

How did it happen that a foreign capital was bombed by United States Air Force and Navy planes during a war of limited means and objectives while the highest officials in Washington simply forgot they had approved the target?

There are two answers to that question. One is short, the other very long.

The short answer is this:

Only one man in the Department of State in late 1966—spending all of his time on the situation in Vietnam—knew both the details of the Marigold initiative and the forthcoming target plans. His name was Leonard Unger. As Deputy Assistant Secretary of State for East Asian and Pacific Affairs, he had little decision-making authority in running the war.

Thus, even if the relationship between the war effort and the secret search for peace had struck him as requiring co-ordination on December 1, Unger would not have been able to cancel or postpone the air strikes on his own. He could have alerted his immediate superior, Assistant Secretary William Bundy, to the possible complications for Marigold if Hanoi were bombed. Bundy, in turn, would have needed approval from Rusk, and probably from the President, to ground the bombers.

The procedures then in effect at the State Department for initiating a stand-down from a scheduled air raid were, officials have since acknowledged, far from ideal.

The long answer involves an explanation of just how the United States government makes national security and foreign policy decisions; how, in particular, it makes Vietnam war decisions.

The answer starts with the fact that Lyndon Baines Johnson has gathered into his own hands more decision-making authority than he can handle. As one frequent White House visitor put it: "The only place important decisions are made here in Washington is in the mind of Lyndon Johnson. And that could happen any time—at four o'clock in the morning, at lunch, in the bathtub."

Deep down within the bureaucracy of the State Department, working under William Bundy's deputy, there is a traditional, though enlarged, kind of "country desk" for Vietnam. It is called the "Vietnam Working Group" and was organized originally as a special task force to oversee the growing American involvement in the war.

Each of the group's ten members studies a particular segment of the Vietnam problem. For example, Heyward Isham, a forty-year-old Foreign Service officer, had the responsibility in 1966 for keeping track of peace possibilities. Isham was kept informed of the Marigold initiative during its early stages but he was removed from the varsity in mid-November when Ben Read "cut the squad."

Charles Conway Flowerree, forty-five, a diplomat who graduated from the United States Naval Academy, was the group's specialist on military matters. As such, he knew of the impending Hanoi raids in late 1966. But he knew nothing of Marigold —at least after the critical stage began—until he read about some of it in the newspapers months after the initiative collapsed.

These two examples indicate that the Working Group had lost whatever real authority it ever might have had in Vietnam decision-making. The group has become in large part a speakers' bureau and propaganda agency for the Johnson Administration. Its members make trips throughout the country, talking about the war to Kiwanis clubs, women's organizations, school assemblies and the like. In addition, the group functions as a service organization, preparing the memoranda and analyses requested by superiors.

"We get all the information about the war," one member said. "We are kept ignorant of a very small amount of information—point 0 0 0, an infinitesimal amount of the total flow of traffic."

The infinitesimal amount missing was precisely the information that counted. It related to the serious peace moves and it prevented the group from coordinating—or even suggesting the coordination of—the military effort with the peace effort. In short, it prevented the group from raising a danger flag on the targeting in the Hanoi area late in 1966.

With this kind of operational paralysis, the State Department has been something less than a fountainhead of innovative diplomacy.[1]

It has added layers of personnel and has buttressed those new layers with organizations outside the normal chain of command.

As a result, one official said: "In the last analysis, the State Department is organized atrociously to handle the Vietnam war. The difficulty arises from the fact that in the last two or three years the Vietnam desk has been moving successively further and further to the top of the government. Now the chief of the desk is Lyndon B. Johnson, the chief of the desk in the Defense Department is Robert S. McNamara and the desk chief in the State Department is Dean Rusk.

"The problem with this is that each one of these men has much more to do than worry only about Vietnam. Despite the fact that they are running the war and seeking the peace, you have to go all the way down to the deputy assistant secretary level until you find someone working only on Vietnam."

At the same time the President and his lieutenants operate

---

[1] One recent report quoted a State Department desk officer for a small country as saying he sometimes needed as many as twenty-nine different clearances to send a routine cable to the American Embassy.

the Vietnam desk, such things as a riot in an urban ghetto, a seizure of a ship by North Korea, a war in the Middle East or a gold crisis intrudes on their time. In fact, such problems have often preoccupied them and the Vietnam war has become secondary in their minds.

The device the top officials in the Johnson Administration have worked out for coordinating their efforts is the "Tuesday lunch," named because it convenes usually—but not always—on Tuesday at one o'clock in the family dining room on the second floor of the White House.

To the extent that the President shares important decision-making at all, he does much of it at the Tuesday lunch with the Secretaries of Defense and State, Walt Rostow and Press Secretary George Christian. Occasionally, General Wheeler, the Joint Chiefs chairman, CIA Director Richard Helms and others sit in.

The Tuesday lunch has long since replaced the Cabinet, the National Security Council or the informal, ad hoc "ex comms" (executive committees) of the Kennedy years as the court of last resort on national security matters, foreign affairs and, particularly, Vietnam.

The President and his aides gather around a mahogany Duncan Phyfe oval table in a room papered with scenes depicting the surrender of Cornwallis at Yorktown. They hold their councils of war and peace—covering a wide spectrum of subjects—while black-coated waiters quietly serve them.

The luncheon group is never more specific than when it turns, as it often does, to consideration of individual bombing targets in North Vietnam. The fact is that no road junction, petroleum storage tank, railroad bridge, factory, warehouse, airfield, antiaircraft gun or missile battery, dock or truck depot in the northern part of North Vietnam is struck by American airplanes without the approval of Lyndon Johnson and his Tuesday lunch partners.

The targets submitted for their approval are selected from a master list in the Pentagon known as the "JCS Target List." This is a compilation kept by the Joint Chiefs of Staff of every possible target in North Vietnam, ranging from the least significant to those, like the harbor of Haiphong, that could provoke the Soviet Union and Red China if they were hit. The targets on the list are suggested by field commanders, analysts of reconnaissance photos at Pacific Fleet headquarters in Honolulu and experts working for the Joint Chiefs in the Pentagon.

These targets are "fixed" or strategic installations in the North that have no direct relationship to the ground fighting in South Vietnam. (Those with such a relationship—infiltration routes, for example—can be struck on the order of the American military commander in Saigon without approval from Washington.)

Before the fixed targets ever get to the Tuesday lunch group, they are researched with excruciating care first by officers on the Joint Chiefs' staff and then by civilian officials in the Pentagon. Finally the Defense Secretary sends them to Ben Read, who feeds them into the State Department information grid for study at several levels. State's interest is to see that the political and diplomatic risks of striking any given target are minimized. The State Department analysts study the possibilities, for example, that the property of third nations might be jeopardized in striking a given target or that foreign diplomats visiting in Hanoi might be embarrassed.

The target suggestions are culled, and those ultimately selected presumably must support the three objectives of the bombing McNamara outlined in testimony in 1966 before the House Armed Services Committee:

> (1) To act to improve the morale of the South Vietnamese forces by attacking the North; there is no question but what the bombing will accomplish that; (2) to reduce the flow and/or increase the cost of the infiltration of men and equipment into the South. There is no question but what the capacity of the system has been cut back. . . .
>
> The third objective was to decrease the will of the North Vietnamese to continue the effort in the South at a time when we had proved to them they couldn't win in the South; that is, *affect their will in such a way as to move them to a satisfactory settlement.* (Italics by authors) We haven't reached that point yet. I cannot guarantee to you that the bombing will be a major factor when we do reach it, but I think it may be.

That statement, repeated often by the Pentagon, points up better than anything else on the public record the essentially political nature of the bombing of North Vietnam. If the bombing, then, in any way inhibits the possibility for a satisfactory settlement, it would appear to be undermining the very policy that sanctioned it.

As a result of all the staff work in the Pentagon and at the State Department, the authorization requests for each target were reduced to a single sheet of paper—a kind of report card—on which the suggested strikes were described in summary. Each individual sheet contained a check list for four items:

1. The military advantage of striking the proposed target.
2. The risk to American aircraft and pilots in a raid.
3. The danger that the strike might widen the war by forcing other countries into the fighting.
4. The danger of heavy civilian casualties.

At the Tuesday lunch, President Johnson and his advisers worked over each of the target sheets like schoolteachers grading examination papers. Each of the men graded each of the targets in the four categories.

The decisions were made on the basis of averaged-out grades.

A steel mill near Hanoi, the lunch group might decide, had a marginal military value, but since both the war-widening danger of striking it and the risk of civilian casualties were low, it would be authorized. On the other hand, dropping mines into Haiphong harbor had a great and obvious military value, but it also had a great and obvious war-widening danger and a high risk to American pilots. So the lunch group refused this authorization.

In this manner the President and his principal advisers, working over a lunch table in the White House, showed their intense concern with individual road junctions, clusters of trucks and structures down to small buildings in a land thousands of miles away. Their obvious concern lent great weight to the contention that never has more care been taken in making sure that limited war-making objectives were not being exceeded.

The Tuesday lunch group operated with such extreme caution that often highly sensitive targets were authorized on a one-time-only basis. If the objective was not knocked out on the first try, the Air Force or Navy had to reapply for a second chance. There were times when the pilots were given only a specific time period in which to accomplish their mission. Most of the time, though, targets were placed on the authorization list and kept there until the military was satisfied they had been destroyed.

Every apparent contingency was accounted for. Except one. Once the targets were placed on the strike list, none of the officials who selected them—that is, none of the Tuesday lunch group members—took responsibility for watching for the exact time when particular targets were to be struck. (There were, of course, exceptions to this, as when President Johnson himself kept vigil the night of the "little monks.")

Once targets were authorized, the Defense Secretary carried the target sheets back to the Pentagon and released the authorizations to the Joint Chiefs. Then the orders flowed down the chain of command through the National Military Command Center in the Pentagon to the Pacific headquarters at Honolulu. There they would be divided among the services and finally the orders sent out to the Yankee Station carriers and, via Seventh Air Force headquarters in Saigon, to the air bases in Thailand.

Depending on the weather and the operational status of the bases and ships, the time between authorization at the White House lunch and the actual strike could be anywhere from a day or two to several weeks. December 2 was the first clear day over the Hanoi area targets after the authorizations were given at the November 15 Tuesday lunch in the White House.

There was a system designed to coordinate the bombing authorizations for fixed targets with any sudden diplomatic activity. It was a fail-safe system that optimally allowed review of weeks-old authorizations in light of the most up-to-date information. But in 1966 it had apparently fallen into disuse.

The fail-safe system worked this way:

Each day the local commanders had to send cablegrams forward through channels, detailing the targets they planned to strike within the following twenty-four hours. The cables from the Thailand bases went to Saigon and from there to Honolulu. The cables from Yankee Station went directly to Honolulu (with copies to Saigon). Fail Safe Number 1 would have been the State Department's liaison man and political adviser on Admiral Ulysses S. Grant Sharp's staff in Honolulu. But no one at Pacific headquarters, including the liaison, knew of Marigold.

From Honolulu, the cables went to the National Military Command Center in the Pentagon, where the State Department kept another liaison man—Fail Safe Number 2. He did not know of Marigold either.

From the NMCC, the message was sent directly to Ben Read, Fail Safe Number 3. Though he knew of Marigold, he apparently did not read the December 1 target cable. After all, these routine daily lists had been coming across his desk for almost two years and there was only so much he could read. If he did read the cable, he did not make the connection between the Hanoi bombing and the Marigold initiative. (The suggestion of a December 6 meeting, one must remember, was not made until December 2 in Saigon.)

From Read's office, the message continued through the national security information grid, going downstairs to Colonel Robert M. Cowherd in Room 6209 of the State Department. Colonel Cowherd was the military assistant to Unger, and Fail Safe Number 4. Though Unger knew of Marigold, Cowherd did not.

One of Cowherd's daily duties was the preparation, from the cable, of an easily understandable list of upcoming targets. He would send this list to the State Department's Operations Center, where the information was transferred to a map. The map, Fail Safe Number 5, would be sent to Read's office, where it was available to anyone with a nodis clearance.

Apparently there was little interest in that map during the first day or two or three in December, 1966. It appears to have been treated as another extraneous piece of paper to be avoided by all bureaucrats.[2]

---

[2] The paper record that is growing in the archives of the State Department may be prodigious but is nonetheless of questionable value. "The more I see of this government," one official commented, "the more I realize no one knows all of what goes into a decision. I mean literally

There is no evidence that the Tuesday lunch group members studied the map as a matter of routine. In fact, some officials said that up to early December, 1966, there was a lack of vigilance. A high appointee of President Johnson recognized this problem when he was asked if the luncheon members did a good job of running the war.

"The Tuesday lunch is a terrible way to achieve effective coordination," he answered. "The problem is that all the people making the decisions at the lunch know the least about Vietnam. Wheeler knows most, McNamara is next and Helms is third. I'm a believer in bureaucracy, in adequately staffing a decision. The people who have the information should participate in the decisions."

What the official did not say is that neither Wheeler nor Helms is invited to all the Tuesday lunch meetings. In fact, they are absent more often than present at those sessions.

He also did not say that neither Helms nor anyone else in the CIA learned of Marigold until its dying stages in December. The CIA, the organization primarily responsible for gathering intelligence in North Vietnam, apparently had no role at all in peace-seeking.

The list of officials and organizations—the CIA, the Vietnam Working Group, the State Department's liaison people with the armed services, the military commanders themselves—not having information about Marigold and/or peace initiatives in general was formidable.

But there was one group that had a surfeit of both information and ideas about peace—it went under the initials "AH"

---

no one. All of the really important decisions are made as a result of unreported phone calls and talks without anything put in writing." Even allowing for exaggeration, that statement is sobering. The official said that the record will not even show when the President himself made decisions. "If the President tells someone he wants something done, that guy isn't going to say in his cables 'the President wants it.' There's no need to. Cables and memoranda," he said, "are often written merely to show one has read a cable he received or to protect one's own position." As an example of the problems involved, he related that when Ellsworth Bunker arrived on the scene as American ambassador in Saigon, he surveyed the burdensome cable flow, and as one of his first actions, he fired off a message to Dean Rusk that said, in almost these words, "Stop telling me how to stop sucking eggs."

on the State Department's organization chart. "AH" stood for Averell Harriman, the seventy-five-year-old peace-seeking old soldier of diplomacy. Harriman and Chester Cooper developed a response for every peace move by North Vietnam or other countries. One observer said of their operation: "They were in charge of dreaming up scenarios, dreaming up ideas, chasing will-o'-the-wisps, pushing, cajoling." Though grand in concept, AH was small in size and had to seek out staff from other offices to do its tedious research work. "It was not a tidy operation," one official commented.

Not many officials in the State Department were thinking of ways to start negotiations. Bundy helped frequently but not always; sometimes Walt Rostow's older but less prominent brother, Eugene Victor Debs Rostow, the Undersecretary of State for Political Affairs, would show an interest. If Nicholas Katzenbach had time, he would participate. Often Ben Read would lend a hand. But generally the Harriman operation withered away as the war deepened, until finally it had become an office concerned primarily with prisoner-of-war care and exchanges.

In October, 1967, Cooper quietly left AH and the government entirely to rejoin IDA, where, though he continued to consult on peace-seeking matters, he busied himself with research on his long-standing interest in the crisis in the nation's cities. His departure was an indication that the existence of AH on the organization chart had become a front, an office bearing a prestigious name, designed to show the nation and the world that the United States had a vast peace-seeking network in operation. In fact, it didn't. AH—the man and the office—had increasingly less to do.

"Harriman is getting older and older, and the care and feeding of Averell is getting more and more difficult," one official in the national security bureaucracy said in late 1967. "He really doesn't have very much to do. The President can't really tell him he's in charge of peace and send him off. It's got to be in Rusk's hands. He can't be Secretary of State and not be in charge of it all. Cooper comes over once a week or so from IDA to check on what's going on and to be ready in case something appears on negotiations."

Another well-placed source implied that what was true after Cooper left was also true from the beginning: that in the balance of forces in Washington, those who were urging the waging of an intense—if limited—war far outweighed those in favor of seeking a negotiated, compromise peace. He said: "It turned out that Harriman had absolutely no mandate. On the one hand you had a carefully organized military machine; on the other there was Harriman with no real mandate. I'd say there was a slight imbalance there."

From all of the above, some conclusions can be reached as to how well the government was organized to seek peace.

It was poorly organized.

Consider:

The President, his Secretary of State and his Secretary of Defense, when discussing Vietnam, spent much of their time dealing with the most minute and precise problems. They spent precious minutes or hours, perhaps, dealing with the fate of a single road junction or cluster of wooden shacks. Along with all their other world-wide concerns and along with the President's domestic concerns as well, this left little time to formulate peace proposals carefully. The bombing program was intended to bring the North Vietnamese to the negotiating table. Yet the American leaders spent so much time planning the bombing, they had difficulty toning it down at a particularly sensitive point to provide the best possible chance for peace negotiations to occur.

The people who had the time to plan such coordination were bureaucratically isolated. Their authority had long since been taken over by the Tuesday lunch group.

The man in charge of finding peace was little more than a figurehead.

The fail-safe system failed because in the last analysis the men who operated it failed.

An Air Force officer involved in planning the raids heard from a State Department official about the original complaints on the December 2 bombing of Hanoi shortly after it occurred. "Jesus Christ," he said, "if you'd have told us about it, we could have stopped the bombings. If you want to work hard enough, you can stop the bombings in an hour."

Nobody remembered to work that hard in December, 1966. A close associate of the President, commenting on the Marigold initiative, said later: "You will never get the inside story."

Why not?

"Because it makes our government look so bad."

CHAPTER FOUR

Grumblings and Murmurings

It was near midnight in the communications room of the concrete-and-glass American Embassy on the Aleje Ujazdowski in Warsaw when the insistent clatter of a teletype machine coming to life jarred the stillness. The paper in the machine jumped forward several lines and the carriage ran freely in place for a while. Then it darted across the paper and the communications clerk read:

FLASH

NODIS

The date was Saturday, December 3, 1966. The first words on the awakened teletype signaled that Ben Read, back in Washington, had completed his realignment of the Marigold information network and was tuning in Ambassador John A. Gronouski for his role. Gronouski might be superseded or later joined by an official from Washington. But as a starter, with the proper instructions, he would talk to the North Vietnamese. Gronouski was enough of a politician, diplomat and intellectual to carry out at least the preliminary arrangements and to set up the early meetings with the North Vietnamese.

His certification as an intellectual was his degrees (B.A., M.A., Ph.D.) from the University of Wisconsin. His political credits included service as a tax research director and tax commissioner in Wisconsin, the organization of John F. Kennedy's presidential campaign there, and his service in Washington as postmaster general. His attributes as an understanding human being were best expressed by his constant good humor and his expansive, enthusiastic Midwestern progressive optimism that made him believe in trying to make dreams come true.

He was almost certainly eased out of his postmaster generalship in 1965 to make way for Lawrence F. O'Brien, a member of the original John F. Kennedy entourage who later became a political adviser to Lyndon Baines Johnson. Mr. Johnson made Gronouski ambassador to Warsaw on September 11, 1965, and if he has since won friends and influenced Polish Communists in favor of the United States, it is not because of his own Polish ancestry. He spoke hardly a word of Polish and picked up almost none after he arrived in Warsaw.

"Gronouski speaks Polish like I speak Chinese," one Polish diplomat said.

But Gronouski was nonetheless respected in his post—his instincts were good, he had a realistic empathy for the Polish people, and as the only American then carrying on official talks with the Chinese Communists, he had learned a thing or two about hard-nosed diplomacy since arriving in Warsaw.

Before he could carry out his Marigold assignment, he had to be fully informed. So Ben Read ordered the entire collection of Marigold papers—five months' worth—fed into the Warsaw circuit. Gronouski had to learn intimately the details of months of deliberations and discussions before he could speak intelligently with either Polish Foreign Minister Adam Rapacki, who was to arrange the first United States–North Vietnamese session, or the North Vietnamese negotiator.

As soon as he saw the nodis heading on the incoming cable, the Warsaw communications clerk knew exactly what to do. He by-passed the Foreign Service duty officer in charge of the embassy that Saturday night and went instead to the desk of the Marine guard on duty outside the elevator on the second floor of the building. He asked the guard to please call the ambassador and inform him a nodis message was arriving. Only the ambassador could receive nodis traffic.

Awakened at his residence, Gronouski dressed, went quickly to the embassy and immediately began reading. He read. And he read. He read, with increasing fascination, throughout the night. He had never before heard of Marigold. Now he was learning he would have a part in it. This was to be the first of many sleepless nights during the coming weeks, and he became excited at the prospect of taking part in an effort to bring peace between his country and the enemy in Southeast Asia. He began suffering, in short, from what others in the State Department have begun calling the "Nobel Peace Prize syndrome." He envisioned himself as a future Nobel Prize winner for helping settle the Vietnam war.

But first he had to absorb the record as it spilled relentlessly out of the teletype. The ambassador's reading continued into the next day. By then he had called in his secretary to help in typing up the messages that came in a seemingly endless torrent from Washington. Sunday night, December 4, he was still reading. In all, except for a few hours' sleep during the period, he read for thirty solid hours.

During that time American airplanes again staged raids on North Vietnam. They flew back into the Hanoi area, striking the Yenvien railway yard six miles northeast of the city, according to the Saigon communiqué, and the Hagia fuel dump, fourteen miles north. The fuel dump was the same one hit in the raid two days before. The Thunderchiefs also hit antiaircraft emplacements. Jacques Maolic, the Agence France-Presse correspondent in Hanoi, later said the planes employed a change in tactics —approaching the city from the northeast, emerging from behind a mountain range, diving through the monsoon overcast, releasing their bombs and sweeping out over the Gulf of Tonkin. The tactics, according to Maolic, caught the North Vietnamese antiaircraft gunners, who had been so effective two days before, off guard, and they reacted slowly.

The North Vietnamese would later charge—and the Americans would deny—that residential areas of the city had been struck during these raids. Since it was not known that a delicate peace initiative was under way, there was no outcry at the time from world leaders or the press about the American raids.

A year later an American official was to say, in discussing why this December 4 raid was not canceled, that the first warning from Lewandowski did not arrive in Washington until after the second raid—the one of December 4. Thus, the American officials said they had no way of knowing that the raids placed Marigold in jeopardy. If the warning did arrive before, he said (admitting it was possible), it did not arrive soon enough for the State Department to have canceled the second raid. If the new raid was going to be canceled, the decision would necessarily have to have been made by Saturday, December 3, in Washington because of the thirteen-hour time difference. The President was off on the Mexican border enjoying a Rio Grande dam inspection; the Secretary of State was accompanying him. William Bundy was preparing for his trip to the Far East. Averell Harriman, the peace-seeker, was visiting Europe on a trip that was part vacation and part business.[1]

Those officials in Washington who were troubled that Saturday by the effect the first raid of December 2 might have on Marigold did not, after surveying the complexity of getting

---

[1] Harriman had left Washington on November 29 to go to London to deliver a lecture memorializing his old friend Winston Churchill. On December 1 he went to Paris to spend five days on holiday. The papers said he did not plan to speak to any French government officials. The trip was, then, all very innocuous, except for one thing. Another visitor who also arrived December 1 was Soviet Premier Alexei N. Kosygin. Coincidence? The official version is yes. But as the Washington *Post* mentioned in a short story announcing the Harriman trip:

Harriman, it was recalled here, went on a vacation to Europe in July, 1965, and returned after conferences with Russian Premier Alexei N. Kosygin, three other prime ministers, four chiefs of state and numerous other European officials.

Averell Harriman is a great one for busmen's holidays. The 1965 vacation to which the *Post* referred, in retrospect, appears almost certain to have been a visit to tell the foreigners that Lyndon Johnson had planned to increase troop strength in South Vietnam.

It is almost too much to expect that Harriman would, by coincidence, arrive in the same city where Kosygin was and not try to talk to him.

a decision from the widely scattered men, think there was time to cancel the second raid. They were also concerned about the effect a sudden stand-down of the bombers would have on the secrecy of Marigold.

The chances are good that Gronouski also did not realize the importance of that new raid—if indeed he had been informed of it—as he finished his background reading at 5:30 A.M. Monday and went home to freshen up before calling on Foreign Minister Rapacki a few hours later. Gronouski expected that day to set a time and place for his first peace negotiation with the North Vietnamese the following day.

The American ambassador easily fell into the spirit of secrecy. He told no one what he was up to. But nevertheless the word spread quickly through the small embassy staff. When the staff members came to work that Monday morning, they learned that the boss had been in his office all weekend. They reasoned that the only issue in the world important enough to keep the ambassador at his desk from midnight Saturday to 5:30 A.M. Monday was Vietnam. They reasoned further—correctly, of course—that if Vietnam was involved, the only possible part Warsaw could play was in negotiating peace.

Despite this good reasoning by Foreign Service officers, staff members, clerks, general services employees, secretaries and even Polish citizens working for the embassy, not a word of the ambassador's comings and goings during the next month leaked out in a way that damaged the initiative. This fact contrasted strikingly with the belief in Washington that American officials cannot keep secrets even when peace is at stake.

To maintain the secrecy, Gronouski even decided to walk, rather than ride, in order to escape the attention that would be shown if his car pulled up in front of the Foreign Ministry building day after day. It takes nine minutes on a cold, early December morning, with a light snow in the air, to walk from the American Embassy to the Polish Foreign Ministry. It is a pleasant walk in one of the few districts in Warsaw that was not leveled by the vindictive Nazi armies during the Polish uprising of 1945. And just before Gronouski reached the ministry, he strode past a little entranceway marked "Mausoleum" in the

Ministry of Education. It is the entranceway to the former Gestapo headquarters, prison and torture chamber for the Warsaw district. The Poles maintain it now as a museum. They cannot easily forget what the Germans did a generation ago or what war means for them. Though there is a great reservoir of good feeling for the United States in Poland, the Poles do see the danger of the Vietnam war widening and involving the two superpowers—one, the Soviet Union, a patron by force and geographical location; the other, the United States, a friend by emotion and national ties—in a world war that would again make their homeland a battleground.

They also fear the Southeast Asian war will detract Soviet interest from Europe, as it has American, and that the Germans (the *West* Germans in the official propaganda line) will take advantage of this to revive warlike ways and their historic drive to recapture their eastern territories.

The secret of the Polish desire to settle the Vietnam war, then, is wrapped up not only in their yearning for a place in the sun—as one diplomat expressed it—but also in their compulsion to avoid a new world war.

Finally Gronouski was sitting in Rapacki's office on the second floor of the red sandstone Foreign Ministry building. Instead of making arrangements with Rapacki for a meeting the next day with the North Vietnamese, Gronouski learned there would be no meeting. Rapacki was vague on just why not. But he did mention in a "fatherly way" that the bombings of the previous weekend were not the kind of acts that could do the United States any good in trying to bring about negotiations. It seemed to Gronouski that Rapacki was only expressing his own offhand opinion and not any feeling of Hanoi's. It was a gentlemanly discussion. Gronouski listened to the warning and replied by noting that such acts of terrorism as the mortaring of Tansonnhut Airfield and a billet in downtown Saigon the day before would not exactly help the North Vietnamese cause either.

The bombings were the first of two points raised at the meeting. The second was the question of clarification desired by the Johnson Administration of the ten points. Gronouski noted that anything as general as the ten points, which the United

States government did not even consider agenda items but, instead, "topic headings," would have to be clarified by the negotiating parties.

Gronouski made it clear that he did not want to clarify the substance of the ten points with the Poles before direct negotiations with the North Vietnamese began. However, he did try, according to one official, to establish the American belief that the ten points could only be considered topic headings for discussion and not the basis for any final agreement.

The United States was never sure Rapacki understood this distinction. And it was wary about entering into any negotiation without that matter being understood perfectly. In fact, it appears that the closer the Johnson Administration came to actual talks, the more wary it grew. Discussing the clarification question a year later, an official said: "We still don't know to what degree we had to subscribe to the language of the ten points. We don't know whether they were topic headings, agenda items, points of departure for discussions or whether we had to accept them as written in blood. We had to make sure that our attendance at a meeting did not create the misunderstanding that we accepted their language."

There were indications later (in the form of news reports inspired by Polish sources) that Rapacki understood Gronouski as saying the United States wanted clarification of the points before it met with North Vietnam. There were even some in the State Department who read the record who said this was the case. But the Americans involved subsequently insisted Gronouski did make it clear that he wished to clarify these points with the North Vietnamese during the face-to-face discussions, not with the Poles beforehand.

The Gronouski-Rapacki talks must have been confusing. Rapacki has been described as "elliptical," and anyone who has ever listened to Gronouski give testimony knows that he is not an articulate extemporaneous speaker.

Further, complications during the next ten days could have developed from the old secrecy bugaboo. Gronouski, to keep faith with his cabled instructions on this point, told no one in the embassy what he was up to and he took no one—not even a translator—with him to the Foreign Ministry meetings. Thus, he had no one to keep notes on the talks. Since his memory for names and dates is questionable, his reports to the State Department could have been confusing.[2]

The first meeting broke up inconclusively. Gronouski was not even sure after the session whether Rapacki was really speaking for Hanoi or on his own authority.

The American, filled nonetheless with hope, went back to his office and sent to Washington the first of the cables he was to describe later as containing "wishful thinking." The only discordant note was the Polish warning on the bombing. In the meantime, he maintained frequent telephone contact with Michalowski to plan for still another preliminary meeting.

The next day, Tuesday, December 6, Gronouski still had hopes he could meet with the North Vietnamese, as Lewandowski had indicated in Saigon four days before. He went back to the Foreign Ministry. Once again he encountered Rapacki's studied obscurity, criticism of the bombing and questioning about just what sort of clarifications the United States wanted on the ten points.

Gronouski discussed the clarifications with him. The most important was over the question of acknowledging the presence of North Vietnamese troops in the South. Gronouski, following his instructions, apparently suggested that if the North Vietnamese did not want to admit their troops were below the 17th parallel, they could simply withdraw them. Rapacki apparently countered by saying there could be no clarification of the ten points at that time, that the United States must accept them as a take-it-or-leave-it proposition.

At this point Gronouski is believed to have noted again that he did not wish to clarify the points *before* meeting the North Vietnamese face-to-face. Their talk was still inconclusive, but

---

[2] Because Rapacki speaks no English and Gronouski no Polish, the two men relied on a translator. They both used Zbigniew Janczewski, who is considered the best Polish-English translator in the Foreign Ministry, although it is standard practice in such situations for each side to have its own translator. In addition to Janczewski, Rapacki was also backed up by Jerzy Michalowski, one of the two directors general of the Foreign Ministry, a Vietnam expert and the man soon to be named Polish ambassador to Washington. Michalowski, too, is fluent in English.

it apparently led to one more cable of wishful thinking from Gronouski.

That same day Henry Cabot Lodge gave a puzzling interview in Saigon. Perhaps he was only trying to protect the secrecy of the Marigold initiative he had nurtured for so long. Perhaps he decided he had been too euphoric the previous Saturday when he drank a ceremonial toast with D'Orlandi and Lewandowski.

At any rate, while Gronouski was trying to set up a meeting with the North Vietnamese, Lodge told newsmen that the war would not end abruptly by negotiation but that it would instead fade out. Militarily, he said, the United States was in a better position than a year ago:

"I think you could say that they cannot win. I think you could say that we cannot lose, we cannot be pushed out. I think you could say we haven't won yet. . . .

"The [Oriental] man makes up his mind one day that this thing that looked pretty good really isn't so very good . . . it's not going to work out so he just decides to fade out and nobody admits anything. There's no treaty, there's no headlines. They don't even admit they were in a war, let alone admit they got defeated at it. And so I think it just might fade, because that's what happened in two other places in Southeast Asia [Malaysia and the Philippines]; but, of course, nobody knows."

Coming from a man who had just been so heavily involved in an effort to bring about a negotiated end to the war and who knew that the effort was still under way, Lodge's reflections were curious.

What was Ho Chi Minh to think as he read a copy of that statement? One wonders if the aged North Vietnamese leader and his advisers have someone who explains to them at times like these that when the occidental man says "yes" he means "maybe" and when he says "maybe" he means "no," and so forth.

While Gronouski met Rapacki in Warsaw, and Lodge granted an interview in Saigon that Tuesday, President Johnson and his advisers apparently reviewed targets at the LBJ Ranch in Texas. McNamara, Deputy Secretary of Defense Cyrus Vance, Walt Rostow and the members of the Joint Chiefs of Staff all went to Texas from Washington. The announced reason for their visit was to discuss with the President the Defense Department's budget for the coming year. It is known, however, that the men at the Tuesday lunch level reconsidered the Hanoi bombings during the days after the first two raids. They reconsidered because there were still two more strikes authorized around Hanoi and they had received the low-keyed warnings from the Polish government in Warsaw and Lewandowski in Saigon.

At this point the United States government had not yet admitted its planes had bombed Hanoi; it was still describing the strikes in terms of the number of miles from Hanoi (never indicating, it turned out later, that the measurements began from the city's center rather than its limits).

But the President and officials at the ranch that day had to know the real facts about where the bombs had struck and of the North Vietnamese public protest that bombs from both raids had fallen within residential sections of their capital city.

Meanwhile, "grumblings and murmurings" about the bombings, especially after Gronouski's first cable containing the Polish warning, were growing in the State Department. They grew into a debate on whether the Hanoi bombing program should be continued. Katzenbach, who was then running the State Department in Rusk's absence, opposed continuing the bombings. Ben Read, who takes a hand in policy-making at times, also opposed them. Chester Cooper, running the peace-seeking operation in the absence of Harriman, opposed them vehemently. Cooper wanted to give the Poles a bit more time to produce, rather than provide the bombings as a possible excuse for them. One associate reported he was "on the verge of blowing his stack" over the possibility that the raids would be continued. Harriman also registered his opposition, apparently in a message from Paris.

But at the ranch, Walt Rostow urged continuation of the bombing—and he was closest to the President's ear. From the Far East, Rusk gave Rostow his support. William Bundy, accompanying Rusk, also went along with the idea even though later he was reported to be generally less hawkish than Rostow in such situations. McNamara's position is not clear.

Those favoring the bombing apparently continued to act out of the belief that if Hanoi really wanted to talk, a bombing raid or two more or less would not hurt the initiative. "When Uncle Ho really decides it's in his national interest to talk, the fact that we bomb here or there is not going to stop him," one official said. "The State Department didn't think the bombing would harm the initiative," another said.

The grumblings and murmurings were clearly being ignored.

Another official said the Polish government was asked specifically whether warnings that the bombings might damage the initiative were its own or Hanoi's. "The Poles said Hanoi had not complained to them about the effect the bombings might have on the initiative, that it was just their view," he continued. At another point, that same official said: "We took the Polish thing seriously even though a lot of people around here didn't believe it. They didn't believe it because the Poles were a funny choice as a channel."

Thus, by December 6, the Administration appears to have decided (a) that Marigold had little chance of succeeding, and (b) that if it were going to succeed, the continued bombing of Hanoi would not hurt it

With his superiors and advisers in the State Department spread out around the world, Gronouski continued to call on the Polish Foreign Ministry, trying to get a decision from Rapacki.

The more Gronouski tried to pin down Rapacki, the more vague the situation grew. The meeting date with the North Vietnamese always seemed imminent. But it was never set. Once Gronouski tried to get some indication that Rapacki really was talking for Hanoi. He kept hoping that somewhere, lurking in the background, maybe even waiting in a room down the hall, was a North Vietnamese representative ready to talk.

On another occasion, Gronouski, the frustration building intolerably, made a special trip to the Foreign Ministry and implored that the talks begin "that afternoon, that night, at three o'clock in the morning." He told Rapacki that if only he could sit down with the North Vietnamese, he could guarantee he would have the bombing turned off in twenty-four hours.

The response from the foreign minister never varied: low-keyed reproach for the bombings of Hanoi, a few cryptic remarks about the clarifications and some excuse why the meetings could not be held that day.

Later Gronouski was to tell a friend: "Doggone, I never could pin him down. I never walked away saying he answered my question. He is very adroit."

The American ambassador never got a clear statement from Rapacki that he was speaking for Hanoi.

In the meantime, Rusk and Bundy, who had left Washington on December 4, the day of the second raid on Hanoi, moved from Tokyo to Taiwan, where on December 4 they received a detailed cable on the mortaring of Tansonnhut Airport in Saigon, the airport at which Rusk was to set down next.

"When we read the cable we considered this a terrible provocation," one of the men traveling with Rusk recalled later.

Asked why the Secretary of State should consider the shelling of an airfield he would be using five days later a provocation while the State Department at the same time felt the North Vietnamese should not consider the bombing of Hanoi provocative, officials merely shrugged.

The security precautions at Tansonnhut were massive as Rusk stepped off the airplane on Friday, December 9, and expressed pessimism over the chances even for an extended year-end truce, much less a lasting peace. Like Lodge, in his interview in Saigon three days before, he gave no hint that negotiations were at that very time under way. In fact, he said: "There is no indication from the other side of interest in moving the problem to the conference table."

And, finally, he went on to restate the standard American position on a bombing halt: "We have told them many times that if they will tell us what they will stop doing, we will consider stopping the bombing."

In case Rusk had forgotten about Marigold at the time he

made that arrival statement, he was reminded of it that night at the American Embassy. He was also reminded of the bombing of Hanoi. Lodge had scheduled a dinner to honor the visiting Secretary of State. Present was Giovanni D'Orlandi.

D'Orlandi and Rusk discussed Marigold during the dinner. The Italian chided Rusk about the timing of the air raids of the previous weekend and wondered about their effect on the peace initiative. Rusk, in turn, raised questions about the course of the negotiations in Warsaw. D'Orlandi, according to the recollection of Americans at the dinner, expressed puzzlement over just what the Poles were up to. He indicated he thought the meeting between Gronouski and the North Vietnamese should have taken place already.

On Sunday, December 11, Rusk and Bundy left Saigon, continuing on the round-the-world tour that would take them via Bangkok, New Delhi and Teheran to Paris for a NATO meeting.

The weekend of December 10–11 passed in Warsaw with Gronouski still tangled in diplomacy with Rapacki. The American would not give up.

Tuesday, December 13, was a turning point. American fighter bombers returned to Hanoi for another run at the same targets they had struck in the first two raids of December. This time they did not even wait for clear weather. The Pentagon told newsmen later "the weather was cloudy and rainy with low ceilings throughout most of North Vietnam." There was a suggestion that the weather might have contributed to pilot errors in spotting targets as well as the obstruction of reconnaissance after the attack.

At any rate, Air Force Thunderchiefs from Thailand struck the Yenvien railroad yards six miles north of Hanoi, and six flights of from eighteen to twenty-four Navy planes each from the carrier *Kitty Hawk* dropped 500-pound bombs and hurled rockets at the Vandien vehicle depot five miles south of Hanoi.

The Associated Press reported from Saigon: "Pilots reported damaging the complex [at Vandien]. Both the rail yards and the truck depot had been hit in previous raids."

A few weeks later Harrison Salisbury, the assistant managing editor of the *New York Times,* visited Vandien. He reported:

"I saw . . . the so-called Vandien truck park on the outskirts of Hanoi—listed as one of the major targets of our December 13 attack. It was not a formidable target when I viewed it from Route Nationale No. 1—just a half-dozen loading sheds, blasted by American bombs. But in attacking these sheds the bombers had wrecked what was called the Polish Friendship School, probably half a mile distant on the other side of the highway. It was perfectly plain what had happened. The planes had come sweeping in on the truck park, and the chain of bombs had continued in a straight line and hit the school as well. I could accept the bombing of the school as an accident. But I was not surprised to find that the North Vietnamese thought it was deliberate. What caused me to wonder was why the truck park had been singled out as a target in the first place. It wasn't much. The action seemed less understandable when I learned from a foreigner who had been down Route Nationale No. 1 just before the raid that there were only twelve or fourteen broken-down buses and trucks in the 'park' undergoing repairs when it was hit. For this kind of target was it worth jeopardizing $2 million planes and the precious lives of American pilots? Was it worth zeroing in through the powerful SAM explosions and the blizzard of conventional ack-ack to destroy twelve or fourteen old motor vehicles that were already out of order? And in the process destroy a fine high school which was supported and aided by the Poles?

"I could not believe this made military sense. It certainly made no political sense." [3]

---

[3] In January, 1968, the authors queried the Defense Department for comment on the accuracy of the Salisbury account of the Vandien bombings. After checking the paragraph quoted above, a public affairs officer said the Department had no information to contradict the report, although, he said, he could not confirm (or deny) that the Polish Friendship School had been hit. He added that Vandien is actually not a single site but three or four sites, each with a half-dozen or so loading sheds, as Salisbury said, and some barracks. The whole "complex" added up to some fifty buildings. He said Salisbury could have seen only one of the clusters and did not realize there were two or three others like it.

If the raid made no political sense to an observer who knew nothing about Marigold, how much sense could it make with the knowledge that it came during a period in which Gronouski was badgering the Poles to produce the promised negotiations and the Poles were telling Gronouski that the North Vietnamese were uneasy about the bombings? (Despite American statements that Rapacki never claimed to be representing the North Vietnamese, the Poles have since maintained they were Hanoi's agents.) The sad irony of destroying a Polish-donated high school—even though accidental—while Marigold was on the table in Warsaw is self-evident.

Gronouski learned of the December 13 raids from a cable. His immediate reaction was despair. He thought it should not have happened.

But it did happen. And this time there was no mistake in coordination. To emphasize that point, on December 14 the planes went back again—the Air Force to the "big" Yenvien rail yards six miles northeast of Hanoi and the Navy to the Vandien truck park five miles south. The ordnance was the same —500-pound and 750-pound bombs and rockets.

By now there was a world-wide uproar over the bombings, with Hanoi charging that in the latest raid 100 civilians had been killed in a residential section of the city.

In Saigon, the American spokesman said the nearest populated area to the Vandien truck park was a village of thatched huts a mile from the park.

But later Harrison Salisbury discovered—and no one was ever to deny it—that a rocket, probably a Bullpup, found its way into Hanoi's diplomatic quarter, where, on a small side street, it hit a tree outside the Rumanian Embassy and exploded, causing damage to the Polish, Rumanian and Chinese embassies. For good measure, it rained splinters at the feet of two Soviet diplomats who had taken cover from the fighter-bombers under a canopy on a terrace at their embassy. The property of all four embassies came together at the spot where the rocket struck.

The Canadian mission to the ICC in Hanoi was also hit that day, Salisbury reported. He said a mission member picked up a fragment and sent it back to Saigon on the ICC courier flight for delivery to American friends, with a note saying: "Look here, chaps, this is going a bit far."

The day of the December 14 raid, in Washington, the State Department finally acknowledged what the North Vietnamese had been charging: that American bombs could be falling inside Hanoi, as most people define a city.[4]

As a result of the uproar, Robert McCloskey, the Department's spokesman, found himself in this exchange with newsmen at his December 14 noon news briefing:

Q: I would like to know from the point of view of policy whether you are in a position to answer the question "Have we bombed Hanoi?"

A: We have not. (Pause) What do you mean by "Hanoi"?

. . . . .

Q: How can you say you don't know anything about the city limits, where they are, and yet you say we have not bombed Hanoi?

A: I took the question to mean that these are civilian targets or population centers, people and the rest, which one generally associates when talking about a city. And what I have said is that so far as I am aware the policy is, so far as targets are concerned, directed against military and militarily associated targets.

. . . . .

Q: But you cannot be definitive as to whether any of these targets are inside the city limits of Hanoi?

A: I just can't answer that. I don't know what one—how one defines what the city limits are.

Q: For the sake of clarification, some of the military targets we have hit in the past have been described as the suburbs of Hanoi.

---

[4] A year later every time the "bombing of Hanoi" was mentioned to an American official, he winced or scowled or did both in disapproval that disappeared from his manner only when the reference was changed to the "bombing of the Greater Hanoi Metropolitan Area."

A: That's possible. I don't know how far the suburbs extend.

Q: Well, "suburbs" is a very general kind of term.

A: I may live in one here and you may live in another, and they may be distances apart. And I'm not trying to be facetious at all here; I just don't know enough about the geography there to be of any help.

If there was semantic confusion at McCloskey's briefing, there was none in Adam Rapacki's office in Warsaw on the morning of December 15. John Gronouski, for once, sensed just what he was going to hear there. He knew it from the time the telephone had rung and Michalowski requested his presence in Rapacki's office. The foreign minister was angrier than Gronouski had ever seen him. He made reference to the raids of the previous two days and said North Vietnam was not going to talk because of these bombings. They had ruined the whole initiative, he said. There would be no talks.

Crushed, Gronouski cabled the news back to Washington. The tone of the message was such that for once the officials reading it realized that indeed a "lot of flak" had been generated in Warsaw that day. But in the next few days it was decided that if the United States and North Vietnam really had been close to talks—and Gronouski was still convinced this had been the case—and if the bombings really had hurt the situation, maybe something could still be done to revive Marigold.

There followed more conversations with Michalowski and Rapacki, more "Nodis/Marigold" cables to the department and a few more sleepless nights.

On December 21, Gronouski and the Department agreed that he should make a trip home for a quick consultation. That set the stage for John Gronouski's little-known jet-powered dash to Washington for one last try to make Marigold work. For all its strategic location as a buffer between Germany and Soviet Union, Poland is not exactly at the crossroads of the world these days. Warsaw's airport is small, and is connected to the city by a two-lane bumpy road down which horse carts still travel with an unworried brazenness that sometimes makes a visitor think they were put there only as hazards for airport limousines. The airport is connected to the outside world almost as poorly as it is to the city.

Airline agents could work out only a cumbersome flight home for the ambassador. Departing Warsaw at 6 P.M., December 21, he flew via Polish Airlines to Frankfurt, where he had a layover. Next he flew to London and had a layover there. Finally he flew to Washington, and landed there some eighteen hours after departure.

His cover story, reported in seven lines of the fifth column on page five of the *New York Times,* December 23, was that Gronouski had flown to Washington "to discuss American economic relations with Poland and Eastern Europe." (He actually did this between Marigold talks, making arrangements while he was home for an agreement to allow Poland to pay part of its debt to this country in nonconvertible zlotys.)

Gronouski spent twenty-four hours talking to officials. Finally he was told that the President had created a circle ten miles in radius around Hanoi in which no bombs would fall for the foreseeable future. The hope was that this would revive the Marigold initiative. Gronouski did not actually see the President, who was at the ranch to spend Christmas in the Texas hill country.

Armed with the piece of paper containing the President's promise, Gronouski left Washington at 6 P.M. on December 23 on the eastbound flight to Warsaw. Once again the route was circuitous.

It was 6 P.M. on a cold, snowy Christmas Eve when a plane from Vienna touched down in Warsaw and Gronouski stepped off to be greeted by Walter Jenkins, his deputy. (Before he left for Washington, Gronouski had initiated Jenkins into the small band of those who knew the Marigold secrets just in case anything should come up during his brief absence.)

Jenkins had alerted the Polish Foreign Ministry to the ambassador's quick return and requested an immediate meeting.

Michalowski tore himself away from Christmas Eve festivities at home (religious holidays are still celebrated nationally in Poland, a devoutly Catholic Communist country) and went to the Foreign Ministry to wait, with Rapacki, for Gronouski's arrival.

At 7 P.M. the American ambassador, in high spirits, presented his compliments and his document to Rapacki. He thought Rapacki expressed some hope that maybe now the North Vietnamese would reconsider their intransigence. Rapacki appeared pleased, but he indicated it might take some time.

Gronouski was drained. He decided to try to spend Christmas with his family on a skiing holiday in Switzerland. He went back to the airport on Christmas morning. It was closed for the holiday. His confirmed reservation had been issued erroneously. There was no flight that day. Disappointed but not undaunted, he took a train to Vienna, expecting to catch a flight from there to Switzerland the day after Christmas. He went to Vienna's airport. It was closed for the day *after* Christmas. Once again he had been given a ticket for a nonexistent flight. Deeply disappointed, he returned to Warsaw.

The ambassador's hopes were buoyed on Tuesday, December 27, when Michalowski called to ask if President Johnson's "circle" had been expressed in statute or nautical miles. Gronouski said he was not sure, that he would query Washington.

A "Flash/Nodis/Marigold" cable brought an immediate reply: It was nautical miles. An hour after he received Michalowski's question, Gronouski called back with the answer. Michalowski took the information and hung up.

Gronouski heard no more about Marigold until late afternoon on December 30, when he was summoned to Rapacki's office. The meeting began at 6 P.M. and was very short.

A grim, crestfallen Rapacki literally threw up his arms and told the ambassador he had been ordered finally and definitively to break off the initiative. North Vietnam would not talk. His government had no choice but to withdraw.

Gronouski thought he detected in Rapacki's voice a note of

sympathy for the United States. The Polish statesman seemed to use a tone which suggested he believed Hanoi should have responded favorably to President Johnson's gesture in creating the bomb-free zone.

The bookkeeping operation was all very tidy. Ben Read was able to take Gronouski's last Marigold cable and close out the active Marigold file with the old year.

CHAPTER FIVE

Diplomacy Needs Pizzazz

In January, 1967, Jerzy Michalowski set off on a quiet trip to the United States and had a round of conferences at the United Nations. His talks were apparently the opening shots in a quiet propaganda war fought in diplomatic circles to assign blame for the failure of Marigold. The Poles were, quite naturally, citing the United States' bombing raids as the cause of the failure.

Soon after his visit, diplomats at the United Nations and highly placed members of the secretariat were trading rumors about the initiative. The same thing was happening in Ottawa, London and perhaps other capitals. The Poles were outraged. But a diplomat's outrage is politely expressed by dropping what seems like a chance remark to a colleague at a diplomatic reception. Actually, the remark is usually as carefully calculated for its effect as a formal note. Those who receive the information early treat it as gossip to be repeated mouth to mouth throughout the diplomatic community and to be reported to their home capitals.

Sooner or later a reporter at one of those cocktail parties is bound to hear a piece of the information. A diplomat unsympathetic to America's policy in Vietnam will give him a lead like this: "It's a shame how the United States always escalates the bombing of North Vietnam just when peace negotiations look so close." Then, after cueing the newsman, the diplomat, nibbling thoughtfully on another canapé and taking another sip of a martini, will add: "Don't say you got it from me, but why don't you look into what happened in Warsaw last month."

What happened in Warsaw last month? Anything to do with peace?

"Well, speak to the Poles. Get it from them. And mind, don't say you talked to me."

Darius S. Jhabvala, the United Nations correspondent of the Boston *Globe,* heard the news of the collapse in Warsaw in this manner from a high United Nations official in January, 1967. Robert H. Estabrook, the UN correspondent of the Washington *Post,* first learned of the story about the same time while on a trip to Ottawa.

It took thirty-four days from the time of the final collapse for the facts of the Polish-Italian initiative—or at least one version of the facts—to reach print. Both Estabrook and Jhabvala published vague accounts about December peace negotiations failing because of the American air raids near Hanoi on December 13 and 14. Estabrook mentioned Poland as the intermediary; Jhabvala did not.

The day after their stories appeared, the two reporters attended a reception at the Indian mission to the United Nations, where the Polish ambassador was seen talking to newsmen. The following morning the Washington *Post* carried a second story by Estabrook. It read:

UNITED NATIONS, N.Y., Feb. 3—North Vietnam definitely agreed last December to an American suggestion for direct discussions toward settling the war, a highly authoritative Western source said today.

The arrangements went so far as to specify Warsaw as the locale of the talks. But after the American bombing raids near Hanoi December 13 and 14—which Hanoi charged damaged civilian areas—North Vietnam withdrew its agreement, accusing the United States of bad faith.

The Western source revealed these diplomatic events

after President Johnson asserted Thursday that there have
been no "serious indications" of a Communist desire to talk
peace. The President's denial has produced considerable
skepticism here about American intentions among those who
profess to be familiar with the details of the effort that
failed. . . .

The first news stories differed in detail but they added up to
criticism of the United States for allowing its bombers to get
in the way of its peace-seekers.

What was one to make of this? Newsmen turned to the
State Department on Monday, February 4, and were told they
should make nothing of it. Carl Bartch was the Department's
spokesman that day at the regular noon briefing. Answering
questions about Estabrook's article, he said there was "no merit
in the position" that the bombings had blocked any United
States–North Vietnamese talks in Warsaw.

Opinion around the world blamed the collapse on the
United States. About the same time these stories appeared in
the Washington *Post* and Boston *Globe,* Italian Foreign Minister Amintore Fanfani privately told visitors he thought the
bombings were at fault. The visitors reported he had warned
the American government of the bombing's effect immediately
after the first two raids of December 2 and 4, and well before
the raids of December 13 and 14.

The United States tried to maintain credibility with its allies
by sending post-mortem accounts to American embassies in
various capitals as well as to the United Nations. The American
diplomats then used the accounts to brief foreign officials on
the American side of the story.

Prime Minister Harold Wilson of Great Britain received
such a post-mortem, but he knew the Polish version of the
story as well. On February 7 he was asked in Parliament about
what had happened in Warsaw. He answered: "It is my view
that what happened then was based on a very considerable two-
way misunderstanding, and that is why I think certain of the
events in December occurred—that is, if you are referring to
the Polish discussions."

In Washington, newsmen got the chance to unearth more

of the Warsaw peace story on February 9 when Secretary of State Dean Rusk held a press conference devoted almost entirely to the subject of peace-seeking.

The secretary involved himself in this colloquy:

Q: Mr. Secretary, this Administration's good faith in trying to reach discussions while bombing and other military activity still go on has been cast into some doubt by stories about the bombing that occurred in mid-December, and arrangements, supposedly, had been made for a meeting in Warsaw. And I think Prime Minister Wilson referred to this in Parliament this week and called it a "misunderstanding" on both sides. Could you elucidate what the misunderstanding was?

A: No, because to do so would, in my judgment, get in the way of the possibility of using existing channels to try to move this matter toward peace. It is not for me to talk about reports of particular channels that might have existed at one time or another or were speculated about. When the full story comes out someday, it will be rather different than some of the things you have heard.

Q: Mr. Secretary, do you accept his implication that part of the blame lies on the United States?

A: I am not accepting or rejecting anything at the moment. I am saying I am not getting into the question of a particular channel that somebody said might have existed.

Clearly, the State Department was handling Marigold in a gingerly fashion, apparently hoping that the matter would die out.

But it didn't. Throughout the spring of 1967 the United States government suffered the diplomatic backlash of the collapse in Warsaw.

Predictably, the refusal of American officials to give details on a story that was leaking out all over the world only whetted the insatiable appetite of newsmen for facts.

In March, Richard Hudson, editor of an obscure monthly called *War/Peace Report,* published an account which for the first time raised the possibility that the raids of December 2 and 4 had been damaging to the peace initiative. There was still no reaction from the State Department.

During these months John Hightower, the distinguished State Department correspondent of the Associated Press, began seeking out the American side of the Marigold story (although he did not know the code name then). Few officials, he found, actually had information about the initiative. He was referred to Dean Rusk for clearance.

Meanwhile, on Saturday night, May 7, Rusk returned to the wealthy New York City suburb of Scarsdale to accept an honor from old friends and neighbors. As president of the Rockefeller Foundation during his exile from government in the Eisenhower years, Rusk had lived in Scarsdale.

After the meeting Rusk and his wife met with representatives of some antiwar demonstrators to receive a petition he could take home with his crystal and parchment honor. The petition asked for a halt in the bombing of North Vietnam, an end to the war's escalation, and negotiations between the United States and all other parties in the fighting.

Rusk reportedly suggested that the group ask North Vietnam to de-escalate as well. The protestors conceded he had a point. Then, according to Herbert Robinson, the group's leader, Rusk said that within a few days the Administration would disclose the details of the failure of the previous December—a statement which later led diplomats and newsmen to think the State Department was on the verge of publishing a White Paper on the Warsaw peace initiative.

Instead, on Monday, May 8, the Associated Press carried a 1,700-word dispatch by Hightower detailing the initiative. Hightower's article quoted "official Washington," and though it was marked for release in newspapers of Tuesday morning, it was distributed on the AP main wire before the State Department's noon briefing on Monday.

Robert McCloskey was questioned about the article and the Scarsdale assertion at the briefing. This was the result:

Q: Bob, on another matter, can you clarify for us whether the State Department or the Administration is planning to put out the so-called full story on the abortive meeting in Warsaw?

A: I know of no intention to do that.

Q: Was the Secretary misquoted in Scarsdale?

A: If that was attributed to him, that was a misquote. I must say it is not clear that that, in fact, was attributed to him by the man who acted as spokesman for the group the Secretary addressed.

Q: Bob, since the fact that there has been a movement, a plan, to get in touch with Hanoi at Warsaw has been disclosed by the Prime Minister of Great Britain, is there any reason why we can't have a story from American sources?

A: Yes, I would think there is probably good enough reason, Joe, that it would not be possible for us to do this.

Q: What is the reason?

A: Well, I think you would have to take my word for that —that there is good enough reason for it.

Q: Bob, there is a rather full story by the Associated Press today. Do you have any comment with that story?

A: I just think I would prefer not to comment on the story.

But, actually, McCloskey did want newsmen to know the State Department considered Hightower's story reliable.

After noting McCloskey's on-the-record reply to the question about Hightower's article, the official transcript shows that something was said on "background." If McCloskey did speak for background, reporters would be forbidden to attribute that remark to the spokesman. It can be reliably reported, however, that an American official questioned that day about the Hightower story said:

"I would have no quarrel with it."

Starting with that assessment, the Hightower article quickly became the gospel-according-to-Washington on just what happened at Warsaw. Washington's bureaucrats have learned to take their cues from both on-the-record and background press briefings as certainly as Soviet officials get their policy line from reading *Pravda* and *Izvestia.*

Told that the Hightower article could be accepted without quarrel, officials would cite it for months afterward as the authoritative story of the initiative. Questioned, for example, about the content of the ten points, officials would say "Hightower had the ten points" when actually he did not.

Rusk, selectively summarizing a secret record, did not tell Hightower some of the essential facts of Marigold. He did not even mention the bombings of December 2 and 4, let alone the possibility that they were the result of poor coordination in the government or that they evoked warnings from the Polish and Italian governments. He—or other sources—indicated the Hanoi bombings were in response to Communist attacks against Tansonnhut Airport in Saigon and an unsuccessful attempt to destroy a bridge in Saigon. Actually, the Communist raids in Saigon came *after* the first American bombings of Hanoi. The Secretary—or his sources—gave Hightower no indication that the United States had been involved in the Marigold initiative for five months. It was made to appear that the involvement was of a short duration.

Through the story, Rusk sought to create the impression that the United States had been bending every effort to mollify the North Vietnamese and to create a congenial atmosphere for productive negotiations. He strongly implied that at the first hint of complaint about the American bombing of the Hanoi area, President Johnson stopped it as an act of good faith.

The exercise was a glaring example of the self-serving leak of classified information, the news management Washington reporters have had to grapple with more and more in recent years.

Explaining why Rusk did not leak a more balanced version of Marigold, an official said: "A guy who's taking off his clothes in public—you can't expect him to make himself completely naked."

Officials tried to steer reporters away from going beyond the Hightower account. When questioned, they would say: "Why, you're plowing pretty old ground there."

The State Department secretariat, under Ben Read, plowed through the Marigold record early and exhaustively to determine what, if anything, had gone wrong. The resulting post-mortem narrative account, some forty pages long, was Xeroxed and distributed to officials for study.

One official said: "Those of us who saw the report agreed that the United States did everything that could have been done to keep Marigold alive, apart from the matter of canceling the air strikes."

Apart from the matter of canceling the air strikes. But that was, after all, no small detail.

The official continued: "Some felt no risk should have been taken until we were certain that Marigold was not going anywhere. Others argued that they were sure Marigold was not for real; therefore, there was no risk in going ahead with the scheduled bombings."

The latter group concluded that if the bombings had not occurred, Hanoi would have found some other excuse for not coming to the negotiating table. Others, apparently a minority, did not suggest that the bombings ruined the initiative. Their point was that because of the bombings, there was simply no way of being sure. They also held that the bombings gave the Poles and the North Vietnamese a pretext to blame Marigold's collapse on the United States. If the bombing had continued as it did during Marigold's first five months—that is, without any strikes in the Hanoi area—some officials argued, the burden for failure to arrange talks would have shifted to North Vietnam. A participant in Marigold commented: "The real pity is that we didn't wait a week or so to test the Poles."

Those officials who insisted the bombings were not a significant factor concluded from the post-mortem that the Poles never had as much authority from Hanoi as they implied. Some even said the Poles had no authority at all, but were merely trying to work out a deal that they could present to the North Vietnamese after ironing out all details with the United States.

The official post-mortem report was filed away, but the matter of assigning blame obviously remained unresolved. More than six months later two officials intimately involved in Marigold privately blamed the failure in Warsaw on Harrison Salisbury and the *New York Times*. Salisbury, in December, 1966, became the first American newsman of stature to visit Hanoi. His reports that American planes had hit civilian targets created a furor in the United States.

One of the officials, in late 1967, said: "When the meetings did not materialize, we thought the Poles had exceeded their authority. However, the latest thinking in the Department is that in early December Hanoi really wanted to talk, but after Harrison Salisbury's copy, they copped out. They realized they had a pretty good thing going and could use American public opinion to get a better deal. We never did for Hitler's Germany what we did for Hanoi. They thought they were something pretty special after that kind of coverage in so influential a newspaper, and they changed their minds."

This well-placed official conceded, it is worth stressing, that Hanoi "really wanted to talk" in "*early* December." The bombings around Hanoi occurred on December 2, 4, 13 and 14. Salisbury's articles from North Vietnam began appearing in the *Times* on Christmas Day, ten days after an angry Adam Rapacki told John Gronouski that the bombings had ruined the prospect for talks and the morning after Gronouski returned to Warsaw from Washington with President Johnson's offer of a bomb-free zone around Hanoi.

Some high officials subsequently denied that the Marigold bombings resulted from a breakdown in coordination in Washington. "I would rather be hung for a knave than a fool," one said.

The Marigold record does suggest, however, that Washington's national security bureaucracy has difficulty coping with the sensitive, tenuous problems of Vietnam diplomacy. One adviser who has studied the secret Vietnam files in the State Department said: "Never underestimate stupidity, lack of judgment and lack of coordination as factors in foreign policy. What appears to be a pattern may not be a pattern at all. Things sometimes simply happen that are not supposed to happen."

One cannot be certain, but the indications are that in this context the December 2 raid, if its possible importance for the success of Marigold had been appreciated, would have been postponed. That first raid could have occurred within hours after President Johnson and his advisers approved the Hanoi strikes on November 15. That would have been two weeks before Lodge and Lewandowski on December 3 committed their governments to setting up a United States–North Vietnam meeting in Warsaw. It was only the monsoon weather that kept the targets on the authorized-but-not-struck list for so long. If the bombing had occurred earlier, it might not have had a damaging effect on the peace initiative.

Despite what were still at that time the extraordinary characteristics of a raid on the Hanoi area (it had been hit only once before, on June 29), the raids did not receive the same extraordinary attention in Washington that accompanied those of the night of the little monks—probably because the Johnson Administration was reluctant to admit that any particular air raid represented an escalation over any previous one. All raids, officials have said, are directed only at military targets and thus each has about the same military value as any other. Acceptance of this belief could lead a functionary to forget that Hanoi—or the "Hanoi area," as the State Department prefers to call it—could be a diplomatically dangerous target if hit at a sensitive point during the Marigold initiative. Functionaries forget that, say, power plants or truck parks have a different symbolic value if situated in Hanoi than in some southern city closer to the war zone. It also could explain the failure in the fail-safe system.

After Marigold, "there was a change in alertness and wariness by Ben Read and others," one official reported. "It always comes down to a question of the people involved when you talk about the effectiveness of such checks." Was this new alertness enough to prevent a recurrence of embarrassing inconsistency between diplomats and bombers?

"Not entirely," one official admitted. For example, in April, 1967, the Canadian government presented a proposal for really demilitarizing the demilitarized zone between North and South Vietnam. The United States took advantage of the offer to put itself forward as a nation sincerely in search of peace. In a bit of diplomatic one-upmanship, it bettered the Canadian offer by proposing a pullback to ten miles beyond the DMZ by both sides.

The announcement of this proposal was scheduled for the State Department noon briefing on April 19. Just before the briefing, one official examined the day's target strike map in Read's office and saw something disturbing. He rushed into Katzenbach's office next door, according to a story that circulated later, and said: "Look, we're going to bomb Haiphong today. That will make our DMZ offer appear insincere. Goddamn it, turn it off!'

Katzenbach was sympathetic, but the official could not get enough of what the bureaucracy calls "pizzazz" behind his demand. Katzenbach told him that because of the shortness of time and other complications, it would be too difficult to stop the raids.

That afternoon the American DMZ proposal was put forward as a first step toward peace.

That night (Washington time), American fighter-bombers attacked two power plants in Haiphong on schedule. The North Vietnamese, as usual, charged civilian damage had also resulted from the bombing.

Thereafter, the State Department received reports that Russian diplomats were noting the juxtaposition of the peace offer and raids, saying, "How can you believe the United States."

Even when the State Department tried to coordinate the bombing with diplomatic events it ran into trouble. The visit of Soviet Premier Alexei N. Kosygin to the United Nations in June, 1967, to try to recoup some of the prestige his country lost during the six-day Arab-Israeli war is an example.

Kosygin arrived on June 17. Fifteen days before, American planes raided the North Vietnamese port of Campha, accidentally hitting the 341-foot-long Soviet freighter *Turkestan*. According to the Soviet protest, two crewmen were injured. The charge was at first denied. But with Kosygin's arrival in the United States, the Johnson Administration stressed conciliation. Some in the State Department felt the Soviet leader might be prevailed upon to help in promoting Vietnam peace negotiations.

The approach to Kosygin was two-pronged. On June 18, the day after his arrival in New York, the United States, citing "new information," admitted that the *Turkestan* had been accidentally struck at Campha. The Pentagon summoned reporters to hand out the embarrassing story.

Second, State Department officials went over the North Vietnam bomb target authorizations in Read's office. They wanted to prevent any awkward coincidences which might irritate Kosygin. They checked to make certain that no dramatic targets such as power plants, harbors, air fields or installations in the Hanoi and Haiphong areas were on the list. They found none. They also tried to make sure the bombing would be kept at a constant level of activity. They wanted "no humps" in the curve, as one official put it. Their research showed there would be none.

But weather played hob with the plans. On June 18, the day the Pentagon apologized for the *Turkestan* incident, exceptionally good weather occurred throughout North Vietnam. The Air Force and Navy bunched up all their outstanding authorizations. They flew the largest number of missions in the year so far—166. The planes struck rail lines, rail yards, sidings, roads, bridges, truck convoys and storage depots, from the southern panhandle and areas near the Laotian frontier to the area between Hanoi and the Chinese frontier.

Newspapers across the United States carried the story of the heavy raids on their front pages of June 19. The story of the Pentagon's admission about the *Turkestan* appeared as a sidelight on inside pages. The officials had sought, by keeping the air war quiet while Kosygin was in New York, to impress him with this country's peaceful intent. Instead, the raids probably reinforced the Communist view of a cynical Johnson Administration speaking peace but waging war.

Some strategists familiar with peace-seeking problems complain about such accident-prone procedures. Instead of only passively checking the authorizations, officials in Washington could have ordered an embargo or limitation on the number of missions during Kosygin's presence in the country.

One official said of the June 18 raids: "They show there is no broad orchestration of a peace initiative. If there were a negotiations high command, we could have the kind of orchestration in which not only targeting but also such things as speechmaking in Congress could be coordinated. A high command could plan things like the postponement of bombing or announcement of troop reinforcements for, say, a week before and two weeks after the announcement of an offer—that kind of thing. Now it's all hit or miss. If a guy like Ben Read remembered, he would go running to Katzenbach's office or Walt Rostow's and pound the desk to stop a bombing raid. If not, it would all go ahead as scheduled."

The extent to which the bombing of Hanoi in December, 1966, may have been self-defeating merits consideration. As Robert McNamara testified, there were three reasons for the bombing—to stop or slow North Vietnamese infiltration to the South, to exact a high price from North Vietnam for its part in the war, and to force it to the conference table. With the possibility of talks near at hand, and considering that two out of the three reasons for the bombing were political, one might well question the timing of the raids. Further, using the Tuesday lunch check list, the advisability of ever bombing Hanoi at all, regardless of whether a peace initiative was under way also, might be subject to challenge. In hindsight, the December, 1966, Hanoi bombings failed in three out of the four check-list categories.

Granting a relatively high military gain for the Americans in the bombings (which may or may not have been the case), the risk of plane loss was high (the North Vietnamese did shoot down a record number during the December 2 raids), the risk of civilian casualties was high (all Western observers who have visited Hanoi agree that civilian targets were hit during the attacks, even if accidentally) and the war-widening risk was present (American munitions did damage the embassies of three Communist allies of North Vietnam).

Inevitably, the matter came down to one of judgment—were the North Vietnamese ready to talk or weren't they? If they were, should the United States have participated or shouldn't it? The Johnson Administration seemed unsure of its judgment. On December 3, when officials in Washington gave Lodge permission to accept the December 6 Warsaw meeting date, they indicated they wanted the talks. But by approving the continued bombing of Hanoi the following week, they gave some sign of having second thoughts. They had, after all, been warned about the harmful effects of the bombings when they made that decision. Then they changed their minds once again later in the month, after the December 13 and 14 raids, when they created the bomb-free zone around Hanoi. In creating that zone, the Administration must have decided that the military reasons for bombing Hanoi were no longer compelling, that it would be advisable to talk with the North Vietnamese and that the bombings earlier in the month had possibly destroyed Marigold.

But by the time they had made that decision, it was evidently too late. Whatever desire Hanoi may have had for a meeting in Warsaw had disappeared.

"All of us were skeptical that the Poles really had Hanoi on the hook, but the structure was interesting and we played it to the hilt," a White House aide said. It would appear that there were periods of skepticism interlaced with periods of "playing it to the hilt." It is also possible that in the end it was the skepticism that came across more clearly to the North Vietnamese, and that this only reinforced Hanoi's own skeptical attitude

After Marigold's failure, the North Vietnamese began emphasizing their demand, made only in passing earlier, for an "unconditional" and "definitive" halt in the bombing of their country before they would "talk" with the United States. (Even with the bombing halt, they did not promise more formal "negotiations.")

Thus, the United States may have paid a high price for the Johnson Administration's management of the Marigold diplomacy: the newly inflexible demand by the North Vietnamese for a bombing halt before talks could (or would, or will, to use all the verb tenses that have been bandied about) begin.

From time to time American officials have treated this attitude as so much sour grapes.

"The object is not *talks*," one official said. "The object is settling the war."

part **II**

Little Gidding
in Vietnam

We shall not cease from exploration
And the end of all our exploring
Will be to arrive where we started
And know the place for the first time.

> —T. S. Eliot, "Little Gidding" Recited
> by Robert S. McNamara as a valedictory
> to seven years as Defense Secretary on
> "Meet the Press," February 4, 1968

CHAPTER SIX

Dean Rusk's Antenna and U Thant

Settlements, unlike talks, can be achieved on a battlefield as well as at the negotiating table. To distinguish between the two possibilities—talks or a settlement—was, in a sense, to reveal the United States' reliance on the battlefield option. Terms and attitudes have since shifted, but in 1964 the dominant view in official Washington was that the United States could not entertain the idea of talks or negotiations until after it applied more military pressure on the enemy.

As a former White House aide later described the mood of that period: "The very word 'negotiations' was anathema in the Administration."

Perhaps U Thant, who as the United Nations secretary general is supposed to be the world's foremost peace-seeker, and the late Adlai E. Stevenson, then the American ambassador to the UN, did not realize this when they became involved in trying to arrange North Vietnamese–American talks. Or perhaps they knew the American attitude but decided they might be able to convince the Administration that it had dangerously misread the situation in Vietnam. Thant and Stevenson involved themselves deeply when hardly anyone with real authority in the United States government appeared much interested.

The ordeal was to drive Thant to despair, and would nag at Stevenson's conscience until he dropped dead on a London street on July 14, 1965, just two weeks before President Johnson ordered large numbers of combat troops into Vietnam.

For almost twenty years administrations in Washington had been seeking a workable settlement for Indochina. Franklin D. Roosevelt knew that the pre-World War II French colonial domination of Indochina was oppressive, and in the months before he died he expressed the hope that the Indochinese people could gain their freedom. Harry S. Truman, faced with the French effort to reassert its shaken control over the Southeast Asian colonies, found himself compelled to give arms and money to France for the task. Dwight D. Eisenhower donated more arms and more money as the French inexorably lost the war with Ho Chi Minh's Viet Minh.

Then, after the 1954 Geneva Conference, Eisenhower pledged aid and advice to the government of Ngo Dinh Diem, but despite this pledge the rebellion against Diem started in earnest in the last years of the Eisenhower Administration. John F. Kennedy, after assuming the presidency in 1961, found that to protect this country's investment in South Vietnam—an investment of men and money for prestige as well as security—he, too, had to keep increasing the commitment.

Finally, in 1964, Lyndon B. Johnson felt obliged to commit, tentatively at first, the nation's own combat forces to shore up a situation that arms, money and advisers had not been able to control in all the preceding years.

All this was done in the hope of making a settlement in Vietnam in keeping with the United States' deep-seated fear of the spread of international communism. By August, 1964, when American airplanes retaliated against North Vietnam for attacks on American ships in the Gulf of Tonkin, the view of the Communist world was in the process of revision in Washington. (The State Department, for instance, had abandoned the term "Communist bloc" as non-descriptive of a splintering Communist community.) But the commitment nevertheless was daily growing larger in Vietnam. France's problem had become America's.

Considering the size of the commitment, the United States government, by 1964, felt it could not very easily settle for anything less than a non-Communist regime in South Vietnam. The neutral government the United States said it would find acceptable in election year 1968 was ruled out in election year 1964, as attested then by William Bundy:

"Some have urged neutralization but the Communist Party in North Vietnam has specifically rejected such a solution for that area. Neutralization of South Vietnam alone would, therefore, simply be a step toward a Communist takeover, as the Communists themselves know in pushing it as an interim course for South Vietnam. Negotiations would serve no purpose as long as Hanoi and Peiping disregard the agreements they signed in 1954 and 1962 on Vietnam and Laos. Expansion of the war outside South Vietnam, while not a course we want or seek, could be forced upon us by the increased external pressures of the Communists, including a rising scale of infiltration."

Bundy's speech was delivered to the Research Institute of Japan on September 29, 1964. Billed as a major foreign policy address, it was accompanied by a background session for American newsmen in which a "reliable American source" in Japan, almost certainly Bundy himself, revealed that contingency plans existed for halting the flow of men, weapons and supplies to the Communist insurgents in South Vietnam by bombing staging bases in Laos and North Vietnam.[1]

As the years passed, the paragraph in the Bundy speech regarding Vietnam took on added significance as a clear indication of two other American policy tenets that would quickly fade with the shifting American positions:

First, it was an open, if somewhat ignored, expression of the American determination at that stage of the war to *avoid* negotiations with the forces the nation was fighting in South Vietnam.

Second, it was a clear indication that despite the dovish election campaign oratory of Lyndon B. Johnson, the United States

---

[1] The source, incidentally, ruled out any major employment of United States ground troops as "disastrous" in giving the image of a "white man's war" to Vietnam. "We are near the Plimsoll line already" with 19,000 ground troops in South Vietnam, the source said, alluding to the line marking the maximum load a ship may take.

was in 1964 thinking seriously about a war expanded beyond the borders of South Vietnam.[2]

Throughout 1964 and into 1965 the political chaos that began with the ouster and murder of South Vietnam's president, Ngo Dinh Diem, and his nepotic, brutal government on November 1, 1963, continued. Whatever semblance there had been of a national coherence in South Vietnam between the signing of the Geneva accords in 1954 and the Diem downfall vanished in the chaos of coups and countercoups. The two months of December, 1964, and January, 1965, were indicative.

On December 19, 1964, the South Vietnamese military high command ousted a legislative "High National Council," and on January 3 installed a civilian regime under Premier Tran Van Huong. On January 20 the cabinet was revised to include four generals (among them were Nguyen Cao Ky, who had assumed the title "Air Vice-Marshal," and Nguyen Van Thieu, both of whom would later rise to supreme power). On January 27, the army decided to take over the government, and in a bloodless coup, ousted Huong, saying he and the chief of state, Phan Kac Suu, could not cope with the violent nationwide Buddhist demonstrations then under way. For the rest of the winter and spring of 1965 the turmoil continued as men with such exotic names for the American ear as Quat, Suu, Khanh, Phat, Minh and Colonel Pham Ngoc Thao (who had been the Saigon government's press

---

[2] Typical of that campaign oratory was a Johnson speech in Manchester, N.H., just one day before Bundy's Tokyo address. The President said: "As far as I am concerned, I want to be very cautious and careful, and use it only as a last resort, when I start dropping bombs around that are likely to involve American boys in a land war in Asia with 700 million Chinese. We're not going north and drop bombs at this stage of the game. And we're not going south and run out and let the Communists take over."

Washington reporters saw some contradiction in those two speeches. Officials, as is often the case, left it to the unflappable Robert McCloskey at the State Department to straighten it out. He blandly labeled the Johnson and Bundy speeches "old themes" that were "not inconsistent" with each other. The President was reiterating that the U.S. wants no wider war in Vietnam, McCloskey said. Bundy's contrapuntal theme was that "Communist aggression is a danger to peace." Taken together, the State Department spokesman said, they express America's Southeast Asian policy.

attaché in Washington before returning home) maneuvered for control.

Therefore, even if the enemy did make the unlikely decision to negotiate, the United States could not, during that period, put forth any strong alternative to the National Liberation Front. Washington officials were wont to explain this in terms of Saigon's "morale." They said that to open negotiations would have destroyed that morale.

One State Department policy-planner said of the Johnson Administration's attitude on negotiations during 1964 and early 1965: "The moment we moved toward negotiations at that stage, it would have been an admission that the game was up." [3]

From September, 1961, when he took over the secretary generalship after an airplane crash in Northern Rhodesia killed Dag Hammarskjöld, until 1964, Thant's prestige continued to grow. In October, 1962, he played a large role in cooling off the Cuban missile crisis that brought the Soviet Union and the United States to the brink of nuclear war. In 1963 he negotiated the end to the Katanga secession from the Republic of Congo. As a Burmese, he had the respect and trust of the growing number of Afro-Asian nations in the UN. As a long-time delegate to the UN, he had developed empathy for the Western world, and his performance had earned him the support of the United States and other great powers. The Soviet government's attitude toward him was ambivalent. At first they opposed his election. They op-

---

[3] There was what one official called a "hostile attitude at the State Department to anything the other side said." As an example, he recalled the criticism everyone automatically made of the formal NLF program for South Vietnam; but in questioning State Department officials he could not find anyone who had read it.

"I had a helluva time finding a copy in this government," he said. "I had to go down several levels into the State Department and finally I found one in Tom Hughes' shop." (Thomas Hughes was the director of the Department's Bureau of Intelligence and Research.) "When I read it, I found very little that I could quarrel with. On the surface, at least, it said the kind of things we had been saying. That doesn't mean the NLF meant it, of course, but the point was that you couldn't argue with most of the language."

posed the actions he took in the Congo. Later, as his neutralism became more apparent, the Kremlin treated him more favorably.

In November, 1963, in the aftermath of the Diem downfall, he suggested to the United States the establishment of a coalition government in Saigon which would take in all the anti-Diem nationalists, including those who had been exiled. The plan foundered because the United States was not interested in such a coalition and because the exiles would not return. But Thant apparently lost no standing in making the suggestion.

During the summer of 1964, while talk of the United States' escalating the war became more prevalent, Thant again made a peace proposal. He called for the reconvening of the Geneva Conference, saying such a move, "even at this late hour, may offer some chance for a solution."

Two weeks later French President Charles de Gaulle suggested, in one of his regally staged press conferences, a summit meeting of the United States, France, the Soviet Union and Communist China to negotiate an end to the fighting in Vietnam and Laos, an evacuation of all foreign forces from the Indochinese peninsula and guarantees by the big powers for the neutrality of the four Indochinese successor states—Cambodia, Laos and the two Vietnams.

President Johnson's election-year response was quick and scornful, but it appeared aimed only at de Gaulle. On July 24, a day after de Gaulle spoke, Mr. Johnson submitted to one of his rare televised press conferences and delivered an opening statement that rejected any negotiations in these words:

"In the continuing discussion of Southeast Asia, let me state American policy once more.

"We are determined to support the freedom and independence of South Vietnam.

"It is true that there is danger and provocation from the North.

"And such provocation could force a response.

"But it is also true that the United States seeks no wider war. Other friends suggest that this problem must be moved to a conference table. And, indeed, if others would keep the solemn agreements already signed at a conference table, there would be no problem in South Vietnam.

"If those who practice terror and ambush and murder will simply honor their existing agreements, there can easily be peace in Southeast Asia immediately. But we do not believe in conferences called to ratify terror, so our policy is unchanged. . . ."

The next day, as if to emphasize the direction Administration policy was taking, the Pentagon announced an increase from 16,000 to 21,000 American military "advisers" in South Vietnam. The increase was another violation by the United States of the "solemn agreements already signed," and symbolized once again the lost meaning of the Geneva accords which all sides had been violating with impunity

The Vietnam war in the summer of 1964 had not yet become the dominant concern of American policy-makers. They had other problems as well. One related to the prestige of the United Nations, which had been declining because of Soviet and French refusal to pay assessments for peace-keeping operations. Thant, in fact, had gone to Moscow in late July to negotiate with the Russians on the matter.

It was against this background that President Johnson invited Thant to Washington for a statelike visit on August 6. Coincidentally, the visit came two days after the American retaliatory raids for the Gulf of Tonkin incidents. A helicopter bearing Thant arced around the Washington Monument and set him down near the White House. On the south lawn of the executive mansion, the U.S. Marine Corps band played for him. There were ceremonial speeches in the Rose Garden and a talk in the oval office of the President. There was a luncheon at the State Department and, that night, a state dinner in the White House. Like any king, president or prime minister, Thant was put up overnight at Blair House. Never in the nineteen-year history of the United Nations had a secretary general been accorded such an honor by the United States.

Intended to bolster the UN's sagging prestige, the visit also served to enhance Thant's stature, and buttressed his belief that he should use his position to do what the UN was created for—to seek ways to make and maintain peace.

At the State Department luncheon, attended by Dean Rusk,

Averell Harriman, William Bundy, Ambassador Adlai Stevenson, Deputy UN Ambassador Charles Yost and Ralph Bunche, Thant's American deputy, Thant reviewed peace prospects. He told Rusk he had been formulating an idea for bringing together emissaries of the United States and North Vietnam for private conversations. He suggested no agenda. He only thought that a face-to-face exchange of views at, say, an ambassadorial level might be helpful. The discussion was all very tentative. Thant gave no indication that he contemplated immediate action. He did not bring it up in a way that would require formal American approval. But nonetheless he was looking for some sign of interest from the State Department, and he thought he saw it in Rusk's reaction.

Back in New York, Thant considered how he could make contact with North Vietnam, which was not a member of the United Nations. He went over all the channels open to him—contacts running through UN members that also had relations with North Vietnam. Finally, though he had been told that same summer by Premier Nikita S. Khrushchev in another context that the Soviet Union could not exert influence in Hanoi, he decided to at least try using the most prestigious of the Communist nations to convey a message to Hanoi. Thant chose to open the channel through a Russian official in the UN Secretariat. He asked the official to request the Soviet mission at the UN to determine—through Moscow and Hanoi—whether Ho Chi Minh would be interested in having an emissary talk with an American. The terms were a guarantee of complete secrecy for open-ended, agenda-less discussions.

In late September, according to versions of the story inspired by Thant, the answer came back from the Soviet government: Yes, Hanoi is interested. Thant immediately notified Adlai Stevenson, who was "favorably surprised." Stevenson told Thant he would report immediately to Washington.

From here on, the story grows murky. One obstacle in reconstructing the events over the next several months is that a key American involved in the Thant initiative—Adlai Stevenson—is dead, and apparently he had not communicated the initiative to Washington in writing. ("Part of the problem," an official recalled, "was that Adlai, talking over the telephone, was vague and imprecise about this matter.") Stevenson, it should be stressed, knew the story from both ends—Thant and Washington. He was the only go-between.

Stevenson relayed to Rusk in late September the word from Thant that Hanoi was interested in direct, secret, low-level exploratory talks. Thant saw Stevenson every two or three days and kept inquiring about a response from Washington. All Stevenson could tell him was that he had heard nothing.

Finally, apparently in mid-October, Stevenson advised Thant to shelve the initiative until after the President's election campaign against Barry Goldwater. Whether Stevenson did this on his own or on instructions from Washington is not clear. (Thant got the impression that Stevenson had not received instructions on this point. By this time, of course, the campaign was in full swing, and Stevenson, himself twice a presidential candidate, could appreciate how difficult it might be to draw the President's attention away from the matter of the moment. Yet Stevenson was to claim in an interview just before his death that he was told by "someone in Washington" to advise Thant to wait until after the election.)

The shape of the campaign was already plain. Goldwater pressed for a tougher military response in Vietnam; the President branded Goldwater as reckless and portrayed himself as a man who could find a solution to Vietnam without expanding the war.

After the election, but still in November, Stevenson informed Thant that Washington, checking through a channel of its own, had not received the impression that Hanoi was willing to talk. Thant asked Stevenson to identify the channel and was told it was the Canadian representative on the International Control Commission. The persistent secretary general checked this on November 30 with Paul Martin, the Canadian foreign minister, when Martin came to the UN for a General Assembly meeting. Martin reportedly told Thant that the Canadian member of the ICC, J. Blair Seaborn, had no access to any member of Ho Chi Minh's cabinet, and that he would not be in a position to know whether the Hanoi hierarchy was interested in talks.

Thant was convinced that his information was far more authentic than anything Seaborn might have passed on to Washington. He told Stevenson of his conversation with Paul Martin and continued, in late November and early December, to urge Stevenson to try again with Washington.

On November 29 Soviet Foreign Minister Andrei Gromyko arrived for the General Assembly meeting. In conversations with Thant December 1, Gromyko verified the message indicating Hanoi's interest in talks which Thant had received through the Soviet official in the secretariat.

Before Gromyko departed for the Soviet Union on December 20, Rusk conferred with him several times in New York and in Washington. One major agenda item was the UN's financial crisis. It would seem likely that Rusk and Gromyko also discussed the Thant-Stevenson initiative at that time.

On December 4 Thant entered a hospital for treatment of ulcers. He returned to his home on December 18, conferred with Stevenson, Soviet Ambassador Nikolai T. Fedorenko and others over the next few days, then departed for a week's vacation on December 31. When Thant returned, Stevenson was away on holiday. Thant asked both Charles Yost and Francis Plimpton, another Stevenson deputy, if they had heard anything from Washington on the initiative. Not only had neither heard anything from Washington, they did not even know what Thant was talking about.

"We had better wait until Ambassador Stevenson gets back," he told them.

A few days later Thant and Stevenson met again. Once more, apparently, Stevenson telephoned Rusk, and once more the reply was that Washington had learned through other channels that Hanoi was not interested in talking. At this point Stevenson apparently moved on his own, perhaps in the belief that he could force Rusk's hand with a more definite proposal. He suggested to Thant that he select a meeting place.

Thant narrowed the choice to four countries where both the United States and North Vietnam maintained diplomatic missions—Cambodia, France, Pakistan and Burma. Rangoon, he decided, was the city most likely to guarantee the secrecy of the meetings. It is the capital of a country that is largely self-isolated. Newsmen have trouble getting permission to visit it. The only resident foreign correspondents represent Tanjug, the

Yugoslav news agency, and Tass, the Soviet news agency. The Western wire services are all represented by Burmese nationals and are thus controllable by the Burmese government.

On January 16 Thant went to James Barrington, the Burmese ambassador to the United Nations, and asked him to inquire if his government would permit a meeting in Rangoon.

On January 18 the Ne Win government replied that if both sides agreed to the talks, it would be happy to be the host. That same day Thant told Stevenson a site had been arranged. On January 30, 1965, Stevenson advised Thant firmly that Washington would not send a representative to any Rangoon meeting. He said Washington felt such a meeting could not be concealed, and that when the news leaked out it would demoralize the Saigon government.

"What government?" Thant is understood to have replied. "Minh, Khanh, Suu, Tri?"

That was the end of it.

Thant knew the South Vietnamese political structure was a shambles, and that the military situation, from the American point of view, was deteriorating. What Thant may not have realized at that moment, and what the American public did not realize, was that the Johnson Administration had been creeping almost imperceptibly toward an enlargement of the war, including the bombing of North Vietnam, and that this policy was about to be implemented.

The President's principal advisers had concluded that bargaining from a position of relative weakness could only produce an unappetizing settlement. The military imbalance, they argued behind the scenes, would have to be redressed before negotiations could be considered.

On February 6 Hanoi received Thant's message on Washington's rejection of talks. On February 7 the United States bombed North Vietnam, ostensibly in retaliation for a Viet Cong raid on the Pleiku barracks.[4] After that Thant told visitors, he was not able to coax Ho Chi Minh into considering talks while the United States continued bombing. Thant believes Ho

---

[4] A discussion of the deliberations in Washington which led up to the retaliatory bombing of February 7 and the start of the regular bombing of North Vietnam appears in the following chapter.

thought there was a relationship between the message reporting Washington's rejection of talks and the bombing. Thant, however, feels the two events were a coincidence. On February 24 Thant openly expressed his disappointment during a press conference at the United Nations. Responding to a question, he rebuked the Johnson Administration by saying: "I am sure that the great American people, if only they know the true facts and the background to the developments in South Vietnam, will agree with me that further bloodshed is unnecessary. The political and diplomatic method of discussions and negotiations alone can create conditions which will enable the United States to withdraw gracefully from that part of the world. As you know, in times of war and of hostilities, the first casualty is truth."

With those words, Thant all but erased the credit he had built up with the Johnson Administration and which had brought him the personal honor that went with the UN prestige-building exercise in Washington the previous August. From that time on, many Washington officials would privately speak of Thant with the same disdain reserved for Charles de Gaulle, Adam Rapacki and other world leaders and diplomats judged to be hostile to America's Vietnam policies.

Thant's seemingly gratuitous affront surprised and angered the White House. Press Secretary George E. Reedy, after checking with the President, told reporters that "there are no authorized negotiations under way with Mr. Thant or any other government. I am not going into any diplomatic chit-chat that may be going forth, or way-out feelers, but authorized or meaningful negotiations—no."

At a press conference the next day Dean Rusk ruled out negotiations until North Vietnam, as he put it, stopped its aggression in South Vietnam. He said: ". . . A negotiation aimed at the acceptance or the confirmation of aggression is not possible. A negotiation which simply ends in bitterness and hostility merely adds to the danger."

The United States had clearly committed itself for the time being to finding a solution on the battlefield.

On February 26 the *New York Times* published a brief report of Thant's efforts to bring representatives of Hanoi and

Washington together in Rangoon. Little public interest was stirred. The report did, however, spur a search that already had been ordered by McGeorge Bundy, then the President's special assistant for national security affairs. Bundy had seen a vague one-sentence reference to a Thant-Stevenson initiative in a secret intelligence document and had asked his staff to find out what it meant. The National Security Council aides scoured their own files and those at the State Department. They were apparently unable after several weeks of searching to find answers for Bundy.

On June 25 Thant received the first astonishing indication that his messages to Stevenson had not reached the President. The secretary general was in the San Francisco Opera House when the President delivered a major foreign policy speech commemorating the twentieth anniversary of the United Nations. Mr. Johnson's speech was a call "upon this gathering of the nations of the world to use all their influence, individually and collectively, to bring to the table those who seem determined to make war."

When they met privately after the speech, Thant told the President he had already undertaken such an effort to arrange a conference, but that his influence did not seem to work on the United States. Thant mentioned the Stevenson initiative. There was no indication of surprise on the President's part as he told Thant he had not been aware of it. Thant could only assume the President had not been informed of the initiative while it was alive but had checked on it as a result of the newspaper reports in February. This would explain the absence of surprise, but the evidence that his messages had not been relayed to the President made a deep impression on Thant.

On July 12, 1965, two days before he dropped dead, at sixty-five, on a London street, Stevenson had a long, gloomy, rambling talk with Eric Sevareid, an old friend, in an upper-floor library of Winfield House, the residence of American ambassadors to the Court of St. James's. Stevenson's despair over the course of American foreign policy and his inability to influence it came through sharply in this post-midnight session. Among other things, he talked of the Thant initiative and of Washington's unenthusiastic reaction to it.

Publication in *Look* magazine the following November of these last thoughts of the dead idol of American liberalism, of a man for whom there had been universal regard, set off an international furor. Stevenson's version gave the impression that the Johnson Administration had plunged into the escalation—what quickly became the Americanization—of the Vietnam war without carefully investigating a possibility for peace.

As Sevareid related Stevenson's version: "Someone in Washington insisted that this attempt be postponed until after the presidential election. When the election was over, U Thant again pursued the matter: Hanoi was still willing to send its man. But Defense Secretary Robert McNamara, Adlai went on, flatly opposed the attempt. He said the South Vietnamese government would have to be informed and that this would have a demoralizing effect on them; that government was shaky enough as it was. Stevenson told me that U Thant was furious over the failure of his patient efforts, but said nothing publicly." [5]

No "diplomatic chit-chat" response from the White House would suffice to stifle the questions Sevareid had raised.[6] The Administration was suddenly confronted not with a vague criticism from U Thant but with a specific and serious, though posthumous, charge from the President's own ambassador. The job of explaining fell to Robert McCloskey at the State Department. On November 15 McCloskey denied (as McNamara angrily did) that there was any truth in the article's references to McNamara. But McCloskey did confirm the essential fact that Thant had advised the United States the previous autumn that North Vietnam was willing to engage in talks.

Why didn't the United States pursue that opening?

---

[5] Stevenson's belief that McNamara, generally thought to have been dovish on the use of military power to find a solution in Vietnam, had squashed the Thant initiative raised many eyebrows in Washington. Though Sevareid did not report it in his article, Stevenson told Sevareid he discussed the initiative with McNamara at a Georgetown party and had gotten a firmly negative reaction.

[6] No one was more surprised at the reaction to his article than Sevareid. He had previously reported his last conversation with Stevenson as a kind of eulogy shortly after the statesman's death. In August the New York *Herald Tribune* and the Manchester *Guardian* had carried relatively complete accounts of the Thant initiative.

McCloskey maintained that there had been no unwillingness by the United States in the fall of 1964 to "enter into
meaningful talks. All our indications were that there was no
serious intent on the other side," he said. "We saw nothing to
indicate that Hanoi was prepared for peace talks and the
Secretary of State said he would recognize it when it came. His
antenna is sensitive."

Reporters, and the American people, were left in the dark
for the moment on what it was Rusk's sensitive antenna had
picked up which enabled the Administration to determine that
Hanoi was insincere when it agreed to talks. Ted Sell of the
Los Angeles Times pursued this question the next day. The
best he could get from a State Department spokesman was:
"You'll just have to take our word for it."

More of an answer was forthcoming from Rusk himself at a
press conference on November 26, one called in an apparent
attempt to quiet the public clamor over the credibility issue and
a possible missed peace opportunity. Rusk said the Thant
initiative was "considered in the light of a great deal of information that we had about the attitude of Hanoi." He mentioned,
without giving details, numerous discussions he said he had had
with officials of other governments, including Communist governments, during the initiative.

"It seemed clear beyond a peradventure of doubt," Rusk
said, "that Hanoi was not prepared to discuss peace in Southeast Asia based upon the agreements of 1954 and 1962 and
looking toward the lifting of aggression against South Vietnam."
He said the Communists felt at the time that they were "on the
threshold of victory. . . . Throughout all of last year the
general attitude of the Communist world was that they might
consider some device to save the face of the United States
while they imposed their will on South Vietnam. Our attitude
was and is that we are not interested in saving face but in saving
South Vietnam." [7]

---

[7] On June 19, 1967, educators attending a Foreign Policy Conference at
the State Department heard still one more explanation of the Thant-
Stevenson initiative by Secretary Rusk. Normally, "background" rules
of the conference would prohibit identifying Rusk as the source, but
Senator J. William Fulbright identified Rusk in a speech on the Senate

The Thant-Stevenson story was not yet over. Publication of the Sevareid article apparently had as sharp an impact on the President as it had on the public. While Dean Rusk and the State Department were given the task of explaining to the public, the President secretly asked Bill D. Moyers, who had succeeded Reedy as press secretary, to undertake an independent investigation of the initiative Sevareid discussed in his article. Many hours went into Moyers' quiet effort to trace the initiative, to determine whether and when the President had ever been informed of it, and to assign a cause for failure. But Moyers was unable to locate all the missing pieces. He satisfied himself that no document dealing with the subject had ever reached the President. This suggested that the initiative had been rejected without the President's knowledge.

What records, if any, Moyers located is not known, but at least one document dealing with the Thant initiative was prepared at the State Department. Whether it was drafted during the life of the initiative or some time later is not clear. Considerable mystery surrounds this top-secret paper. It was a two- or

---

floor on April 18, 1968. Here, from the official State Department transcript, is what Rusk said:

"You've heard about the end of '64–beginning of '65 business when peace was about to break out in Rangoon [laughter]. The only contact there was a Russian member of the secretariat. During that period I myself had several long talks with Mr. Gromyko. So it's not surprising that I would consider my information from Mr. Gromyko more relevant, more authoritative, than anything that came from some relatively junior member of the secretariat.

"In any event, Hanoi denied there was ever any such contact, and other denials have come into the picture. . . .

". . . Really, what happens on these matters is basically this: There are an awful lot of candidates for the Nobel Peace Prize running around the world these days [laughter and applause]. . . . They don't understand what they hear. And if the ladies will forgive me, they frequently come out of Hanoi or some other contact eight months pregnant [laughter]; and then when we check it out with Hanoi, we find that there's nothing in it." [Laughter, applause]

"Now I realize that the photographers in Washington tell me I look like the neighborhood bartender [laughter], but I assure you that I'm not the village idiot [laughter]; and we would not be doing our job if we were not following up day and night every clue, every allusion, every hint through any channel anywhere that would help open this thing up to a peaceful settlement. You, at least, ought to carry a presumption that maybe what I said is correct." [Applause]

three-page memorandum, over Dean Rusk's signature, which made clear that the State Department did not think much of Thant's proposal. The memorandum went to McGeorge Bundy, who then controlled most of the flow to the President of papers dealing with national security issues. Bundy later returned the memorandum to Rusk with this notation: "As per our conversation."

What Bundy and Rusk said to each other, and to what extent that conversation may have influenced the Administration's response to the Thant initiative is locked in the minds of those two men. The disposition of that document also may bear on the extent, if any, to which the President was advised of the initiative by his subordinates when it was still alive.

Nothing could be found by the authors to contradict the President's statement to Thant the previous June that he had not known about the initiative.

On November 26, 1967, Moyers, who had left the White House to become the publisher of *Newsday,* and Richard N. Goodwin, a former colleague of Moyers on the White House staff, discussed on a television program Goodwin's contention that the Administration had overlooked several opportunities for negotiations. The following exchange occurred:

Goodwin: ". . . The opportunities are on the public record. . . . In 1964 U Thant said they offered to meet us in Rangoon —Hanoi did, and that offer was refused by the American government. And you can go through a series . . ."

Moyers: "Look, Dick, I think you should point out that as also the public record shows, that that particular thrust, or parry, or whatever you choose to call it, was dealt with at a lower level than the President, and having been in the White House at the time, I think both of us were at that time—I don't recall that ever coming to the White House, and I don't think that—well, I'd like to know whether you do or not."

Goodwin: "I don't recall it, but I think it's a rather embarrassing fact. . . ."

Almost a year after the Sevareid article, in October, 1966, the story took another surprising twist. The President, on a speech-making visit to New York, called on Thant in the secretary general's thirty-eighth-floor office at the United Nations. He was accompanied by Dean Rusk. Inevitably, the conversation turned to the Thant-Stevenson initiative, and once again the President told Thant he had not been informed of it.

"The President sat in that very chair and said he had never heard of it," Thant was to tell visitors later. "He said it was a new book."

Then Rusk added the new twist. The Secretary of State told Thant that Stevenson had not been authorized to reject the Thant approach. Thant and UN officials were stunned. They could not conceive that Stevenson would have taken it upon himself to cancel the Thant initiative. Yet that was the clear purport of Rusk's statement. Had Stevenson, in fact, become so discouraged by Washington's unresponsiveness to the Thant proposal that he finally told the secretary general to just forget the whole idea?

How would that compare with the Sevareid account?

How would it compare with the recollection of a close Stevenson associate, who said: "While I don't think Adlai was convinced beyond any doubt that this was real, Adlai told me he had been inclined to follow it up, to check it out rather more assiduously than Washington did."

How would it compare with the Administration's confirmation of the initiative after the Sevareid article and the official explanations of why the Administration had rejected it?

The Johnson Administration has, in private, offered still another explanation for Washington's wary treatment of the Thant proposal. At some point, perhaps during the UN General Assembly meeting in December, 1964, Thant was told by a Washington official, believed to be Rusk, that the initiative was a KGB (Soviet secret police) operation, and therefore tainted. Thant insisted that the initiative was his and that the Russian official's connection with the KGB was irrelevant.[8] He told the

---

[8] In the view of experts on such matters, the fact that the Russian official was a KGB member would make him a more reliable channel. The elite of the Soviet government belong to the KGB. In a sense, KGB training in Moscow is the equivalent of a Harvard or Yale law school background in the United States Foreign Service. "Calling a Russian in the UN Secretariat a KGB man is like calling Kosygin a Communist," one official said.

During the Cuban missile crisis of 1962, Alexander Fomin, a coun-

American official that he had verified through Andrei Gromyko that his message had been transmitted.

The Administration seems to have shifted ground in trying to explain—publicly and privately, before and after Stevenson's death—why the Thant initiative failed. But to a former White House official, the explanation is not all that complicated:

"That was the last great opportunity for talks before the bombing of North Vietnam and the inevitable escalation on both sides. We let the opportunity slide by. We miscalculated. The bombing did not improve our position."

---

selor at the Soviet Embassy in Washington, made contact with John Scali, American Broadcasting Company correspondent covering the State Department. Fomin relayed to the Kennedy Administration through Scali a message that was in large part responsible for breaking the Soviet–U.S. impasse. Fomin was then considered by the Administration as the top-ranking KGB man in the United States. As far as is known, no one at the State Department complained that the Fomin-Scali channel was a KGB operation. The Department, facing a nuclear crisis, was delighted to receive the message.

CHAPTER SEVEN

The Three-Month War

By the time Adlai Stevenson rejected U Thant's peace effort, President Johnson, according to some reports, already had maps and aerial photos of North Vietnam spread out on the big Cabinet Room table in the White House and was memorizing the locations and characteristics of possible targets in Ho Chi Minh's country. He was supervising the final stages of the meticulous planning that had been going forward on a contingency basis in 1964. Although he had endured great agony over the decision, his mind was all but made up to carry the war northward.

Caught in this steady push toward heavier American involvement were Leonid I. Brezhnev and Alexei N. Kosygin, who had, in October, 1964, led a peaceful Kremlin coup which deposed Nikita S. Khrushchev. Brezhnev and Kosygin came to power with two foreign policy objectives—to maintain, if possible, the trend toward more peaceful coexistence with the United States and to heal, if possible, the ever-deepening rift between Khrushchev's Soviet Union and Mao Tse-tung's China. They learned within a month of their accession to power that rift-healing on any basis acceptable to the Soviet Union would be impossible.

Lyndon Johnson, however, appeared only too eager to oblige with improving Soviet-American relations. In his 1965 State of the Union message, the President invited the Soviet leaders to the United States and also suggested that the leaders of each of the two superpowers address the people of the other on nationwide television. The Kremlin did not react unfavorably to the suggestions, although it tempered its good words about the President's message with the warning that the United States was still meddling too much in the affairs of other nations. The allusion to Vietnam was inescapable.

In January, 1965, while Mr. Johnson and his advisers were considering heavier military involvement to rescue the increasingly desperate situation in South Vietnam, the Soviet leaders decided to see if they could reassert the Kremlin's influence in North Vietnam. In 1964 Khrushchev had written off North Vietnam as well as North Korea as areas in which he could not compete successfully for influence with Mao. From all appearances, Khrushchev's successors decided to encircle, if possible, Red China with Russian influence. Thus, Alexander N. Shelepin, the former secret police chief and perhaps the main challenger of Brezhnev and Kosygin at the time for Kremlin power, made a ten-day visit to Mongolia on China's northern frontier to help put down a pro-Chinese revolt in the Mongolian Communist Party. As Shelepin completed his visit, the Soviets signed a new trade agreement with Japan, gave prominence to reports of technological assistance to Indonesia, flattered Ceylon beyond necessity on the occasion of its national day and sent a deputy premier to India to celebrate the tenth anniversary of the Soviet-Indian Friendship Treaty. Most important, Kosygin himself made a long, tedious flight to Hanoi to visit four days with Ho Chi Minh. On the way he stopped in Peking to talk to Chinese Premier Chou En-lai, who received him coolly. The Kosygin trip, following exchanges of good sentiments between Moscow and Washington, raised the possibility that the Soviets would urge Ho to make a settlement with the United States. If Kosygin were to do this, however, it would have to be done cleverly. To try to force Ho into a settlement would leave the Soviets vulnerable to ever-increasing propaganda blasts from Peking that Moscow was the handmaiden of Washington in trying to rule the world. It was taken for granted, therefore, that Kosygin would also have to reassure Ho that as a fraternal socialist power, the Soviet Union would aid North Vietnam in the event of any American attack.

While the Soviet leaders were planning Kosygin's trip, President Johnson decided on one last move to make certain it really was necessary to begin an air war in North Vietnam to save the situation in the South. He dispatched a high-level delegation headed by McGeorge Bundy, his then special assistant for national security affairs, to Saigon to investigate.

Traveling with Bundy were Chester Cooper, John T. McNaughton, Assistant Secretary of Defense for International Security Affairs, and Leonard Unger; Lieutenant General Andrew Goodpaster represented the Joint Chiefs of Staff.[1]

The White House sought to create the impression that the Bundy mission was not portentous and reflected no great change in the Administration's strategy. At a press conference on February 4 Mr. Johnson explained the trip as one in a series of consultations Ambassador Maxwell Taylor had been having with Washington officials every two months or so. Normally, he acknowledged, Taylor came home, but conditions being what they were, it was felt that the ambassador should not leave Saigon.

"I only want to reassert this morning our determination to continue our present policy, the policy of our government from the beginning, to try to help the people of Vietnam help themselves to preserve their freedom," Mr. Johnson said. There was nothing in his remarks or in any background information given reporters in Washington to suggest that McGeorge Bundy had gone to South Vietnam for one last look before a momentous

---

[1] Goodpaster served as military aide to President Eisenhower before 1960 and was used regularly by Mr. Johnson as a liaison between the White House and the former President. Goodpaster received briefings at the White House and Pentagon and then traveled to Gettysburg or wherever General Eisenhower might be to update him on national security matters. He also carried back to the White House suggestions from the general. Mr. Johnson has frequently emphasized General Eisenhower's support of his Vietnam war policy. In April, 1968, Mr. Johnson named Goodpaster deputy commander of American forces in Vietnam. He was to become a full general.

change in policy. In fact, quite the opposite impression of the trip was created.

Bundy arrived in Saigon the same day the President held his news conference. On February 7, the day after Kosygin arrived in Hanoi, enemy guerrillas broke through the defense perimeter around the big American air base at Pleiku in South Vietnam's Central Highlands, and using mostly captured American weapons, mortared the flight line and some American military barracks. When the fifteen-minute attack was over, eight American soldiers were dead and 108 wounded. Six helicopters and a transport plane were destroyed. Several other aircraft were severely damaged. The attack, one of three conducted simultaneously, came two hours after the annual Tet (lunar New Year) truce had expired.

"Bundy went up there to inspect," a former White House official recalled later. "He saw the hospital and the other areas, and the scene had a terrific impact on him emotionally. A man from the ivory tower was suddenly confronted with the grim horror of reality. Mac got mad and immediately urged a retaliatory strike."

But even before the retaliation came, there was a hint that a regular program of bombing the North was under consideration. Dispatches from Saigon reporting the Pleiku raid noted that Westmoreland and other military men in Saigon favored an air war against North Vietnam. The dispatches gave no indication that the decision had all but been made in Washington before Bundy left. In his book *Lyndon B. Johnson and the World,* Philip L. Geyelin quotes a high State Department official as saying, the week before the Pleiku attack, "Almost all the cable traffic between here and Saigon is on going North." The immediate question on February 7, however, was that of instant retaliation for Pleiku.[2]

---

[2] The quick reaction to Pleiku was in striking contrast to the absence of any response following an attack on Bien Hoa Air Base on November 1, 1964, one week before the Johnson-Goldwater election. Viet Cong forces mortared Bien Hoa, killing five Americans, destroying five B-57 bombers and damaging twenty-two others. The B-57s had been sent into South Vietnam after the Gulf of Tonkin incident as a symbol of American air power. Ambassador Taylor urgently recommended a reprisal

Rowland Evans and Robert Novak, in their book *Lyndon B. Johnson, The Exercise of Power* reported the aftermath of the Pleiku raid this way:

> "McGeorge Bundy . . . joined Ambassador Taylor and General Westmoreland in recommending instant retaliation in telephone talks with the President from the communications headquarters in Saigon. With McNamara and the Pentagon generals making the same recommendations in Washington, the President personally selected the first targets from hundreds of choices clearly marked in the large-scale map of North Vietnam pasted together, section by section, from the reconnaissance photographs."

That same day airplanes based on three carriers[3] in the Gulf of Tonkin bombed and strafed the North Vietnamese military base at Donghoi, north of the 17th parallel. The next day American and South Vietnamese planes attacked a communications center in the Vinhlinh area. The White House said the retaliatory attacks were against "barracks and staging areas . . . actively used by Hanoi for training and infiltration of Viet Cong personnel into South Vietnam." Though these first strikes of 1965 were officially called "retaliatory," it was to become clear in just a few weeks that they in fact marked the beginning of the United States' air war against North Vietnam.

As one source recalled: "On his way back to Washington Mac Bundy prepared a memo urging a steady program of bombing the North . . ."[4] Another source familiar with what

---

against North Vietnam, and Geyelin reported that Taylor later expressed "frank puzzlement, in private conversations, at Johnson's failure to do anything in response to Bien Hoa." Geyelin argued that the failure to respond, taken together with the President's election campaign statements, left North Vietnam in doubt about American resolve to get tough in Vietnam.

[3] At that time the United States usually kept only one of the 7th Fleet's attack carriers on station off Vietnam and left the other two free for patrolling elsewhere. The presence of all three seemed to be further indication that the strikes had been anticipated before the Pleiku attack.

[4] This source felt that instead of waiting for a North Vietnamese bid for negotiations as a result of the bombing pressure, the United States should have sought negotiations quickly. He said: "From the start of the bombing, a few of us in the Administration believed it was essential to get into talks fast. Otherwise, combat troops would have to

was then happening behind the scenes said: "Mac felt that within three months of the start of bombing, Hanoi would give up and seek peace. He thought bombing was the way to avoid sending combat troops. He was dead wrong."

The possibility that the Pleiku raid was timed to provoke a response from the United States that would embarrass Kosygin has not been altogether discounted. An Eastern European correspondent who traveled to Hanoi with Kosygin, for example, felt that the Chinese instigated the Pleiku attack during the Kosygin visit, confident that the United States would retaliate. The retaliation, in turn, would show up Kosygin as a paper tiger unwilling to help North Vietnam. It would also undercut whatever effort Kosygin might be planning to turn Hanoi in the direction of negotiations, and it would complicate relations between Moscow and Washington. The correspondent said that in Moscow he had heard mysterious references among Chinese about the "welcome" their country was planning for Kosygin in Hanoi. He also reported seeing dozens of MiG airplanes on alert at the airport of Nanning, just north of the North Vietnamese–Chinese frontier. The Chinese, he thought, exerted enough influence in the South Vietnamese National Liberation Front to arrange such an attack by the NLF's military arm, the Viet Cong.

The idea of such successful Chinese planning and anticipation of Mr. Johnson's reaction seems far-fetched, but it has nonetheless never been completely dismissed by American officials. Another view was that the North Vietnamese encouraged the Pleiku attacks while Kosygin was in Hanoi to stimulate more aid from the Soviet Union.

Kosygin was caught in a difficult position by the air raids. New in his job, he was still establishing his power. He could not make major pronouncements without consulting the Kremlin. He had not yet developed the self-assurance that a year later would enable him to play the middleman in a largely successful effort to quiet passions that had brought India and Pakistan to war over Kashmir.

Publicly, while in Hanoi, he reacted to the bombings with

---

follow, and then the inevitable escalation on both sides. But we couldn't get anything going."

silence. He went about the business of negotiating a new economic and military air agreement with the North Vietnamese. But he must have been furious at the insult. According to one report, he had gone to Hanoi with a maximum and a minimum aid authorization and had been empowered, according to his judgment of the situation, to give aid between those limits. After the attack he gave the maximum. The question of military aid, when he arrived, was of secondary importance, although he did have military advisers with him who, by their positions, appeared qualified to discuss antiaircraft defenses. After the raids and after his assurances that the Soviet Union would never let its North Vietnamese comrades down in the face of American attacks, military aid became more important. Any opportunity Kosygin might have had to press Hanoi on peace talks evaporated after the American bombings. Some thirty-six hours after the air raids, the Soviet Union reacted, saying it would stand with "its allies and friends . . . to safeguard the security and to strengthen the defense capability of the Democratic Republic of North Vietnam." On his way back from Hanoi, Kosygin again stopped in Peking. Where he had received a cool reception from Chou En-lai a few days before, he was now greeted warmly by Mao Tse-tung. As it turned out, the good feeling between the Chinese and Soviets was only transitory. But for a time it appeared as if the bombing had not only risked destroying whatever value Kosygin had as a peacemaker, but had also fostered Soviet–Chinese cooperation.

Virtually every American official realized that bombing North Vietnam while Kosygin was there represented a serious complication. Many considered it a bad mistake. One official who helped plan the raid said: "We certainly realized . . . it could be embarrassing for Kosygin but we decided to go ahead with it anyhow. We knew it would put him on the spot to a degree, but we couldn't hold off." Other officials felt the raid could have been delayed.

"It was bad manners," said one. "The timing of the bombing was unfortunate," said another. "Personally I think it was a mistake," said a third. "We caught hell from the Russians."

On February 10 the Soviet government permitted students to stage a huge demonstration in front of the American Embassy. Thousands of Russians, aided by Chinese and Vietnamese, hurled paint, ink, bricks, bottles, ball bearings and ice at the large building. When it was over, 202 windows had been shattered—a record for such demonstrations in Moscow. A few days later Kosygin arrived home. Word was passed through the diplomatic community that the Soviet Union was incensed at the affront. American diplomats in Moscow were castigated at every opportunity. Kosygin voiced his anger in a message to the French government just prior to a visit by French Foreign Minister Maurice Couve de Murville to Washington. Couve, it is believed, told the President and Dean Rusk of Kosygin's message—understood to have contained a warning against further bombing of North Vietnam.

Meanwhile, in Washington, planning went forward for a program of regular bombing of the North. Despite the denials by President Johnson that this was in prospect, all the military arrangements were being made. And a political justification—a State Department White Paper intended to document North Vietnam's domination of and aid to the National Liberation Front's insurrection—was also being drafted.

On February 26 Kosygin went before a nationwide Soviet television audience to make a somber report on his trip to Asia. "An end to the U. S. aggressive actions against the Democratic Republic of Vietnam is needed, first and foremost, to create conditions for the exploration of avenues leading to the normalization of the situation in Indochina," he said. He called for a withdrawal of U. S. troops from South Vietnam and South Korea but did not say this was a condition for the beginning of negotiations. He warned that the war could widen and revealed that the Soviet Union already had started sending military aid to North Vietnam. He also made it plain that improved Soviet-American relations, no matter how desirable, "cannot be reconciled with [United States] actions spearheaded against the Democratic Republic of Vietnam."

The next day the United States published a sixty-four-page

White Paper designed to prove "above all [that] the war in Vietnam is *not* [italics in original] a spontaneous and local rebellion against the established government. . . . In Vietnam a Communist government has set out deliberately to conquer a sovereign people in a neighboring state. And to achieve its end, it has used every resource of its own government to carry out its carefully planned program of concealed aggression. North Vietnam's commitment to seize control of the South is no less total than was the commitment of the regime in North Korea in 1950.

"This report is a summary of the massive evidence of North Vietnamese aggression obtained by the government of South Vietnam. This evidence has been jointly analyzed by South Vietnamese and American experts."

The evidence was, in fact, something less than massive, as State Department officials themselves realized. Later one official was to admit the White Paper was an embarrassment [5] and to compliment I. F. Stone, the acerbic pamphleteer of the left, for a masterful job of dissecting and debunking the hyperbole. The paper showed, for example, that 179 weapons of North Vietnamese, Czech, Chinese or Soviet manufacture had been captured during the eighteen-month period from June, 1962, to January, 1964. Stone was not impressed. He obtained from the Pentagon a statement that "we" captured an average of 7,500 enemy weapons each eighteen months. Thus the 179 would be only 2.5 percent of the total. Presumably the others were all weapons the enemy stole or captured from the South Vietnamese.

Similarly, to support the charge that North Vietnam had embarked upon a conquest of the South, the White Paper said some 37,000 "military personnel"—19,500 "confirmed" and the remainder "estimated"—had been infiltrated from the North between 1959 and 1964. Stone noted that the document cited only six case histories of native North Vietnamese who were captured or who defected in South Vietnam in those six years.

On March 2, three days after the White Paper was published, 160 American planes bombed an ammunition dump at

---

[5] The embarrassment was such that William Bundy later added a bright New York lawyer, Dan Davidson, to his staff to prevent a recurrence.

Xombang, ten miles inside North Vietnam, and the harbor at Quang Khe, fifty-five miles north of the demilitarized zone. The raids were the first that were conducted without any alleged specific provocation by the North Vietnamese. They committed the United States to an escalatory course to improve the military situation. They also foreclosed any Soviet intercession for peace at that time.

The day after the raids a nineteen-nation Communist conference in Moscow, called to repair the Sino-Soviet rift, issued a statement condemning "open aggression" and "barbarous acts" by the United States. On March 4 some 2,000 students, led by Asians, attacked the American Embassy. Police could not control them. Troops were called out. The battle lasted three hours. The new shattered-glass record surpassed that of the February 10 demonstration. Almost every window on the front of the ten-story building was broken. When Ambassador Foy D. Kohler called on Foreign Minister Gromyko to protest, the Soviet official dryly told him that U. S. air attacks on North Vietnam "are incompatible with professed American desires to improve its relations with the Soviet Union." [6]

Throughout March the Johnson Administration received an increasingly heavy barrage of criticism from those at home and abroad who opposed the air war. The answer was determination not to negotiate and the dispatch, for the first time, of Marines to South Vietnam—to protect American bases. Those 3,500 Marines were, in fact, the first American combat troops to go ashore in South Vietnam. The dissension was underscored by a speech in Philadelphia by Canadian Prime Minister Lester B. Pearson, a Nobel Peace Prize winner for his role in settling the Arab-Israeli war of 1956. Pearson did no less than recommend that the President order a bombing pause so that Hanoi might negotiate "without appearing to do so as the direct result of

---

[6] If the demonstration had any salutary effect, it marked the renewal of the violent Sino-Soviet dispute. Several militant Chinese students were injured by police trying to subdue the demonstrators. Peking protested and two days later staged a demonstration at the Soviet Embassy in the Chinese capital. China also recalled most of its students from the Soviet Union.

military pressure." Such advice from the leader of a foreign government while on American soil was taken as an affront by the White House. During lunch at Camp David the next day the President treated Pearson frostily. Yet while the President was apparently spurning the advice of his critics, he was planning a major foreign policy pronouncement to be delivered at Johns Hopkins University in Baltimore.

The Administration was still not ready to call for negotiations. McGeorge Bundy's three-month bombing plan had not yet run its course. North Vietnam had not been sufficiently softened up to seek negotiations. Pressure for a peaceful gesture was mounting, however. The speech writers, in an official atmosphere that considered a call for negotiations a sign of weakness, had a difficult time drafting a message that would placate the critics.

The President began the speech by noting that the week before "seventeen nations sent their views to some two dozen countries having an interest in Southeast Asia." He never mentioned that the seventeen nonaligned nations had urged a "peaceful solution through negotiations . . . without posing preconditions." He said, instead: "We are joining those seventeen countries and stating our American policy, which we believe will contribute toward peace in this area of the world."

The speech presented the American objective as "the independence of South Vietnam, and its freedom from attack." It blamed North Vietnam for the aggression. It said the shadow of Communist Chinese aggression was in the background. It warned that the United States "will not be defeated . . . will not grow tired . . . will not withdraw, either openly or under the cloak of a meaningless agreement." It proposed one billion dollars for a grandiose economic development plan for Southeast Asia in which, it was hoped, North Vietnam would participate after peace had come.

In the original drafts, the speech did not explicitly place the United States on record as favoring negotiations, saying only: "We will never be second in the search for . . . a peaceful settlement in Vietnam. There may be many ways to this kind of peace: In discussion or negotiation with the governments concerned; in large groups or in small ones; in the reaffirmation of old agreements or their strengthening with new ones.

"We have stated this position over and over again, fifty times and more, to friend and foe alike."

The lack of a call for negotiations in the speech disturbed several on the President's staff. Finally, the night before the address, the President consented to the insertion of one more sentence at the end of the passage quoted above. Richard Goodwin and Bill Moyers drafted this sentence: "And we remain ready, with this purpose, for unconditional discussions."

The President would allow them to go no further than "discussions." The State Department—a colleague of Moyers and Goodwin said—was unhappy even with that. "We thought the word 'discussions' was a great triumph," this official continued. "We got busy telling everybody that 'discussions' really meant 'negotiations,' that the United States was willing to enter into negotiations. Actually, it wasn't until the President's July press conferences that the words 'discussions' and 'negotiations' began to fuse." [7]

The Johns Hopkins speech failed in both its endeavors—to placate the President's critics, and to induce Hanoi to signal it was willing to negotiate on the President's terms. The clamor for a bombing pause, which had quieted somewhat immediately after the speech, grew louder once again. At noon Washington time, May 12, the bombing stopped without any announcement. [8]

In Moscow, Ambassador Kohler received a message from Dean Rusk to deliver to North Vietnamese diplomats in the

---

[7] At his July 28 press conference, the President said the United States was ready "to negotiate with any government, any place, any time." He also disclosed he was increasing "almost immediately" the troop level in Vietnam from 75,000 to 125,000, including the dispatch of the First Cavalry (Airmobile) Division. The announcement came after Defense Secretary McNamara returned from Saigon and reported a deterioration in the military situation.

[8] The pause was not announced until May 15, when officials in Washington revealed bombing had been suspended temporarily for "operational" reasons—to permit reconnaissance and damage assessment. Thus, though they dropped no bombs, American planes continued to fly over North Vietnam during the pause.

Soviet capital. Kohler asked Soviet Foreign Ministry officials if they would deliver the note. "Deliver it yourself," he was told.

American officials spent a day on the telephone trying to set up a meeting between Kohler and the North Vietnamese ambassador. The North Vietnamese would not receive him. On the second or third day of the pause, one of Kohler's subordinates drove to the North Vietnamese Embassy with the message. He knocked on the door. An unidentified man responded. The American proffered he envelope. The North Vietnamese took it.

The message from Rusk said nothing about negotiations. It only told the North Vietnamese that a bombing halt had started which would continue into the following week. It suggested that Hanoi reciprocate by "significant reductions in . . . armed actions." It seemed to discourage negotiations before a slow-down in the fighting in this manner:

> The United States must emphasize that the road toward the end of armed attacks against the people and government of [South] Vietnam is the only road which will permit the government of the United States to bring a permanent end to their air attacks on North Vietnam.

The day after the note was delivered—the third or fourth day of the pause—it was returned by messenger to the American Embassy.[9] An apparently identical American note was transmitted about the same time to the North Vietnamese government in Hanoi by the British Consul General there on May 17. It was similarly returned on May 18.

At 5:30 A.M. Washington time, May 18, less than six days

---

[9] As far as Kohler and his staff could discern, the North Vietnamese had returned the envelope unopened. But the presumption was that it had been opened and resealed. The envelope was sent to Washington for a laboratory examination. Kohler never learned the results.

The North Vietnamese messenger dropped Rusk's message into an outgoing mailbox at the American Embassy. Officials have since mused about the possibility that if it had not been discovered by chance, the message would have been carried off in the next mail pickup and the United States might not have learned that it had been rejected.

Any lingering doubt about whether North Vietnam knew the contents of the envelope was removed on December 10, 1965, when Hanoi Radio broadcast the text of Rusk's message. A paraphrased version of the note had been published in a British White Paper the previous August.

after the bombing had stopped without prior announcement, it began again, suddenly. American officials took the view that rejection of the notes in Moscow and Hanoi was clear proof of North Vietnamese intransigence. Yet many believed the United States could not have reasonably expected Ho Chi Minh to accept with alacrity the demand made in Rusk's note to lay down his arms.

In the last hours of the bombing pause, Mai Van Bo, the North Vietnamese representative in Paris, went to the Quai d'Orsay for a meeting with Etienne Manac'h, the director of Far Eastern affairs for the French Foreign Ministry. Sources said Bo was skeptical about his visit. It was understood he simply reiterated the four points Premier Pham Van Dong had proposed as the basis for a settlement at the same time Lyndon Johnson made his Johns Hopkins speech. But Bo apparently suggested that the withdrawal of American troops demanded in the four points would not have to precede a settlement.

Was this a diplomatic nibble by the North Vietnamese at Rusk's message? In Paris it was not treated that way. One official said: "There were only hours left before the bombing resumption. The message [relayed by Manac'h to the American Embassy] was not clear. . . . Bo did not give the impression of urgency in the way he handled it. He kind of ambled into Manac'h's office. Our embassy did not handle it with any urgency. I'm not sure whether the message got to Washington before the bombing resumed." Another source said it did not get to Washington until a day or two after the bombing resumption.

There was an inconsistency in the policy of an administration that produced simultaneously a bombing pause and a message to the enemy that discouraged negotiations. One explanation is Hanoi's: The United States masked its escalatory moves with peace talk that was all sham. Another, more subtle and complex, was indicated by the experiences of the French Vietnam expert, Professor Philippe Devillers, during and just after the May pause. A widely recognized authority on Southeast Asia, Professor Devillers had gone to Washington to meet American Vietnam policy-makers personally. The day before the bombing pause ended, he visited Walt Rostow, then chairman of the State Department's Policy Planning Council. The professor was shaken by the hardness in Rostow as he slapped the desk with his palm and said of Vietnam: "It is on this spot that we have to break the liberation war—Chinese type. If we don't break it here we shall have to face it again in Thailand, Venezuela, elsewhere. Vietnam is a clear testing ground for our policy in the world."

This is the kind of attitude that could produce the note Rusk sent the North Vietnamese. Four days later the professor encountered the kind of attitude that could have been responsible for the pause. He went to the executive offices of the President and met with Chester Cooper and James C. Thomson Jr., then both members of McGeorge Bundy's National Security Council staff. Cooper told the Frenchman: "The President is very anxious to end the war. He is so obsessed with the war and there are so many problems at home to be dealt with . . . Try to convey the message that the President is eager to grasp any opportunity. Help the President find a suitable way out." [10]

Was there enough time in the May pause to allow the North Vietnamese to react carefully? The Administration thought so. In July, Dean Rusk told a Voice of America interviewer the bombing had been resumed after a "very harsh, very harsh" reply from Hanoi. Such a reply has never been released and, in fact, Rusk himself cast doubt on its existence in the same interview, when he said: "We've asked the other side on more than one occasion what else would stop if we stopped the bombing.

---

[10] Devillers saw two faces of one government again the following August 26 in New York. In the morning he met UN Ambassador Arthur Goldberg, who said the United States was just waiting to respond to a peace signal from Hanoi. In the afternoon William Bundy flew from Washington to meet Devillers in a motel room and tell him "there is no point in negotiations until we rebuild South Vietnam." Devillers chose to believe Cooper and Goldberg and indeed did try a hand at mediation to "help the President find a suitable way out." He discovered, he said later, that it was the Rostow-Bundy view and not the Cooper-Goldberg view that prevailed. He felt the United States had let him down and that his credibility with Hanoi's representatives in Paris had been damaged.

What else will stop? Are you going to stop sending those tens of thousands of men from North Vietnam into South Vietnam? Are you going to stop attacking those villages and killing off thousands of innocent civilians? What else will stop? And we've never had any reply."

On August 9 Robert McNamara dealt with the length of the pause this way in a television interview: "It was long enough for North Vietnam to make perfectly clear that they didn't plan to do anything as a result of our stopping other than what they had previously been doing. They wouldn't talk. They wouldn't stop the aggression in the South. They wouldn't agree to talk in the future, so all I can say, we stopped and maybe sometime in the future . . ."

He never finished his answer. His interviewer never challenged him on just what the United States had proposed during the five-day pause simply because at that time the proposal Rusk made was not known.

The pause was not undertaken with an offer to negotiate. It seemed instead a test of the thesis that within three months of bombing, Ho Chi Minh would sue for peace. The test had failed—and so had an attempt at direct diplomacy. It soon became time for an ascetic Florentine politician to see if mediation based on Biblical precepts might not work.

CHAPTER EIGHT

Savonarola, Circa 1965

The Monastery of San Marco in downtown Florence is one of the secondary tourist attractions in the city where the Renaissance was born. You do it only on a leisurely tour after the Duomo, the Baptistry, the Medici Chapel, the Piazza della Signoria, the Palazzo Vecchio, the endless museums, the hilltown environs, the Ponte Vecchio and the leather shops. Which is to say that only the most intrepid tourists ever see the monastery built by the Medici family and decorated by Fra Angelico. The Dominican friar Girolamo Savonarola was elected Prior of San Marco in 1490, and from his position he preached zealously against the simony of the Holy See and the moral degeneration of Renaissance Italy. He was the conscience of his time.

Just a few steps from the cell in which the prior's hair shirt, rosary and other relics are on display, Giorgio La Pira, a modern-day Savonarola, has occupied ascetic quarters for over thirty years. Though not a clergyman, he has preferred the monastic quarters.

He lived there before World War II as a law professor at the university and the publisher of an anti-Fascist magazine. He moved out during the war to go into hiding when the Fascists made him a wanted man. He took up residence again after the war. He lived there while he dominated Florentine life as the mayor of the city from 1950 to 1957 and again from 1960 to 1964, with all the drama that characterized Savonarola's rule from 1490 to 1498.

La Pira's is not an imposing residence. You step through a doorway cut into a side wall of the monastery and down one step into a hallway. The first thing you notice is a red silhouette bas-relief, hanging on a wall, of Fra Bartolomeo's famous profile of Savonarola. Two of the three rooms are for work. In one a group of volunteer women sit typing La Pira's voluminous correspondence while his student followers carry on quiet, earnest discussions in the corners.

La Pira does not in any way physically resemble the stern, handsome, sharp-featured prior. He is a small man whose lively eyes are magnified by thick, rimless spectacles. His clothing is nondescript. His voice is squeaky, not at all like that of the prior, which, it is said, used to shake the thick green-and-white marble walls of the cathedral when he railed against the false popes in Rome.

Savonarola was only forty-six when he was martyred at the stake in 1498 after Pope Alexander VI and the Franciscans conspired to put down the Dominican's moralistic revolt against the status quo. La Pira's martyrdom came at the ballot box in 1965, when, at sixty-one, he was finally turned out of power partly because of a trip he made that year to Hanoi to talk to Ho Chi Minh. He wanted to see if his political philosophy, which is based on making the Sermon on the Mount come true, could help bring peace to Southeast Asia.

La Pira's adventure in Hanoi developed out of a forty-year friendship with Italian Foreign Minister Amintore Fanfani. Years ago Fanfani had been a student of La Pira's at Catholic University in Milan. After World War II La Pira helped Fanfani organize the Christian Democratic Party, which was to be the liberal bulwark against the powerful Communist Party in Italy. La Pira worked as deputy labor minister to Fanfani in the late 1940s and served as a member of Parliament. In 1950, when the Communists seemed certain winners in municipal elections in Florence, La Pira retired from the national scene to lead the Christian Democratic ticket in that city. He won a thankless job. Florence was still paralyzed. The vital Arno River bridges destroyed in the war had not been rebuilt. Schools for the children, homes for the families, jobs for the workers: all were sadly lacking as a result of the war.

La Pira described what he did this way: "I looked into the laws—and between them—and found an old law that said I could take the villas that were empty and give them to the homeless. The laws allowed me to requisition industry. We put people to work building bridges and schools. All this without money you don't do. Mathematics is like a balance, but what is spent is always less than what is gotten for the money. We didn't use the money to dance. We used it to give the people what they needed. It was Keynesian economics."

By 1957 he had presided over an "economic miracle" for Florence, but was, as often happens with political reformers, turned out of office. He said he was the victim of "Socialist Democrat McCarthyism." By 1960 he was back in office. During his years in local politics he also gratified his desire to act on a larger stage. He held conferences for mayors from all over the world. He kept in touch through a ceaseless correspondence with leading figures in both the Communist and non-Communist camps. He envisioned his beloved Florence, with its great cultural heritage, as a spiritual center and as an active force in bringing peace to the world. His endeavors were not successful. He brought Arabs and Jews together in an attempt to settle the Arab-Israeli dispute and only succeeded in stirring up more enmity. An effort to solve the French-Algerian war also foundered.

His anti-Communist credentials were impeccable. In the 1950s he turned down invitations to visit both the Mayor of Moscow and Ho Chi Minh, saying they should instead come to Florence, where he had more freedom than they in their cities.

La Pira was an ardent supporter of John F. Kennedy and had, he has said since, no great objection to the late President's foreign policies. He assumed that Lyndon Johnson would carry on those policies. He was still confident after the August, 1964, Gulf of Tonkin incidents and rebuffed a complaint cabled to him then by Chou En-lai about the American activities. Not until after the February, 1965, air raids on North Vietnam did his mind change. He stepped up his letter-writing activities and convened a seminar of foreign policy experts in Florence, who drafted a document calling for a reconvening of the Geneva Conference and a settlement. The document was sent to all the parties involved. It was generally ignored by all but the North Vietnamese, who sent an answer condemning the United States.

In May, 1965, President Johnson encouraged Fanfani to help the United States seek a negotiated settlement. In the following months Fanfani discussed the situation with his old friend La Pira. Fanfani suggested that La Pira travel to Hanoi to explore prospects for negotiation. While Ho was turning down requests for visits by a British Commonwealth peace mission and Kwame Nkrumah, then president of Ghana, La Pira sought an invitation from Ho. He received it on September 7, 1965.[1]

La Pira, then a professor of Roman law at the University of Florence, and Professor Mario Primicerio, a young mathematician, set out for Hanoi on October 20, in an atmosphere of great secrecy. They traveled by way of Warsaw, Moscow and Peking, staying in each of those cities as the guests of the North Vietnamese. When poor weather forced them to remain two days in Siberia, the North Vietnamese government paid the bills there as well.

La Pira and Primicerio reached Hanoi on November 8 and embarked on a two-day round of visits to churches, a university and some political groups. On the third day they met Ho Chi Minh, Pham Van Dong and two representatives of the National Liberation Front of South Vietnam for an hour and a half. The group talked at length about peace negotiations. La Pira was certain Ho considered him as a representative of the Western powers and a man authorized to convey terms for negotiations.

---

[1] After La Pira received his invitation he wrote Harry S. Ashmore, executive vice-president of the Center for the Study of Democratic Institutions in Santa Barbara, California, to ask him if there was anything he could do while in Hanoi for the Center's planned Pacem in Terris Conference. Ashmore empowered La Pira to deliver invitations to the Chinese and North Vietnamese. Ashmore himself, while delivering such an invitation to a subsequent conference, was to get involved in a peace feeler over a year later.

The North Vietnamese gave him no written documents, but La Pira took careful notes and said later he paused several times to check various points with his hosts.

The interview ended with Ho asking: "Well, Mr. La Pira, how do you think? What will happen?"

La Pira said he answered: "We are only one swallow. It is true that one swallow does not make a spring. But nevertheless we are a swallow. Maybe there will be more."

The next morning La Para attended a 5 A.M. requiem mass in a Catholic church for a dead priest. Then the two Italians left Hanoi, retracing their path to Rome.[2]

The two arrived in Rome on November 15 and sent a cable to Fanfani in New York, summarizing their findings in Hanoi. Then Primicerio flew to New York to report to Fanfani, who was serving as president of the United Nations General Assembly. Fanfani conferred with Ambassador Arthur Goldberg on November 19, and the following day wrote a letter to President Johnson about the La Pira–Ho talks. The important two paragraphs of the letter said:

> On Thursday, November 11, in Hanoi, Ho Chi Minh and the President of the Council, Van Dong, expressed to two persons (known to me) the strong desire to find a peaceful solution to the conflict in Vietnam and, in summary, stated—according to what they wrote me—that "in order for the peace negotiations to come about, there will be necessary (a) a cease-fire (by air, by sea, by land) in the entire territory of Vietnam (north and south); cessation, that is, of all belligerent operations (including therefore also the cessation of debarkation of further American troops); (b) a declaration according to which the Geneva Agreements of 1954 will be taken as the basis for the negotiations —a declaration made up of the four points formulated by Hanoi, points that are in reality the explanation of the Geneva text which, therefore, can be reduced to a single point: application, in other words, of the Geneva accords."

---

[2] By the time the two men arrived in Hanoi, they had spent all of their money, La Pira recalled later, and had to request 200,000 lire (about $300) from Ho for incidental expenses on the way home.

The text of the communication which I have received adds that "the government in Hanoi is prepared to initiate negotiations without first requiring actual withdrawal of the American troops."

To the same interlocutors, Ho Chi Minh said: "I am prepared to go anywhere; to meet anyone."

The words attributed to Ho were almost identical to statements President Johnson had made from time to time.

With Fanfani's letter to the President, the report of two amateur diplomats became grist for the professionals. Fanfani took over for La Pira. Dean Rusk handled matters for the President. On November 29, unknown to La Pira, Arthur Goldberg and Fanfani met in New York, and Goldberg told Fanfani that a letter would be forthcoming shortly from Rusk. Fanfani received the letter December 6. It said:

1. The United States was reaffirming willingness to enter discussions or negotiations without any preconditions.

2. It would be willing to negotiate on the basis of the Geneva agreements without qualification or conditions.

3. It did not agree that Hanoi's four points—particularly the reference to the NLF program—were an authentic interpretation of the Geneva agreements, and that Hanoi's "apparent insistence" on a prior declaration accepting them seemed inconsistent and a precondition. The United States would be prepared to discuss the four points as well as other points it, South Vietnam or other governments wished to advance.

4. A cease-fire would have to be mutual.

5. It saw significance in Hanoi's failure to demand withdrawal of troops prior to negotiations but still saw problems in items two and three. As a result: "We are thus far from persuaded that statements by Ho Chi Minh and Pham Van Dong quoted by your Italian sources indicate a real willingness for unconditional negotiations."

On the day Fanfani received Rusk's letter, he summarized it in a letter of his own to North Vietnamese officials, which he gave to representatives of a third country, believed to be

Poland. The letter reached Hanoi by December 13. On that day Fanfani informed Rusk of the letter's arrival in Hanoi. None of this was made known to the inhabitant of the San Marco monastery

On Saturday night, December 4, a telephone rang in a restaurant in Strasbourg, France. Professor Giorgio La Pira was calling from Florence. He wanted to talk to Peter Weiss, an American copyright attorney from New York who, he knew, was dining there. Weiss came to the phone and found himself being urged to come to Florence. It was, La Pira told him, a matter of war and peace. Weiss had just completed a long business trip and was looking forward to returning to New York the next day. He resisted. But not for long.

"You know, when you're talking to La Pira," Weiss recalled, "it's like you're talking to an emissary of the Almighty, because of his kind of faith. He's a man driven by faith. And it comes through. He's a hard man to turn down."

La Pira knew Weiss as a participant in those early attempts at Florentine mediation of the Arab-Israeli dispute. Weiss, a well-known liberal activist, had attended two of the sessions. He was also an acquaintance of Ashmore. La Pira, not realizing Fanfani had already been promised a reply from the Americans, had grown dejected over the lack of response. He saw signs that the war was escalating and feared that the Johnson Administration was not taking advantage of the opening he had provided. He wanted to put pressure on the Administration. He had placed a call to Weiss in New York and learned the lawyer was in Europe. He traced him from Paris to Strasbourg and then from Weiss' hotel to the restaurant.

Two and a half hours after the call Weiss was on the midnight train to Florence. The next day, a Sunday, he spent four hours in La Pira's quarters at San Marco discussing the Hanoi visit with La Pira and Primicerio. As active and literate members of the anti-war movement in the United States, Weiss and his wife had studied the course of Vietnam diplomacy carefully. Thus, he was not impressed with the newness of what La Pira was saying. "It was more or less of a piece with everything that had happened within the previous years or eighteen months," Weiss recalled. "I thought it was important that Ho Chi Minh and Pham Van Dong spent all that time with him. I thought the one new thing was possibly the warning that if Hanoi or Haiphong were bombed, it would close off the possibility of peace negotiations." (That warning had not been included in Fanfani's letter to the President.)

La Pira urged Weiss to spread the word of his effort among influential Americans. Weiss returned to New York and called Ashmore, who, in turn, arranged a meeting between Weiss and Arthur Goldberg on December 8. Weiss told the ambassador of his conversation with La Pira. Goldberg told him the government had already heard about La Pira's journey to Hanoi from Fanfani and that Rusk had already replied. Goldberg did not tell Weiss of the nature of the reply.

Weiss had also drafted a memo covering his conversation with La Pira, which included the warning about bombing Hanoi and Haiphong. He left one copy with Goldberg and sent out five copies, four of them through intermediaries who knew the recipients. He personally delivered one to Representative Jonathan B. Bingham of New York. The others went to McGeorge Bundy at the White House, Supreme Court Justice William O. Douglas, Senator J. William Fulbright and Senator Robert F. Kennedy, who was included at La Pira's demand.

On December 15, two days after Ho received Fanfani's letter, a flight of four to six Thunderchief fighter-bombers dropped some twelve tons of bombs on the Uongbi power plant fourteen miles from downtown Haiphong. It was described as the first raid on a major industrial target in North Vietnam. The next day Defense Secretary McNamara said the raid was "appropriate to the increased terrorist activity in Vietnam" and "representative of the type of attacks we . . . will continue to carry out." Uongbi's 24,000 kilowatts of generating capacity represented fifteen percent of North Vietnam's power supply. Apparently the bombers failed in knocking it out completely. They attacked again on December 20.

It is not known whether the warning about the effect of

such a raid in Weiss' memorandum was considered at the Tuesday lunch level before the Uongbi air strike was approved.

All of this was happening in the weeks following publication of Eric Sevareid's story of the U Thant–Adlai Stevenson peace initiative. Public interest in the subject of peace talks was high. The third week in December, Richard Dudman, a St. Louis *Post-Dispatch* Washington correspondent, acting on a tip that interesting peace feelers were being passed from Mai Van Bo to Etienne Manac'h in Paris, began making inquiries. One of his calls went to a recipient of the Weiss memo. Yes, Dudman learned, there was something doing but not in Paris. The source had a memo on his desk. Dudman could have a copy. Dudman checked the memo with an Administration source on December 16 and was told the initiative was not being taken seriously in Washington. Dudman learned nothing of the Rusk correspondence with Fanfani. The source who had given him the Weiss memorandum told him the Administration had "rejected" the initiative. The bombing the day before of the Haiphong power plant in the face of the warning in Weiss' memorandum appeared to Dudman to confirm that there had been a rejection.

He filed a story for the December 17 editions of his afternoon newspaper, saying the United States had rejected the initiative. The morning of the seventeenth, still in time to make his first edition, Dudman called James Greenfield, then the Assistant Secretary of State for Public Affairs, and Weiss, for comment. Weiss asked him to kill the story because he thought the initiative was still live. Greenfield said the story would destroy the La Pira channel. After checking with his superiors, Greenfield told Dudman he could see the entire La Pira file if he held up the story. But by this time the presses were running in St. Louis. The story created a world-wide sensation. Goldberg accused Weiss of leaking the story to Dudman and publicly implied the *Post-Dispatch* had ruined the chances for peace in Vietnam. Weiss had never met Dudman and both agree the New Yorker was not the source of the story. To make his charge against the *Post-Dispatch,* Goldberg had to discount both the sentence in

Rusk's letter about how "far from persuaded" the Johnson Administration was of Hanoi's willingness to talk and the Haiphong power-plant raid.

Within hours after Dudman's story was on the streets in St. Louis, the State Department released the Rusk-Fanfani correspondence. Robert McCloskey denied the "rejection" of the proposal, saying: "It is now up to Hanoi to determine whether it wishes to move this question from the battlefield to the conference table. We would welcome a straightforward expression of Hanoi's views. We await Hanoi's reaction."

The following day the North Vietnamese issued a statement denouncing talk of a peace probe as "sheer, groundless fabrication." This was to be expected. Weiss' memo had said it would happen if the initiative became public. The statement generally went on to confirm the message La Pira and Primicerio had brought home from Hanoi.

The United States had obvious reservations, but it nevertheless took La Pira's initiative seriously. The death of the initiative had an explosive aftermath in Italy.

In late December, Fanfani defended the efforts of his friend La Pira in the face of much criticism from those in Italy who felt that Fanfani had meddled in something that should not have concerned the Italian government. About the same time Mrs. Fanfani was approached by the editor of the right-wing magazine *Borghese* and asked if she could set up an interview with La Pira. Mrs. Fanfani agreed, thinking La Pira could charm *Borghese*'s editor and thus steer the magazine away from its criticism of him and her husband. La Pira was quoted as calling Italian Premier Aldo Moro "sad and soft," the Socialist Vice-Premier Pietro Nenni "extinct" like his party, and Dean Rusk one who "doesn't know anything, doesn't understand much." Fanfani interpreted this as an insult to his Christian Democratic Party by his friend. He resigned his job, ostensibly to save Moro from embarrassment. Actually Fanfani, an astute political infighter, seized on the incident to challenge Moro's authority. In January the whole incident was smoothed out, with Fanfani

back in office—but not until the Italian press enjoyed a long
spell of big headlines over it.

By the end of 1967 Giorgio La Pira was running his letter-
writing operation from his three simple rooms in San Marco,
unencumbered by the worries of high office. He had returned to
teaching. His students, most Florentines and even, begrudgingly,
his detractors, all considered him something of a saint. He was
brooding more than ever over the future of the world.

He cited John F. Kennedy's speech at the United Nations on
September 25, 1961, in which the President reminded nations of
their responsibilities for the next 10,000 years. "Mankind must
put an end to war or war will put an end to mankind," Kennedy
said. To this La Pira added: "I stand for ten thousand years of
peace for all, for the idea that war is impossible and peace
inevitable, for the construction of economic bridges for everyone.
It's quite sensible and it corresponds to the Biblical vision of the
world.

"And you can't say to me, 'Well, you are a dreamer'—I
know they call me a dreamer. I say you are wrong. Johnson is
a dreamer. You can see that he put himself in a position and
now he can't get himself out.

CHAPTER NINE

Four, Fourteen or Forty

Down on the Texas range they have a form of entertainment that is as big as life. They call it a "fandangle" and it has just about everything in it—barroom brawls, shoot-outs, singing, dancing, herds of cattle, fireworks. A fandangle is a sight to behold, as rancher Lyndon B. Johnson well knows. He has brought Texas fandangles to his LBJ Ranch, in sparse hill country forty-eight miles west of Austin, to entertain important guests. Even the most sophisticated come away impressed.

In the wake of all the publicity in December, 1965, on the collapse of the Giorgio La Pira mediation effort and the controversy over the U Thant–Adlai Stevenson initiative, President Johnson decided to try fandangle diplomacy. He launched a loud peace offensive, seemingly designed as much to prove to the world that he really wanted a negotiated settlement to the war as it was to bring about that settlement. The effort was accompanied by an enormous amount of publicity. The travels and sayings of special American peace emissaries the world over dominated the headlines much of the time.

Some professionals, encrusted in the traditions of diplomacy, were disparaging of a search for peace made publicly. They thought the only diplomacy the Communists take seriously is that conducted in secret. But not all that happened during Lyndon Johnson's fandangle surfaced on page one.

The peace offensive had its roots in a suggestion made by Defense Secretary Robert McNamara in November, 1965, that the bombing of North Vietnam be stopped for an extended period to test Ho Chi Minh's willingness to talk. The President began to give the suggestion careful consideration after the brouhahas over the La Pira and Thant-Stevenson episodes. The plans of the President were still in the making while world leaders such as Thant and Pope Paul VI were calling for extended truces in the fighting during the Christmas, New Year's and Tet holidays of December, 1965–January, 1966.

The President quite evidently was disturbed by the adverse publicity on the peace initiative disclosures. For instance, on December 20 he held a state dinner for West German Chancellor Ludwig Erhard but did not invite the chairman of the Senate Foreign Relations Committee, J. William Fulbright. The senator had criticized the May, 1965, bombing pause as too short, and had continued to press for a more meaningful halt in the air war. For this (as well as for his assault on the Administration for intervening in the Dominican Republic rebellion), he received a presidential cold shoulder.

The scheduled Christmas bombing pause started at 5:30 A.M. Washington time, Friday, December 24. There was no official word that it would be extended beyond the thirty-hour truce announced by military headquarters in Saigon. The bombers were grounded after carrying out the fourth raid in six days against the Haiphong area industrial complex. The first hint that something unusual might be developing came in reports from Washington the day after Christmas that an "air of mystery" surrounded the fact that no bombing missions had yet been carried out after the expiration of the Christmas truce. On December 28 a Pentagon spokesman acknowledged that the continued bombing pause was for "diplomatic" and not "military" reasons. While public awareness of the attempt to achieve negotiations came slowly, some diplomats were hard at work behind the scenes. They were trying to establish direct and secret contact with the North Vietnamese.

The key locale was Rangoon, where the American ambassador, Henry A. Byroade, despite the isolationism of Burma's leader, General Ne Win, had established good relations. The decision to try Rangoon was partly based on the preliminary work U Thant had done the previous January in getting Ne Win's approval for face-to-face meetings between the Vietnam adversaries. On December 29 Byroade received a message from Washington, with instructions to find a discreet way to deliver it to the North Vietnamese mission in Rangoon.

Formerly a brigadier general in the Army and an assistant secretary of state, Byroade, at fifty-two, was a direct individual who knew how to use authority. Other diplomats might react overcautiously to the instruction to be discreet by seeking out a circuitous channel to the North Vietnamese. Byroade simply telephoned the North Vietnamese consulate. He said he had a message from his government to deliver to Vu Huu Binh, Hanoi's consul general in Rangoon, and asked for an appointment. Several hours later he was told Binh would see him. That afternoon Byroade drove his private car to the North Vietnamese consulate at 40 Komin Kochin Road. Binh offered Byroade a beer. Byroade accepted. Then they talked.

According to one source, the note Byroade gave Binh informed the North Vietnamese that the bombing pause had started and said the United States "expected" some kind of response. A week or ten days later, according to Rangoon sources, Byroade received an answer. The North Vietnamese considered the note an ultimatum. (The objection, it was reported, was the use of the word "expected" rather than a more conciliatory term like "hoped for.") The United States, it was understood, had Byroade deliver still another message to Binh at a third meeting. The timing of a reply to that message was to assume some importance.

While Byroade was quietly developing a direct channel in Rangoon, the President raised the curtain on his peace fandangle. Before anyone realized it, Averell Harriman was aloft in a Boeing 707 presidential jet bound for Warsaw. The move took everyone by surprise, including the American Embassy in Warsaw and the Polish government. Ambassador John Gronouski was in Poznan to visit a trade fair. The plane was already airborne when Gronouski's deputy, Albert W. (Bud) Sherer, Jr., received instructions from Washington to inform the Polish government of their impending visitor and to make arrangements for the landing. Sherer and Mieczyslaw Sieradski, the deputy director of the North American department in the Polish Foreign Ministry, worked through the night to prepare for Harriman. Meanwhile, Gronouski was roused from bed in Poznan and ordered back to Warsaw. He caught a night train that got him back to the capital with just enough time left to clean up before he went to the airport to meet Harriman. The plane was only about two hours from touchdown when Sherer and Sieradski completed the arrangements. With the Harriman plane passing Bornholm Island in the Baltic Sea and only minutes to spare, the Polish Air Force sent word to its outlying bases not to scramble against the unidentified aircraft approaching the coast.

Reports at the time said Harriman was traveling with a retinue of seventeen aides. Actually, the group included two seven-man flight crews. The roving ambassador had with him only a specialist on Hungary and one on China, as well as a personal staff member.

Almost immediately after landing, Harriman, with Gronouski, called on Foreign Minister Adam Rapacki. Jerzy Michalowski, one of Rapacki's principal deputies, sat in on the conversation. Harriman's message, as was that of all the presidential envoys spreading out around the world, was a general one. The United States wanted to talk to the North Vietnamese. It was willing to talk on almost any terms. In fact, there were several ways in which the talks could be carried out. Within a few days the White House would make that message public in a statement entitled, "The Heart of the Matter in Vietnam." It listed fourteen points, under a subheading, "U. S. Contributions to the Basket of Peace":

1. The Geneva agreements of 1954 and 1962 are an adequate basis for peace in Southeast Asia;

2. We would welcome a conference on Southeast Asia or on any part thereof;

3. We would welcome "negotiations without pre-conditions" as the seventeen nations put it;

4. We would welcome unconditional discussions as President Johnson put it;

5. A cessation of hostilities could be the first order of business at a conference or could be the subject of preliminary discussions;

6. Hanoi's four points could be discussed along with other points which others might wish to propose;

7. We want no U. S. bases in Southeast Asia;

8. We do not desire to retain U. S. troops in South Vietnam after peace is assured;

9. We support free elections in South Vietnam to give the South Vietnamese a government of their own choice;

10. The question of reunification of Vietnam should be determined by the Vietnamese through their own free decision;

11. The countries of Southeast Asia can be nonaligned or neutral if that be their option;

12. We would much prefer to use our resources for the economic reconstruction of Southeast Asia than in war. If there is peace, North Vietnam could participate in a regional effort to which we would be prepared to contribute at least one billion dollars;

13. The President has said "the Viet Cong would not have difficulty being represented and having their views represented if for a moment Hanoi decided she wanted to cease aggression. I don't think that would be an insurmountable problem."

14. We have said publicly and privately that we could stop the bombing of North Vietnam as a step toward peace although there has not been the slightest hint or suggestion from the other side as to what they would do if the bombing stopped."

The drafters of the fourteen points appended one more sentence that verged on whimsy: "In other words, we have put everything into the basket of peace except the surrender of South Vietnam."

Harriman's presentation to the Poles was convincing. And he got the opportunity to make it not only to Rapacki but also to Wladyslaw Gomulka, the first secretary of the Polish Communist Party. Usually Gomulka, like all Communist Party leaders, is inaccessible to Western diplomats and statesmen. But Harriman had long experience in dealing with the Communist world, including service as ambassador in Moscow during World War II. For Harriman, Gomulka relented. Such meetings were so rare that the session with Harriman was the only time Gronouski met the man who really ran Poland.

When Harriman related why he had come, Gomulka answered, according to Communist sources: "You are gangsters, but we are willing to deal with gangsters to stop the war."

Harriman left Warsaw not knowing what the Poles would do and flew on to Yugoslavia to see Marshal Josef Tito. Gomulka and Rapacki may have indicated they would try to sound out the North Vietnamese, but they did not specify in what manner. They decided, in fact, to dispatch Jerzy Michalowski to Hanoi. Michalowski, as a former Polish representative on the International Control Commission, was no stranger to the North Vietnamese capital. While Harriman was taking off from Warsaw's airport on December 30, Michalowski also was there, waiting for a flight to take off for Hanoi. When Michalowski heard the Harriman party was arriving, he boarded his own plane early to avoid detection.

Harriman went on to complete a ten-nation, seventeen-day, 30,000-mile itinerary, arriving in Saigon on January 15. Michalowski went to Hanoi, and apparently tried to cajole the North Vietnamese into taking up the American offer to talk. He remained away from Warsaw eighteen days. The Poles tried to keep the trip secret. The Foreign Ministry put out a story that he was ill. All social engagements he had accepted for the New Year's season were canceled. His wife, Mira, a former researcher for *Time* magazine, well-known author and social lioness in the capital, went into seclusion rather than appear in public and risk inadvertently giving her husband's secret away.[1]

Harriman's trip had all the earmarks of improvisation. When

---

[1] Michalowski almost encountered Harriman on January 13 when they were both in Vientiane, the capital of Laos. The Pole was talking with Laotian Premier Souvanna Phouma when he learned Harriman was due in an hour. He bid the premier a quick farewell and left the palace before Harriman arrived.

he landed in Belgrade he told reporters he would leave the next day for Paris to make a rest stop before returning to Washington. Instead, he hurtled off to New Delhi and Peshawar to carry messages to Indian Prime Minister Lal Bahadur Shastri and Pakistan's Mohammed Ayub Khan. From there he zigzagged around the globe to Teheran (where he told reporters, "This is as far as I go on this mission"), Cairo, Bangkok, Tokyo, Canberra, Vientiane and Bangkok again before going to Saigon. He remained in Saigon from January 15 to January 19 before returning to Washington via Manila.

Harriman was not the only special emissary on the move. McGeorge Bundy flew to Ottawa to give the Canadians the fourteen points. Thomas C. Mann, Assistant Secretary of State for Inter-American Affairs, went to Mexico City. Arthur Goldberg, summoned from a vacation in the Bahamas, raced to Rome on December 30 to confer with officials in the Vatican and the Italian government. Then he went to Paris for a New Year's Eve talk with President de Gaulle—telling the Frenchman the war "can only be settled at the conference table without prior conditions"—and finally on to London for a New Year's Day meeting with Harold Wilson, who interrupted a Scilly Islands vacation for the session.

G. Mennen Williams, Assistant Secretary of State for African Affairs, also was enlisted. Home in Detroit to celebrate the New Year, Williams received a call from Dean Rusk at 11 A.M. on December 31 to return to Washington immediately. He made a 2 P.M. commercial flight. He was briefed at the State Department that afternoon and spent New Year's Eve aboard another of the presidential jets en route to Morocco. He covered fourteen nations in seven days. To maintain that kind of schedule, not only did his plane carry alternating flight crews but a back-up plane was sent to Africa in case anything happened to the primary craft. The pace was so hectic that some in the Williams party, fully occupied while in the air with the drafting of cables and memoranda for the State Department, would occasionally step off the plane not quite sure where they had landed. Williams sought out Kenyan leader Jomo Kenyatta at the resort city of Mombassa on the Indian Ocean. He intruded on the Ivory Coast leaders just as they were beginning an important meeting of their political party's national committee. The meeting was postponed. Wherever he went Williams engendered enthusiasm as leaders of the emerging nations were given the feeling they could participate in bringing peace to Southeast Asia.[2]

The President also made Hubert Humphrey part of his peace-seeking team. The vice-president went to Tokyo on December 28 to talk with Premier Eisaku Sato, and reportedly gave him a document detailing 190 different conversations Dean Rusk had had on the subject of peace negotiations with various diplomats and other persons. In January, Harriman visited Tokyo to urge Foreign Minister Etsusaburo Shiina to use what influence he could on the Soviet Union to get talks started.

In addition to Michalowski's trip to Hanoi and Byroade's meetings in Rangoon, there were indications of other secret efforts to initiate talks. For instance, in Algiers, President Houari Boumediene conferred with North Vietnamese and the National Liberation Front representatives. Something apparently was afoot in Moscow as well. Several months after the bombing of North Vietnam was resumed, a Soviet ambassador told a Western diplomat that talks had occurred in Moscow during the pause, and that the Soviet government was furious because the bombing resumption destroyed those contacts. The ambassador would not specify whether there had been direct United States–North Vietnam talks in Moscow or whether the Soviet government had been the intermediary in the exchanges.

For a time it appeared that Budapest, like Rangoon, might become a locale for talks. Janos Peter, the former clergyman turned foreign minister of Hungary, had, in the fall of 1965, made a United Nations speech saying the North Vietnamese would talk if the bombing stopped. He later told Rusk the same thing in a meeting, according to Janos Radvanyi, the senior Hungarian diplomat in the United States who since defected

---

[2] Ghana's Kwame Nkrumah was so taken with Williams' presentation that he decided to go to Hanoi to see if he could mediate. While he was flying from Rangoon to Peking, en route to Hanoi, on February 24, the Ghanaian Army, assisted by air force and navy units, seized control of Accra and deposed the fifty-six-year-old leader. Nkrumah never made it to Hanoi. The North Vietnamese canceled his visit. He went into exile in Guinea.

and settled in California. Radvanyi wrote in *Life* magazine in March, 1968, that on December 23, 1965, Rusk called him to the State Department to present to him what was later published as the fourteen points. This set off a series of meetings and cablegrams in which Peter tried to arrange talks between the United States and North Vietnam in Budapest. Rusk tried to keep the contacts limited to Rangoon, Radvanyi said, but agreed to Budapest if necessary. Radvanyi said the Johnson Administration would only meet National Liberation Front representatives as members of a North Vietnamese delegation. Peter persisted in trying to arrange a meeting that included the NLF. Throughout January the State Department nagged Radvanyi for word from Budapest. None came despite his cabled urgings.

While the fandangle diplomacy was in full swing, the Soviet Union was going through another prestige-building phase in Asia. On December 21 Soviet leaders had signed a new economic and technical aid agreement with the North Vietnamese in Moscow. Then Leonid Brezhnev, the Soviet Communist Party chief, went to Ulan Bator to strengthen ties with Mongolia, the buffer state between Siberia and Red China, and made a speech saying the United States wanted negotiations now simply because it realized the "hopelessness" of its situation. All it had to do, Brezhnev said, was recognize "the justness of the Vietnamese people's demands." Alexander N. Shelepin, another Soviet presidium member, led a friendship mission to Hanoi on January 7. His delegation was weighted with military experts, giving the impression that the Kremlin was planning to increase its military commitment to North Vietnam. But Shelepin approached his task cautiously, making certain to offer just enough support so that the Chinese could not accuse the Soviets of conspiring with the United States[3] to sell out the Vietnamese people, but also, apparently, exerting influence on Hanoi to seek a negotiated settlement.

There were signs that Shelepin and his colleagues in Moscow

---

[3] Harriman did not include Moscow in his peace offensive itinerary primarily because the Johnson Administration did not want to give Peking the pretext to charge Soviet-American collusion.

were treating the American peace offensive far more seriously than the North Vietnamese, who had—publicly, at least— dismissed it as a sham. The communiqué issued by Moscow and Hanoi after the meeting, rather than expressing agreement on a condemnation of the American escalation, said this instead:

> The Soviet delegation and the North Vietnamese ex- changed views on the serious situation created by the escala- tion by the American imperialists of the aggressive war in Vietnam and Southeast Asia.

That vague sentence, ignoring the American diplomatic efforts, held open the possibility that the Soviet side at least recognized the opportunity to correct the serious situation peacefully. If not, the communiqué easily could have con- demned the peace offensive as the North Vietnamese did on January 4:

> The United States authorities' talks about peace are in complete contradiction with their war schemes and acts. While making noise about its "peace efforts," the United States is making feverish preparations to double the United States military strength in Vietnam.

On January 2 Lyndon Johnson moved his headquarters back to the White House from his Texas ranch, where he had been recovering from gall bladder surgery on October 25. One by one the peace emissaries came home to report. Arthur Goldberg reported to the President on January 4 and then told newsmen the pause was designed to show that "actions speak louder than words." The next day he circulated a letter to U Thant and other United Nations diplomats, asking them to use "any appropriate measure" to "advance the cause of a peaceful settlement."

On January 12 the President delivered his State of the Union message, and amid all the proposals designed to expand his Great Society, he had a passage pledging the United States would stay in South Vietnam "until aggression has stopped." But he said: "We will meet at any conference table, we will discuss any proposals—four points or fourteen or forty—and we will consider the views of any group. We will work for a cease-fire now or once discussions have begun. . . .

"We may have to face long, hard combat or a long, hard conference, or even both at once. . . ."

The President noted that the bombing pause, then twenty days old, had not yet produced any response from the North Vietnamese.

During January there was some indication that the bombing pause was slowing down the war in South Vietnam. Although Viet Cong units remained active, military contact with North Vietnamese troops fell sharply. On January 13 the President told reporters: "The number of incidents have dropped off markedly. I don't say there is any connection with that and our peace moves, but that is a fact."

The United States nevertheless went ahead with plans that obviously had been in the making long before the pause started to reinforce its troops in South Vietnam. At the end of December another 4,000 troops had arrived at Pleiku in the Central Highlands. In mid-January, after the President's remark to reporters, at least 7,000 more were added. This raised the total of U. S. forces in South Vietnam to about 190,000. On January 21 Senator Richard B. Russell, chairman of the Senate Armed Services Committee, said he favored and expected the eventual American troop complement in South Vietnam to reach 400,000 to 500,000 men. Arthur Goldberg had said at the White House that actions speak louder than words. Yet during a period when the United States was scouring the world for peace talks and when military "incidents" in South Vietnam had dropped "markedly," the Administration chose to increase its armed force in the South by six percent or more.

Despite the fall-off in contact with North Vietnamese main force units, the allies were not entirely quiescent on the ground during the bombing pause. On January 8 the so-called Iron Triangle, an enemy stronghold near Saigon, was struck by 8,000 American, South Vietnamese, Australian and New Zealand troops. Toward the end of the month, when it appeared the Administration had concluded that its peace probes had failed, an even larger action was mounted. Some 20,000 men of the U. S. First Cavalry Division, supported by South Vietnamese and South Koreans, staged Operations Masher and Double Eagle—search and destroy missions that included the largest amphibious landings since the Inchon landing of the Korean War

On January 11 in Tashkent, capital of the Soviet Republic of Uzbekistan in Central Asia, Indian Prime Minister Shastri died of a heart attack several hours after he and Ayub Khan had signed an accord claming the Indian-Pakistan dispute over Kashmir. Soviet Premier Alexei Kosygin, who had shown up Western skeptics by successfully mediating the conference, accompanied Shastri's body to New Delhi. The funeral for Shastri provided the opportunity for American and Soviet leaders to discuss Vietnam during the bombing pause away from Moscow and without triggering a Chinese charge of collusion. On January 13, Humphrey, Rusk and the American ambassador to India, Chester Bowles, met for two hours with Kosygin.

After the funeral Rusk went to Saigon to join Harriman in mollifying the South Vietnamese government. The Saigon leaders had grown to fear that the peace offensive would lead to negotiations that would undercut their interests. On January 16 the United States and South Vietnamese governments issued

---

⁴ In a lighter moment, Humphrey tried to charm Kosygin. Spotting the Soviet premier and his daughter strolling in the grounds of the Presidential Palace, Humphrey sent an aide to fetch a set of cuff links and a bracelet bearing the vice-presidential seal. Humphrey always keeps a supply handy. He presented the bracelet to Kosygin's daughter and the cuff links to Kosygin. The daughter put the bracelet on her wrist immediately; Kosygin was reluctant. He explained he was not sure he should wear the cuff links considering the state of Soviet-American relations. Humphrey told the premier to put the cuff links in a drawer. When Kosygin did put them on, Humphrey said, the vice-president would take that as a signal that relations had improved. Kosygin smiled and accepted the gift. Whether he has ever worn them is not known.

a communiqué pledging to continue the war and noting there had been no indication that the enemy wanted peace. The communiqué appeared to be a turning point. Rusk and Harriman flew home. They were the last of the emissaries to return. Fandangle diplomacy came to an end. Now the Johnson Administration waited for word or acceptable deed from Hanoi and began to chart its future course.

Jerzy Michalowski returned to Warsaw from Hanoi on January 16 with perhaps the first sign that North Vietnam would remain intractable. British Ambassador George Clutton asked him how things had gone in Hanoi. Michalowski's reply was at once cryptic and revealing. He said:

"God damn those Chinese."

The remark was reported to Washington.

On January 21 U Thant called on the United States to continue the bombing pause and asked that the National Liberation Front be given a role in a coalition government for South Vietnam. Opinion began to polarize. Many foreign governments—including such allies as the British and Japanese, as well as the French—called on the United States to extend the bombing pause at least beyond the Tet holidays, if not for a much greater period. American diplomats began circulating the idea that only the bombing, not the war, had been suspended.

Working against this pressure was the desire of the military leaders and some conservative powers in Congress to resume bombing. General Earle G. Wheeler, chairman of the Joint Chiefs of Staff, told the Senate Armed Services Committee on January 18: "If you stop bombing, in effect you throw one of your blue chips over your shoulder." The President showed he was cognizant of all the reasons for a bombing resumption in answering seventy-six Congressmen who asked that the Vietnam matter be referred to the United Nations. The President said there would be "no abandonment of our peace efforts" but "it is quite another matter to close our eyes to the heavy weight of evidence which has accumulated during the past month" that the other side was not interested in negotiations.

On January 25, with the bombing pause thirty-one days

old, Senator Fulbright urged the President to promise the NLF a place at the negotiating table. He and Senator Mike Mansfield, the majority leader in the Senate, asked the President to continue the pause. Fulbright said thirty-one days was not enough. Fulbright's statement came after Rusk was put through a tough interrogation at an executive session of the Senate Foreign Relations Committee.

"The poor guy had a pretty hard time between the hawks and the doves," Senator Joseph Clark told reporters. "I don't know which gave him the hardest time. The hawks were unhappy, the doves were unhappy, and Rusk was unhappy."

By the following day all signs pointed to a bombing resumption. Fandangle diplomacy had given way to another of Lyndon Johnson's favorite tactics—announcements that the President was closeted with his top national security advisers in a full-dress review of the war. News reports described the "gloomy and somber" mood in the capital. At the State Department, Robert McCloskey said there had been "no interested or affirmative replies to American peace overtures." At the White House, Press Secretary Bill Moyers said after a two-and-half-hour National Security Council meeting that the President had not made up his mind to resume the bombing. On January 27 reports circulated that the Joint Chiefs of Staff, former Ambassador Maxwell Taylor, Deputy Undersecretary of State U. Alexis Johnson, Ambassador Henry Cabot Lodge and probably Dean Rusk favored a renewal of bombing. Undersecretary of State George Ball and Arthur Goldberg were said to be opposed, although Goldberg was reported "not at the vital center" in decision-making. McNamara and McGeorge Bundy were said to be in the middle.

While the President was making ready for a bombing resumption, the North Vietnamese, on Friday, January 28, broadcast the text of a letter Ho Chi Minh had sent the previous Monday to the leaders of all Socialist countries and the heads of some other nations.[5]

---

[5] North Vietnamese diplomats in Moscow called on the British Embassy the day after the letter was broadcast with a copy for "Her Britannic Majesty." The British diplomats politely explained that the Queen maintains a staff of ministers to run the government for her.

Ho ridiculed the American peace offensive, saying:

> The Vietnamese people will never submit to the U. S. imperialists' plot. At the very moment when the U. S. government [puts] forward the so-called new peace effort, it is frantically increasing U. S. strength in South Vietnam.
>
> It is stepping up the terrorist raids, resorting to the scorched-earth policy, burning all, destroying all, killing all, using napalm bombs, poison gases and toxic chemicals to burn down villages and massacre the civilian population in vast areas of South Vietnam.
>
> I sternly protest against such extremely barbarous methods of warfare. . . .

After this invective, Ho said, in the Hanoi Radio English version: "If the U. S. government really wants a peaceful settlement, it must accept the four-point stand of the DRV government and prove this by actual deeds. It must end unconditionally and for good all bombing raids and other war acts against the DRV. Only in this way can a political solution to the Vietnam problem be envisaged."

The Ho letter came when the President, "confident and relaxed" on the last Saturday in January, had decided to resume the bombing but was, according to one report, "moving slowly and deliberately, searching the globe for last-minute evidence that North Vietnam is prepared to seek a negotiated settlement rather than a more violent war." A presidential order to resume bombing two days hence went out to the U. S. command in Saigon that day, but it could, of course, have been rescinded if there were a sudden break on the diplomatic front in the interim.

On the previous day, as part of the final "searching-the-globe" process, Rusk telephoned Janos Radvanyi to ask if there was any word from Foreign Minister Peter. Radvanyi cabled Budapest, warning that in his opinion a resumption of bombing was only hours away. He asked for an immediate answer, but received none.[6]

---

[6] Radvanyi learned some of the background when he visited Budapest the following summer. He wrote in *Life* magazine:

> Janos Peter had kept the Soviets and the Poles fully informed of

There was one piece of "last-minute evidence" in Warsaw which caused a stir. On that Saturday morning, January 29, Foreign Minister Adam Rapacki summoned British Ambassador George Clutton and "Bud" Sherer, Gronouski's deputy (Gronouski was in Germany having a tooth pulled), to the Foreign Ministry for individual appointments. He referred each to Ho's statement on the four points, reading it in French. As he read it, the United States had to "recognize" rather than "accept" the four points in a peace settlement. He told both diplomats that sentence was significant. In London and Washington the difference between "accept" and the less compelling "recognize" was spotted immediately. The possibility was considered that a misunderstanding over a translation error might prevent peace talks. In Washington, according to one source, "the best damn linguists in the government" attacked the problem that weekend. The cable traffic between the State Department and Warsaw was heavy. The Department also asked the British to check with the North Vietnamese Embassy in Moscow, which had delivered a copy of the letter.

On Sunday morning British newsmen playing broomball, a cross between ice hockey and soccer, on the frozen-over tennis court at the British Embassy in Moscow, noticed a North Vietnamese diplomat arrive. They were told he had delivered a copy of Ho's letter. Actually, he had been summoned to discuss the translation problem. The British asked him whether the English version distributed by Hanoi Radio—the "accept" version of the letter—was as official as the French. He said it was. He pointed out that the Vietnamese verb "cong nhan" can be translated as either "accept" or "recognize," that there was no dis-

---

my exchanges with Rusk, and he had also forwarded my messages to Hanoi. The Hanoi response had been completely negative. . . . The Hungarian chargé in Hanoi was told that Janos Peter "misunderstands the peace trickery of the American imperialists."

When he asked on what basis Peter had been proposing a direct meeting between North Vietnam and the United States, Radvanyi said he was told "the whole move was without any basis" and was urged not to "pry into the affair."

Radvanyi said he asked Peter what he could say to Rusk and Bundy. "It is not necessary to say anything," Peter was quoted as replying. "The Americans think anyhow that the Chinese at the last minute stopped our action."

tinction between the two. A Vietnamese-English dictionary in London verified this. The English were skeptical because *Pravda* used a Russian word that clearly meant "recognize" and not "accept." But then, in Warsaw, where the whole controversy started, the Polish Communist Party paper *Trybuna Ludu* published a version that used the Polish word for "accept." Why, Rapacki was asked that Sunday, had the newspaper used "accept" while he was saying the word was "recognize"? It developed that the Foreign Ministry had relied on the French version of the letter while the Polish News Agency had used Hanoi Radio's English text to render its translation. Rapacki blandly told the British that the news agency had been mistaken and the Foreign Ministry was right.

Washington decided the whole business was a teapot tempest. On Monday, January 31, after thirty-seven days of bombing pause and in bad weather, American planes again attacked North Vietnam.

Ever since, the Poles have complained that the British check in Moscow was with a junior official who did not realize that Hanoi really did mean "recognize." The Poles claimed that if the United States had only authorized Warsaw to check directly with officials in Hanoi, the outcome would have been different. Substantiation of such a claim would now be difficult, at best. In any case, the strong indication is that Lyndon Johnson had already made up his mind.

The United States did not even wait for a reply from Hanoi to the last message Henry Byroade had given Vu Huu Binh in Rangoon. It arrived in Rangoon several hours (one source said five hours) after the bombing resumed, but because of the communications problem in the Burmese capital, it seems highly probable that the reply was en route long before the bombing resumption.

Unless North Vietnam was willing to cut in Peking on the exchanges, Binh could not transmit Byroade's messages by cable directly to Hanoi. The only telegraphic connection possible was through facilities of the Chinese Embassy. The only secure method was by diplomatic pouch, and that was an arduous undertaking. The pouch had to go either by train from Rangoon to Kunming and then, after a change, to Hanoi, or it

could travel the same route by air. In either case, the turn-
around time involved several days at least.

The belated answer to Byroade apparently was as intractable
as Ho's letter to the heads of government. But to one Western
diplomat who learned part of what transpired in Rangoon, and
who had become disillusioned with U. S. policy in Vietnam, that
wasn't the point:

"When the reply for Byroade arrived in Rangoon, the North
Vietnamese representative there did not even know the bombing
had been resumed five hours earlier. The reply, as it turned
out, would not have been considered satisfactory [to the United
States]. But the point is that it didn't make any difference what
it said because Washington resumed bombing before they knew
what the message was. How can you expect tensions which have
risen to the level of hostilities suddenly to decrease to a level of
fruitful talks during that short period of time? To me it in-
dicates a deliberate attempt to continue the fighting."

Administration officials rejected such a judgment as harsh
and narrow, and urged instead a broader perspective of the
entire period, as reflected in President Johnson's statement upon
the resumption of bombing:

> . . . For thirty-seven days no bombs fell on North Viet-
> nam. During that time we have made a most intense and
> determined effort to enlist the help and support of all the
> world in order to persuade the government in Hanoi that
> peace is better than war, that talking is better than fighting
> and that the road to peace is open. Our effort has met with
> understanding and support throughout most of the world,
> but not in Hanoi and Peking. From those two capitals have
> come only denunciation and rejection. . . .
>
> The answer of Hanoi to all is the answer that was pub-
> lished three days ago [Ho Chi Minh's letter]; they persist
> in aggression, they insist on the surrender of South Vietnam
> to communism. It is therefore very plain that there is no
> readiness or willingness to talk. . . . The end of the pause
> does not mean the end of our own pursuit of peace.
>
> That pursuit will be as determined and as unremitting as
> the pressure of our military strength on the field of battle.

In the days immediately following the bombing pause, President Johnson went to Honolulu to meet with South Vietnam's leaders, Nguyen Cao Ky and Nguyen Van Thieu. The meeting resulted in a Declaration of Honolulu, a Ky statement promising elimination of Communist influence in South Vietnam by the end of 1967, and a Ky-Thieu press conference suggestion, which they did not urge on the President, that the port of Haiphong be bombed. In the months ahead, the big peace offensive gave way to a bigger war.

Prime Minister Lester B. Pearson was among those heads of government to receive Ho Chi Minh's letter of January 24. Even prior to that, Canada, a member of the moribund International Control Commission, had been thinking of ways to find a more meaningful role for the ICC—perhaps a role in mediating a settlement. The Pearson government was uncomfortable about the resumption of bombing in the North and the prospect of almost certain enlargement of the war in the South. The Canadians thought Ho's letter, which would require an answer, provided an opportunity for exploration.

After full consultation with Washington, the Canadian government summoned out of retirement Chester Ronning, one of the most experienced Asian hands in the Western world. Robust and sharp-witted at seventy-one, Ronning agreed to undertake a special peace mission to Hanoi. The pretext, if one was needed, was that Ronning would hand-carry Pearson's reply to Ho.

Ronning was born in China of Lutheran missionary parents, and was fluent in Chinese. He had befriended Ho Chi Minh and some of his lieutenants—including the man who was to become premier of North Vietnam, Pham Van Dong—either in China or at the 1954 and 1962 Geneva Conferences. Most Western delegates shied away from Dong and his colleagues in Geneva, but when Ronning would see them alone in the gardens he would approach and engage them in conversation. Since Ronning did not speak French, he was able to converse with some North Vietnamese in Chinese.

Ronning took Pearson's reply—which was understood to have emphasized the urgency of peace talks—to Hanoi on

March 7. For four days he conferred with Pham Van Dong and other members of Hanoi's hierarchy. Canadian officials later reported that the main message Ronning brought back from Hanoi on the March visit was that a cessation in the bombing was the key to talks.

Upon his return, Ronning met in Washington with a number of high officials, including William Bundy. The briefings went on in secret over several days. In reports to his government, Ronning observed that both sides had become hard-headed, that both were so confident of "victory" that neither was prepared to make concessions. Administration officials told Ronning the bombing would stop when Hanoi was ready to reciprocate.

From March to June there were intermittent discussions, in which Ronning participated, between Ottawa and Washington on the possibility of arranging talks with North Vietnam. With the Administration's support, Canada decided to send Ronning back to Hanoi in June to determine whether North Vietnam would offer some reciprocal step for a bombing halt. Ronning was in Hanoi from June 14 to 18 and met with, among others, Foreign Minister Nguyen Duy Trinh. His talks were wide-ranging, going beyond the immediate question of cessation of bombing and reciprocal military de-escalation. But on the issue of reciprocity, which was of primary concern to the United States at that moment, North Vietnam remained adamant.

Ronning cabled a preliminary report to Canadian Foreign Secretary Paul Martin while en route home. The Canadians passed the information to Washington and urged the United States to avoid an escalatory bombing until the Ronning mission could be assessed.

On June 21 William Bundy secretly flew to Ottawa for a personal report from Ronning. Bundy, Martin, Ronning and other officials met for some seven hours in a downtown hotel room. The meeting broke up at 11 P.M. In terms of hard and immediate substance, the United States concluded that the Ronning missions had brought no change. Pearson and Martin did not dispute this view but stressed the long-range good that could flow from the channel. They felt their government could nurture the contact and use it again. Whatever Bundy said allowed Pearson and Martin to infer the United States would not escalate the war in the near future. American officials said no such commitment was intended or made.

On June 28, Washington and Ottawa time (June 29 in Vietnam), one week after the hotel meeting with Bundy, American bombers struck the Hanoi area for the first time in the "little monks" raids. The Canadians were dismayed, even bitter. The Ronning initiative was finished. Later Ronning told associates the Johnson Administration had stubbornly refused to accept the fact that the Soviet Union and China would not permit North Vietnam to be defeated militarily, and that a political compromise was the only realistic solution.

The day American bombers closed the Ronning channel, Marigold was born in Saigon as Henry Cabot Lodge met with Giovanni D'Orlandi.

Six months later Hanoi was bombed again and Marigold died a controversial death in Warsaw in December. The New Year, 1967, brought a new and major effort in the search for peace, this time in London and Moscow.

part **III**

Channels and Phases

Then, when he had done enough to inspire fear, he turned to mercy and proffered the allurements of peace.

—P. Cornelius Tacitus
Agricola

CHAPTER TEN

The Inviting Mood of Ho Chi Minh

For North Vietnamese President Ho Chi Minh, the receiving of visitors from abroad during the month of January, 1967, was of great importance. The seventy-six-year-old, physically frail, politically ruthless leader had an important message he wanted to get across to his antagonists in Washington. Maybe the visitors could help.

It appeared that Ho felt the time had come to begin talking about ending the Vietnam war. He had, however, an important condition. He demanded that Lyndon Johnson cease "unconditionally" [1] the bombing and all other acts of war against North Vietnam before talks could begin.

This was the message Ho relayed to the small stream of visitors to the Presidential Palace in Hanoi, the former official residence of the French governors general where Ho himself now lived.

Perhaps the most notable of those meetings occurred on January 17 when three elderly pacifist clerics were ushered into the ornate reception room of the palace to talk, under the

---

[1] There is some question as to whether Ho was demanding during this period that any bombing halt be "permanent" as well as "unconditional."

gilded ceiling, with Ho and Premier Pham Van Dong. The three were the Right Reverend Ambrose Reeves, the sixty-seven-year-old Bishop of Chichester, England; the Reverend A. J. Muste, an eighty-two-year-old pacifist, who would die at home in New York within a few weeks; and Rabbi Abraham L. Feinberg, a sixty-seven-year-old American citizen who had years before moved to Toronto, Canada. The three guests sat side by side on a big, square-cut velvet-covered couch. Ho sat on the edge of a second couch placed at right angles. Pham Van Dong sat low in a similarly styled easy chair. The meeting was cordial. The guests were served tea and wine. They all drank a toast to the Vietnamese people. Then Ho presented to each a hand-carved walking stick fashioned by North Vietnamese artisans. Finally there was substantive conversation, which, among other subjects, touched on the United States' bombing of North Vietnam. It had to stop, Ho told his visitors. At one point the North Vietnamese president broke into the English he had learned as an assistant to the famous Chef Escoffier at London's Carlton Hotel to deliver this message:

"Let Mr. Johnson come with his wife and daughters, his secretary, his doctor, his cook, but let him not come with a gun at his hip. Let him not bring his admirals and generals.

"As an old revolutionary I pledge my honor that Mr. Johnson will have complete security." [2]

---

[2] The three pacifists returned from Hanoi by way of London, where, on January 23, they held a press conference and revealed the invitation. In Washington, a State Department spokesman said Rabbi Feinberg had gone to North Vietnam after being denied permission by the government and thus might be subject to prosecution. He was not prosecuted. Instead, Philip M. Kaiser, the deputy chief of the U. S. Embassy in London, telephoned him and respectfully invited him to an interview on what he had learned in Hanoi. Kaiser cabled a report to Washington after the interview. On January 28 Feinberg, while stopping at the Hotel Alrae in New York en route to Toronto, underwent another governmental debriefing. First, Lieutenant Colonel Anthony A. Caffri of the Air Force, stationed at the Pentagon, questioned him about American war prisoners to whom he had talked in North Vietnam. Then William R. Smyser, the head of the North Vietnam section in the State Department's Bureau of Intelligence and Research, had a long conversation with the rabbi. "He seemed very interested in my impressions of the North Vietnamese leaders," the rabbi

The old revolutionary's symbolic invitation was not delivered on impulse. The proposal for talks after a bombing cessation was a theme that ran through conversations he and other important North Vietnamese leaders had during the beginning of 1967. On January 12 Ho met with Harry S. Ashmore, of the Center for the Study of Democratic Institutions, and William C. Baggs, editor of the Miami *News* and a director of the Center. They had gone to Hanoi to invite a North Vietnamese representative to a Pacem in Terris convocation the Center was staging in Geneva the following May. In return, Ho issued an invitation of his own to them: to keep in touch with him or to have representatives of the United States government keep in touch with authorized representatives he had in several places around the world.

On January 10 Egon Lutz, a reporter for the *Nürnberger Nachrichten,* wrote in his paper that Ho had told him in an

---

reported a year later. While in New York the rabbi placed a phone call to Arthur Goldberg. The ambassador happened to be in Washington for conferences at the State Department when the call came. The ambassador's secretary, however, immediately put the call through on a government line to Washington and the rabbi relayed Ho's invitation to the President. The rabbi later said Goldberg had promised to pass the message to the President. After talking to Goldberg, the rabbi returned to Toronto and kept busy the next several days answering phone calls from officials at the State Department and Pentagon. His treatment by the government was most cordial. Then, on February 21, he received a letter from the State Department asking him to mail in his passport for violation of the travel regulations. Instead of complying, he called an American consular official in Toronto, who came out to his house and picked it up. The loss of the passport was, for many months, no inconvenience. As an American citizen he was still able to travel freely from Canada to the United States. On June 2, 1967, the State Department wrote offering him a passport if he signed oaths pledging to obey all existing travel regulations and any that might be promulgated in the future. He felt he could not, in good conscience, sign such oaths, and ignored the offer. Inquiring at the American consulate in Toronto, he was told he could make a standard application for a new passport and that Washington would consider it even though it was still officially demanding the oaths. On February 2, 1968, he applied through normal channels, using only the standard forms. As March ended, the State Department canceled travel restrictions. At this writing, Feinberg was still awaiting the government's decision in the hope that he could soon take his wife to Jamaica for a holiday with friends.

interview that if the United States was prepared "to give up its policy of aggression and to withdraw its troops from Vietnam, we will gladly invite them to tea."

The most important invitation of all during that period came through the reportage of Wilfred G. Burchett, an Australian journalist with close connections in the Communist world, who suddenly began writing articles late in January that seemed more like diplomatic *aides memoire* than material for news columns.

"Halt the bombings, come and talk," Burchett reported he was told by high officials in Hanoi.

Burchett explained the sudden readiness of North Vietnamese officials to begin talks in early 1967 this way: "When I asked why a move was not made earlier—and it's open knowledge that a number of Socialist-bloc countries were urging such a move over a year ago—I was told that if talks were offered a year ago, the United States would have taken that as a sign of weakness and bombings would have been intensified." Now, he continued, Hanoi's offers were made from a position of strength.

The United States decided to follow up the invitations. The outcome might not be a tea party in Hanoi for Lyndon Johnson and Ho Chi Minh, but, conceivably, the follow-up could lead to low-level talks somewhere in the world between representatives of the two nations fighting to exert their will in South Vietnam. The State Department alerted the American Embassy in Moscow to try to arrange direct contact with the North Vietnamese Embassy. The American officials wanted to make another attempt to revive the Marigold initiative that had collapsed in Warsaw the previous month. In early January the State Department received a cable from its Moscow Embassy reporting North Vietnamese diplomats had given indications they would meet with Americans.

It must have appeared to the President and his advisers that maybe the bomb-free circle they had established around Hanoi to coax Marigold back to life was beginning to have some effect. They quickly gave the Moscow cable flower treatment—it was code-named, marked "nodis" and placed on a special list to be seen only by a select few, all of them known to the President. Then they sent orders to the embassy in Moscow to proceed with arrangements for a meeting.

Ever since the United States began its bombing of North Vietnam in February, 1965, while Soviet Premier Kosygin was visiting there, Moscow had been a difficult place in which to do diplomatic business relating to the Southeast Asian War. At almost every opportunity American diplomats, including Ambassador Kohler, sought indications that the Soviet government was willing to play a role in bringing the Vietnam war under control. Each time the Americans asked the Soviets to intercede they received the same do-it-yourself answer Kohler had gotten in May, 1965, when he wanted the Soviet Foreign Ministry to transmit a letter from Dean Rusk to Ho Chi Minh. Clearly, the Kremlin leaders meant to continue their hands-off attitude toward the problem. As far as they were concerned in 1965 and 1966, no good could come of getting caught in the middle between Ho Chi Minh and Lyndon Johnson. The Chinese Communists could make good use of such a situation to score propaganda points.

But early in 1967 a change in attitude in Moscow reflected Hanoi's apparent willingness to begin talks. The manner in which the American Embassy in Moscow received the signal that the North Vietnamese would consider direct contacts is still secret.

It is unlikely, however, that the signal came directly from the North Vietnamese to the Americans. Kohler had been trying ever since the May, 1965, incident to establish face-to-face talks, and he had always been rebuffed by the North Vietnamese —except once. The exception came in 1966, when he did succeed in setting up a meeting at the North Vietnamese Embassy. It was a complicated, stiffly formal affair that lasted almost three hours. Though Kohler and Le Trang, the North Vietnamese chargé d'affaires, might have talked face-to-face in either French or Russian (with occasional help from translators), Trang insisted on talking Vietnamese, which a colleague translated into Russian. Kohler stuck to the formality, employing a translator to render Trang's words from Russian into English. Then he replied in English, which was subsequently translated into Russian and then retranslated into Vietnamese for Trang. Kohler's attempts to follow up that meeting and to keep the channel open were in vain.[3]

Reflecting the change in Ho Chi Minh's attitude, Le Trang was a far more approachable person in January, 1967, than he was in 1966. The task of arranging a meeting with him fell to John Connaughty Guthrie, a tall, lean, handsome, taciturn bureaucrat who, as deputy chief of the United States Embassy in Moscow, had been in charge until Kohler's replacement arrived.

Guthrie has been termed the Gary Cooper of the United States Foreign Service. At fifty-one, he was serving his third tour in Moscow during his twenty years as a diplomat. His first tour was in the late 1940s, during the height of the post-World War II Stalinist excesses. His second tour was in the mid-1950s, during the rise to power of Nikita Khrushchev. And

---

[3] While Kohler worked hard to establish secret contact with the North Vietnamese, he publicly ignored them. Protocol demanded this posture because of the absence of diplomatic relations between the two countries. For example, there was the great "doyen crisis" of 1965 when the ambassador from Afghanistan finally left his post. He had been the senior ambassador in Moscow in length of service, and thus the doyen, or dean, for years. His departure meant that the title of doyen would automatically fall to the next man in seniority, Nguyen Van Kinh, the North Vietnamese ambassador who had served since 1957. Kohler and most of his Western colleagues refused to recognize either Kinh or the second in line after him, East Germany's Rudolf Dölling. They reached down to number three on the seniority list and named Hippolyte Cools of Belgium the "rump doyen" and proceeded to take their cues on protocol from him.

In late 1965 Kohler was attending a reception at which the wife of an American correspondent brought Hoang Thinh, the friendly correspondent of the (North) Vietnam News Agency, over to a group to introduce him. Kohler was in the group. When the woman introduced Thinh to the ambassador, Thinh extended his hand. Kohler turned abruptly and walked away. The embarrassed woman downed two big whiskies neat.

By the time the White House gave the order to the embassy in Moscow to follow up the possibility of opening a channel in January, 1967, the problems of protocol had eased. Kohler had returned to Washington in the fall of 1966 to finish his diplomat's career as Deputy Undersecretary of State for Political Affairs. Furthermore, Nguyen Van Kinh, it turned out, was an absentee doyen. More often than not he was away from Moscow. Even when he was in town, he seldom made public appearances.

now he was back in the post-Khrushchev era of collective leadership. His knowledge of communism's practice in the Soviet Union, then, spanned a whole range of conditions and atuned him well to the nuance by which political movement is judged in such a society. Additionally, he was particularly well prepared for the assignment he received in January, 1967, because of his knowledge of the Far East. After earning degrees from Williams College and Columbia University, he shipped out to China to take a teaching job in 1939 at Lingnan University in Canton. When the Japanese captured Canton, he fled with the university to Hong Kong. When the Japanese invaded that colony, he joined the British Army, then was captured as the Japanese overran the island. He spent most of World War II as a prisoner. After his second Moscow tour, he went to Bangkok to serve three years as the political counselor in the American Embassy there.

On January 10, ambling and unexcited as usual, a trace of a bemused smile on his placid face, John Guthrie stepped out of a back door of the American Embassy and into a waiting car in the shabby courtyard.

The car moved out through a narrow archway and past the blue-coated Soviet militiamen standing guard. The guards nodded, as they always do to those entering and leaving the compound. It is their job to note who comes and goes, and report those movements. Guthrie ignored them as all the Americans always did. The car made a right turn into the twelve lanes of traffic on Ulitsa Chaikovskovo, the broad "garden ring" road surrounding downtown Moscow. Almost at the Moscow River the car turned right into the section of town generally reserved for Moscow's best hospitals and medical schools. A mile and a half from the American Embassy it pulled up in front of an ocher-colored stone villa of pre-revolutionary design at Ulitsa Bolshaya Pirogovskaya 13. The car passed through an open iron gate and into a small parking lot. Guthrie alighted, went around to the front door, knocked, quickly got a response and entered.

Inside the North Vietnamese Embassy, he found himself facing a large portrait of Ho Chi Minh staring down from a point high up on the reception hall wall opposite the doorway. He was led into a room off the hall and there, in an atmosphere of quiet, polite formality, he proceeded to make the United States' case to Le Trang for direct American–North Vietnamese meetings. With any luck, the Moscow channel was now open. With any luck, John Guthrie, or someone replacing him at a future date, might finally conduct the negotiations that had eluded Ambassador Gronouski in Warsaw the month before. Perhaps, if the situation grew really hopeful, the negotiator might be Llewellyn E. Thompson, one of the most respected men in the entire Foreign Service, who was arriving the next day to take his post as President Johnson's ambassador to the Soviet Union

That night in Washington, many hours after the Guthrie-Trang meeting, Lyndon Johnson went for a ride in his capital. It was nighttime when the big black presidential limousine moved out of the White House grounds into Pennsylvania Avenue for the two-mile trip to the Capitol. The President, unlike Guthrie earlier, was on no peace mission. He was going before a televised joint session of Congress to deliver his constitutionally required annual report on the State of the Union.

Although Mr. Johnson unquestionably received immediate word earlier that day of the outcome of Guthrie's talk in Moscow, he could not spend much time away from the speech thinking about the next move in the new channel. Neither could he mention the extremely secret meeting in his speech. The President stood on the rostrum in the chamber of the House of Representatives that night and, in his most somber tones, delivered this passage on the Vietnam war:

"I wish I could report to you that the conflict is almost over. This I cannot do. We face more cost, more loss, and more agony. For the end is not yet. I cannot promise you that it will come this year—or the next. Our adversary still believes he can go on fighting longer than we and our allies are prepared to resist him."

That Mr. Johnson was settling down for the long pull in Vietnam was evident. He called for a six percent income tax surcharge and, in a little noticed omission, he did not even use the term "Great Society" that he had applied with so much pride to the tremendous legislative accomplishments of the years 1964–1966.

The Great Society had gone to war.

The following morning, in his spacious Moscow apartment, when he awoke half a world away from Washington, John Guthrie must have read with interest the United States Information Agency wireless report on the President's speech. Guthrie was a man who went by the book. He knew the rules of diplomacy. He realized that even if the President had seen a glimmer of hope for peace, the night before was not the time to broadcast it. There was nothing for Guthrie to do but wait and judge the rhetoric on Capitol Hill against his own private instructions.

The day he received the State of the Union report, John Guthrie took another ride. This time, with the American flag flying from the fender of a big black limousine, he drove out to Sheremetyevo Airport to greet the newly arrived Llewellyn Thompson. The embassy staff had been awaiting him eagerly. Some of the more adventurous souls had even taken the trouble to construct a new poker table for the embassy snack bar. "Tommy" Thompson was known in the Foreign Service and in Washington for his great skill at the poker table as well as in international affairs. He liked to play for high stakes.

Publicly the propaganda organs of Hanoi treated the Vietnam passage in the State of the Union message as an ominous declaration of a decision to intensify and widen the war. But, privately, the North Vietnamese leaders made the decision to keep the Moscow channel open, thus indicating they understood President Johnson had as much use for broadcast rhetoric as Ho Chi Minh. At some point during the ten days after the State of the Union, Guthrie and Le Trang arranged another meeting at the North Vietnamese Embassy.

Guthrie, of course, was in no way his own master on these matters. Thompson was a strong, well-informed man who, before he came to Moscow, had served importantly in the innermost councils of government. During the Cuban missile crisis of 1962 his cool, self-assured analysis of Nikita Khrushchev was one of the factors John F. Kennedy used in determining not to blink first in the face-down that could have led to nuclear war. Thompson could be counted on to instruct Guthrie carefully on his every move. Additionally, there was no shortage of high-level policy-makers in Washington.

There the peace-seekers had before them the record of the Marigold initiative in Warsaw. They tried to revive something along its lines. The ten points—over which Gronouski had agonized with such frustration the month before—contained possibilities that could be renewed, although this time the language would be formulated by Americans. They decided that Guthrie could serve up a variety of possibilities for discussions—a "whole smorgasbord," to use the image of one of the officials who drafted Guthrie's instructions—to test the reaction in Hanoi to direct contacts. That process began at Ulitsa Bolshaya Pirogovskaya on Friday, January 20.

"Guthrie gave him a list of things we were willing to talk about and the order we would like to discuss them in. We asked them what they wanted to talk about and in what order," one official said of the messages Guthrie delivered.

Much of what really happened at this meeting and those that were to follow in Moscow is still a mystery. One of the points of mystery, for example, is the question of how many written notes Guthrie handed Le Trang. Standard practice in such cases would be for a diplomat to make a so-called "oral *démarche*"—read aloud from a carefully prepared text called, in the diplomatic trade, a "talking paper" or a *"peu de papier"* —and then, to make sure his views were properly transmitted, leave behind either the informal talking paper or a more formal *aide memoire*.[4]

While Guthrie and Thompson waited for Le Trang to send the U. S. proposals to Hanoi, the new American ambassador began reintroducing himself to Moscow, where he had served as ambassador at the end of the Eisenhower years. Thompson had

---

[4] Guthrie, according to one official familiar with the Moscow channel, left more than one formal note—perhaps as many as four. All of them, he said, could be described as formal *aides memoire* and not as the less formal, more easily disavowed talking papers. Another official indicated Guthrie initialed the notes.

been sent back for the second tour as a man who knew and understood the Soviet mind. He arrived as a man respected by Soviet officials. If any American diplomat could improve relations with the Soviet Union while the Vietnam war worked to harm them, it was Thompson.

It did not take Lyndon Johnson long to realize Thompson's mission would be a difficult one. On Monday, January 23, the first working day after the second Guthrie-Trang meeting, Thompson went downtown to the Great Kremlin Palace. In a room formerly used for imperial audiences when the Czars were visiting Moscow, the American presented his credentials to the figurehead in the Soviet collective leadership, the rotund, chain-smoking president of the Soviet Union, Nikolai V. Podgorny. Thompson had arrived in Moscow carrying a special message from President Johnson to the Kremlin leadership, but he did not present the note to Podgorny. He apparently wanted to discuss it with a real power in the Soviet leadership. Instead, he made a short statement urging cooperation between the two superpowers to ease the burdens of the world arms race and to join in aiding underdeveloped countries improve their lot. After the ceremony the two men conferred privately for an hour.

Later Western spokesmen said the Podgorny-Thompson conference had been "friendly" but that the Soviet president had expressed "apprehension" that the Vietnam war presented a "serious obstacle" to improved relations between the two countries.

Thompson failed to get an appointment with Premier Kosygin until one month after he presented his credentials. By then he had already quietly given the letter to Foreign Minister Gromyko. Clearly, the Soviet government was not interested in making things easy for the United States or in Soviet-American cooperation while the war against communism in Southeast Asia raged. The men in the Kremlin appeared unwilling to go any further than the men in Hanoi's Presidential Palace would allow them to go.

On January 27 Guthrie went back to the North Vietnamese Embassy to see Le Trang. The American had been instructed to seek a response from the North Vietnamese to his earlier visits. Trang very carefully informed Guthrie that what would follow was not to be considered an answer to his January 20 message, which the Hanoi government still had under consideration. The North Vietnamese diplomat then launched into the kind of propaganda diatribe Communist diplomats have developed into an oratorical art form. A cascade of bombast rolled over the placid Guthrie. He duly recorded the message, as he had been trained, and left to make his report on this "denunciatory reply," this "answer that wasn't an answer."

It would be up to the officials in Washington to decide what Trang's diatribe meant for the future of any negotiations.

CHAPTER ELEVEN

"Just Almost Any Step"

At 8:50 P.M. Eastern Standard Time on January 27, within hours after Trang delivered the diatribe to Guthrie in Moscow, the world-wide information-monitoring system of the United States government began picking up a strong, clear English-language radio-teletype dispatch from the (North) Vietnam News Agency International Service. It began: "Hanoi, 28 January—Nguyen Duy Trinh, DRV foreign minister, has granted an interview to Australian journalist Wilfred Burchett. Questions and answers follow."

Within minutes the text of the report began moving on teletype machines at the Central Intelligence Agency, which in turn fed it to the State Department Operations Center, the White House Situation Room and the National Military Command Center at the Pentagon.

The beginning of the interview consisted of typical denunciation and was probably similar to what Trang had unloosed on Guthrie in Moscow. It began by talking of the "perfidious . . . maneuvers of the U. S. imperialists. . . ."

One part of the interview, however, was more than just propaganda. It presented in clear, authoritative language the

terms on which the North Vietnamese leaders would sit down
for "talks" with the United States:

> *Question:* The United States has spoken of the need for
> dialog or contact between itself and the DRV. Would you
> comment on this statement?
>
> *Answer:* The United States has made such statements, but
> in its deeds it has shown the utmost obduracy and perfidy
> and continues the escalation, stepping up and expanding the
> aggressive war. If it really wants talks, it must first halt un-
> conditionally the bombing raids and all other acts of war
> against the DRV. It is only after the unconditional cessation
> of U. S. bombing and all other acts of war against the DRV
> that there could be talks between the DRV and the United
> States.

Previously the terms had been conveyed only through intermediaries with no official standing. Now they were coming from
North Vietnam's foreign minister. Four hours later VNA distributed a front-page commentary from Hanoi's Communist
Party newspaper, *Nhan Dan,* repeating the foregoing Trinh-
Burchett exchange with instructions that the last two sentences
of the answer be underlined.

Trinh, as foreign minister, was of course aware of what had
been going on between Guthrie and Trang in Moscow. Yet
rather than use the secret channel, the North Vietnamese government had decided to broadcast an apparent reply to the Guthrie
approaches. (The possibility that the diatribe Trang delivered
to Guthrie contained some indication of the terms for talks
cannot be ruled out. On several occasions the United States
has privately informed the North Vietnamese of new proposals
before making them public.)

The North Vietnamese during the next several days mounted
a world-wide propaganda campaign to draw attention to Trinh's
stop-the-bombing-and-talk message.

Trinh's call for an "unconditional halt" to the bombing was
not new. It had been made by various North Vietnamese on
several occasions during the two years since the air war in North
Vietnam had started. But the interview marked the transition
from emphasis on such political matters as the four points of

Pham Van Dong or the five points of the NLF to the purely military matter of demanding a bombing halt that "could" bring "talks." It was a signal—perhaps unrecognized at the time—that nothing fruitful could come from Guthrie's messages while the bombing continued. It made crystal-clear the symbolism in Ho Chi Minh's invitation to Lyndon Johnson to come calling but without a gun at the hip.

Though the Trinh interview became known in official Washington the night of January 27, its significance was not discovered by newsmen until January 31. When Robert McCloskey, the State Department spokesman, was asked for comment, his response was almost predictable. The State Department, he said, was considering carefully the Trinh statement and the commentary in *Nhan Dan*.

While the Johnson Administration was investigating the import of the Trinh interview, Senator Robert F. Kennedy was on a speaking and fact-finding tour in Europe. The senator's repeated statements that the next few weeks would be "critical and crucial" to the search for peace in Vietnam received wide publicity. It could not help but nettle the President, whose relationship with the brother of his predecessor had been difficult, at best. On January 31, Kennedy spent seventy minutes in Paris with President de Gaulle, one of the world leaders who were becoming the bane of Mr. Johnson's existence. On February 1 Kennedy went to the Quai d'Orsay to talk about Vietnam with Etienne Manac'h, director of Far East affairs in the French foreign office and a man with eight years of experience in Indochinese affairs.

Manac'h had at his command the benefit of all the records and insights of the French experience in Vietnam. The archives began with the first invasion of 1857. By 1859 the French had conquered Saigon. By World War I they completely dominated the country. By 1930 their rule had grown so repressive that, as Professors George McT. Kahin and John W. Lewis point out in *The United States in Vietnam,* they had as many French civil servants administering the colony as Great Britain had Britons in India, which had a population twelve times as large. Thus, by the time of their eviction in 1954, the French had amassed a wealth of experience, and even after the withdrawal, maintained good channels of intelligence into North Vietnam. France and North Vietnam keep diplomatic missions in each other's capitals. Limited numbers of French doctors, scientists, teachers, labor leaders and newspapermen—Communist and non-Communist—travel regularly to Hanoi. An overseas colony of some 30,000 Vietnamese live in France and many try to keep in touch with family and friends in Vietnam. Frenchmen, in fact, have quietly relayed messages from American prisoners in North Vietnam to their families in the States.

For this reason Paris has become the kind of Vietnam war listening post for the United States that Swiss cities were during World War II or Vienna and Berlin were during the Cold War years. The Central Intelligence Agency station in Paris, well staffed and well informed on Vietnamese affairs, has an obviously important mission. John Gunther Dean, a forty-one-year-old first secretary and Vietnam expert in the American Embassy, has had, since he arrived at his post in July, 1965, an equally obvious role as one of the State Department's peace-seekers. He seemed well equipped for his job. The holder of a Ph.D. from the Sorbonne, he was fluent in French. A native of Germany, he had a feeling for the continental manner. A veteran of six years' service in Vietnam and Laos as a diplomat and worker in the American foreign aid program, he understood the nature of the United States' problem.

Etienne Manac'h became John Dean's principal contact at the Quai d'Orsay. The two held frequent, informal conversations during which Manac'h would put forth a variety of ideas for diplomatic settlements that were based solely on his own knowledge of the situation. At no time during these meetings would Manac'h ever claim the French government was offering a plan or proposal for a Vietnam settlement. Those would be left to the more important figures in the government—Foreign Minister Couve de Murville or President de Gaulle himself. Actually, the French were smart enough to realize that any plan they might advance, considering the nature of Franco-

American relations in recent years, would arouse reaction ranging from suspicion to hostility in the Johnson Administration.[1] Some important American officials operate on the firm premise that French advice on Vietnam simply cannot be trusted, that de Gaulle is only too eager to see the Americans fail as his proud France failed in its fight with Ho Chi Minh.

Despite the uncomfortable turbulence in the upper echelons of their respective governments, Dean and Manac'h found their relationship salutary. This was to become apparent on February 1 when Dean accompanied Kennedy to the Manac'h meeting. Manac'h had an important communication for the United States government from the North Vietnamese government. He had received it within the previous two or three days from Mai Van Bo, the chief of North Vietnam's diplomatic mission in Paris.[2] The message was this:

The Hanoi government wanted the Johnson Administration to realize that the interview Nguyen Duy Trinh had given Wilfred Burchett was important. Trinh had been sincere in saying talks "could" follow an unconditional cessation of the bombing. The interview did indeed represent a shift in the bargaining position of the Hanoi government.

Manac'h had held this information to himself for a short

---

[1] The state of Franco-American relations had fallen to such a low in 1967 that Charles Lucet, the French ambassador to Washington, was understood to have complained to friends in Paris that he had the feeling he was being treated as a security risk by the Johnson Administration.

[2] Bo was the senior North Vietnamese diplomat outside the Communist world. He was a natural focal point for direct contacts between Hanoi and Washington, but he had made himself a difficult man for Americans to see. Only a few Americans, most of them Vietnam war dissenters, and none of them, as far as was known, officials, had obtained appointments with him. He avoided American diplomats. At one reception, for instance, Bo entered a room in which Dean and another American were talking in a corner. As soon as he saw them, Bo spun around and left the room. Bo and Manac'h, however, met every week or ten days. Any message Bo wanted transmitted to Washington could be started on its way through Manac'h. Another good contact of Manac'h's, incidentally, was Wilfred Burchett, with whom the Frenchman talked every time Burchett made one of his infrequent visits to Paris.

time rather than relay it immediately to Dean so that it could be delivered in Kennedy's presence. He might have felt that transmitting the message with Kennedy's knowledge would assure that it received the greatest possible consideration in Washington.

Ironically, though Kennedy had been saying that a "critical" period for negotiations was at hand, he very nearly missed the point of his meeting with Manac'h, as one source recalled later. The senator, of course, was unfamiliar with the intricate details of Vietnam diplomacy and he had difficulty following the conversation in French which Dean was translating for his benefit. But Dean grasped the possible significance immediately. In fact, he interrupted Manac'h to make sure he had not misunderstood.

Was Manac'h saying that Bo had said the statement was "important"? Dean asked.

Precisely, Manac'h replied.

That point settled, Manac'h went on to discuss ideas for a three-stage peace negotiation. Some confusion developed over whether this was a North Vietnamese proposal, but American officials later said they understood from the beginning that these were simply Manac'h's own ideas of what might be acceptable to Hanoi for a long-range solution in Vietnam.

The meeting over, Dean left Kennedy and hurried back to the embassy to draft a memorandum on the conversation. He returned to Manac'h's office later in the day, showed him the memorandum and told him it would be transmitted to Washington. He asked Manac'h to read it carefully. Manac'h verified the account and then reiterated that Bo had attached great importance to the Trinh interview. That night Dean cabled a two-page memorandum on the meeting to the State Department. A more detailed five-page report went off to Washington by diplomatic pouch later in the week.

By the time Kennedy and Dean ended their meeting with Manac'h, Dean Rusk, in Washington, had come to a few conclusions about the Trinh statement. He went before a panel of British newsmen to record an interview that would appear on television in Great Britain. Rusk was asked if the United States would be prepared to stop the bombing in exchange for the possibility of talks. Rusk firmly rejected the idea.

Before the United States grounded its bombers, he said, the Johnson Administration must know what the reaction would be from the other side. He left the clear implication that the United States had decided to meet the Trinh proposal with a demand for reciprocal military de-escalation by the enemy in Vietnam. It was a signal that the Johnson Administration considered the Trinh proposal only a bargaining position from which Hanoi should be prepared to negotiate a compromise.

Rusk did indicate, however, that the United States was prepared to give a little on a previously hard position involving representation of the National Liberation Front at peace talks. He said the enemy had been informed the Administration was prepared to discuss acceptance of the NLF as a "full negotiating party," but was not willing to elaborate.

"Quite frankly," he said, "I'll be prepared to discuss that with someone who can end the shooting, so I don't see much point in negotiating that point with you because you can't stop the shooting. But it's perfectly—it's been made known—that we're prepared to discuss the problem with the other side."

Rusk was almost certainly referring to the meetings Guthrie had been having with Trang in Moscow. In fact, the next day, February 2, Guthrie went back to the North Vietnamese Embassy in Moscow for the fourth time in twenty-three days to continue spreading the "smorgasbord." If the public utterances of American officials at the time were any indication, Guthrie's presentation ignored the proposal in the Trinh interview. Even so, the North Vietnamese kept the channel open.

The same day Guthrie met with Trang, the White House staff was deep in the preparation of Lyndon Johnson's first televised news conference of the year. The conference was coming against a background of intensified reporting, comment and speculation on the Administration's Vietnam policies. With the annual truce for the Tet holidays—the lunar New Year celebrated in the Orient—approaching, more and more voices around the world were proclaiming the desire for lengthening the truce or expanding it into a cease-fire.

The Trinh interview had been responsible for some of this. So had criticism of the President's bombing policy by the Senate Foreign Relations Committee. Robert Kennedy's "crucial period" observations had helped stimulate discussion, as had indications from Pope Paul that he was about to renew his appeals for peace.

Excitement over the press conference grew during the day. The East Room of the White House—where Dolley Madison had hung her laundry during the War of 1812, where Federal troops had been quartered during the Civil War, and where the bodies of Abraham Lincoln and John F. Kennedy had lain in state—began to fill early. Hundreds of reporters stepped gingerly over the snaked television and radio cables and sat under the intense blue-white lights. Shortly before 3 P.M., a presidential aide appeared and placed an indexed black loose-leaf notebook on the rostrum. Then the President walked purposefully into the room, appearing from behind the battery of television cameras at the entrance.

Without any hesitation he began reading a statement on the need for Senate approval of the Soviet-American consular treaty then under consideration on Capitol Hill and under strong attack by right-wing elements in the country. Although he did not say so, his plea was another effort to keep Soviet-American relations as cordial as possible during the war.[3]

The consular treaty plea finished, the President nodded almost imperceptibly to Frank Cormier, the White House correspondent of the Associated Press, for the first question.

Cormier asked: "We are reading and writing a good deal lately about diplomacy aimed at a Vietnam settlement. I wonder if you could give us your assessment of the peace front at this time?"

The President obviously had a carefully prepared statement on the subject in the black notebook, and now he delivered it

---

[3] The United States Senate, after long debate, gave its consent in the spring of 1967. But not until May 4, 1968, immediately after the United States agreed to hold formal talks with North Vietnam in Paris, did the Soviet government suddenly announce ratification of the treaty.

—not only to the newsmen, not only to the millions of Americans listening, but to the world statesmen interested in negotiating peace and to the government in Hanoi. He said:

"Mr. Cormier states a question that I know is on the minds of all the people here today and all the people of this country.

"As you know, I have underlined over and over again the very deep interest of the United States in a prompt and peaceful settlement of all the problems of Southeast Asia.

"I have said many times that we are ready to go more than halfway in achieving this result.

"I would remind all of you that we would welcome a conference in Southeast Asia. This might be a Geneva conference. It could be an all-Asian conference, or any other generally acceptable forum.

"We would be glad to see the unconditional discussions to which I referred in my statement of April, 1965, at Johns Hopkins.

"We would participate in preliminary discussions which might open the way for formal negotiations.

"We are prepared today to talk about mutual steps of de-escalation.

"We would be prepared to talk about such subjects as the exchange of prisoners, the demilitarization of the demilitarized zone, or any other aspect which might take even a small step in the direction of peace.

"We would be prepared to discuss any points which the other side wishes to bring up, along with points which we and our allies very much want to raise ourselves.

"Or there could be preliminary discussions to see whether there could be an agreed set of points which could be the basis for negotiations.

"It is against this background that we study very carefully all of the public statements made which appear from time to time and which bear upon Southeast Asia, and all the views which we receive from or through other governments.

"It would not be helpful to me—and I do not intend to do so—to comment on any particular channel or communications at this point. You may be sure that we are diligent in our search for the possibility of peaceful settlement.

"In all candor, I must say that I am not aware of any serious effort that the other side has made, in my judgment, to bring the fighting to a stop and to stop the war."

The President's lengthy reply was full of so-called "signals" to Hanoi. As Signal Number 1, it invested with presidential authority the privately transmitted positions Guthrie had been presenting in Moscow. For, indeed, though the correspondents in the East Room that day and the television-watching public had no way of knowing, the President was hitting the highlights of the secret Guthrie messages in his answer.

Signal Number 2, in his reference to "mutual steps of de-escalation," was an implicit rejection of the Trinh offer for talks only in exchange for a bombing halt. Mr. Johnson was responding that any American bombing halt must be met with North Vietnamese de-escalation.

Signal Number 3, in the President's stated lack of awareness of "serious" effort by the other side, was an implicit invitation to North Vietnam to make a new offer.

What kind of offer? The President dealt with that six questions later, responding to this query: "Are you prepared at all to tell us what kind of other steps the other side should take for this suspension of bombings?"

He answered: "Just almost any step.

"As far as we can see, they have not taken any yet.

"We would be glad to explore any reciprocal action that they or any of their spokesmen would care to suggest.

"We have made one proposal after the other. We would like to have a cease-fire. We would be very glad to stop our bombing, as we have on two previous occasions, if we could have any indication of reciprocal action.

"As of now they have given none. I assume they are willing to give none until I hear further."

Here was a restatement of Signal Number 2, the demand for reciprocity, and of Signal Number 3, asking for a new proposal.

Reporters, however, did not recognize the hard line on reciprocity implicit in the President's answers. They seized on four little words, "just almost any step," and wrote stories interpreting the President's remarks as a loosening of the American position. In fact, even in the United States government there were policy-makers promoting the idea of negotiations who saw the President's remarks as a relaxation of his demands on Ho Chi Minh.[4]

One of those policy-makers was Chester Cooper, the deputy peace-seeker to Ambassador Averell Harriman, who was getting ready to leave for England. About the time the President was holding his news conference, Cooper was making a final inspection of the peace file in Ben Read's national security information grid. He checked the status of the Guthrie-Trang channel in Moscow. He also reviewed a draft of a letter under preparation for the President to send to Ho Chi Minh. He found nothing incompatible with his instructions. Unannounced and unnoticed, Cooper left for London that evening to counsel Prime Minister Harold Wilson during the impending meetings with Premier Alexei Kosygin. Kosygin would be arriving the following Monday, February 6, for a state visit, which just happened to coincide with the advent of Tet. Considering that, considering the Trinh offer, considering all the peace talk in the air, considering the Soviet Union and Great Britain were co-chairmen of the 1954 Geneva Conference, the Vietnam problem was expected to receive priority attention.

North Vietnam's leaders reacted to the President's press conference with a speed that made it appear they were monitoring Mr. Johnson as he spoke. With Hanoi a half-day ahead of Washington, it would already have been early Friday morning, February 3, when the news conference was aired. Later that day Burchett sent off a dispatch from Hanoi to *Yomiuri,* an English-language newspaper in Tokyo, that said:

> For the moment, Hanoi is confident it has demonstrated its good will and is still hoping despite Johnson's press-

---

[4] That press conference also offered a poignant insight into the torment the war was causing Mr. Johnson. Asked how he felt those days about his job and "about us in the press" in light of all the current criticism, he answered, in part: "I go to bed every night feeling that I failed that day because I could not end the conflict in Vietnam. I do have disappointments and moments of distress, as I think every President has had. I am not complaining. If you can endure it in the press, I will try to endure it in the presidency."

conference remarks that Washington will show some modicum of good will. . . .

Hanoi's statement on talks was made to test the sincerity of Washington's frequent expressions of a desire for peace negotiations, etc. Hanoi feels it has opened the door with Nguyen Duy Trinh's statement and that it is up to Washington to make the next move.

If Johnson is really going to stick to his earlier pronouncements, he must definitely halt the bombardments, start the talks and see what steps are possible next.

If anyone in Washington thought the North Vietnamese were making their offer from a position of weakness, Burchett warned this would be a "major blunder." He said: "Hanoi is prepared for such a hawklike reaction."

In Moscow, Tass distributed a commentary on the Trinh offer and the President's press-conference response. Tass said, in part:

The statement of Nguyen Duy Trinh about the possibility of talks between the DRV and the United States, provided bombings are unconditionally stopped, is a new manifestation of good will by the DRV government.

The unwillingness of United States ruling circles to stop the criminal bombing of the DRV can only be regarded as a refusal to meet around the conference table, and as a sign of their determination to further escalate the aggressive war in Vietnam.

Tass made a point of its belief that the Trinh offer was the kind of reciprocal indication the United States was seeking and that Mr. Johnson, in his news conference, had ignored it.

Kremlin-watchers saw in this a signal that the Politburo was disturbed because Trinh's offer had brought no favorable response from the President. Reading the Tass and Burchett dispatches together that weekend before Tet, it must have been apparent to officials in Washington that Ho Chi Minh thought he had already taken "just almost any step" and that he would remain as intractable in his position of refusing military reciprocity as the President was in demanding it.

In this highly charged atmosphere, Richard N. Goodwin, an aide to both John Kennedy and Lyndon Johnson before he had grown disenchanted with the nation's Vietnam war policy, and Walt Rostow, the President's hard-line special assistant for national security affairs, met to debate that policy before a conference of college newspaper editors in Washington on Saturday, February 4.

Goodwin charged the Johnson Administration had let opportunities to negotiate a settlement "go by."

Rostow denied the charge. "Nothing has yet happened that would justify us as saying we have a serious offer to negotiate," he said. But then he lifted the veil surrounding the secret diplomacy just enough to let the nation know something was indeed occurring:

"This is an extremely interesting or delicate phase in what is or might turn out to be a negotiating process."

CHAPTER TWELVE

Wilson Took It Like a Man

Chester Cooper arrived in London on Friday, February 3, with the latest version of a negotiating scenario secretly designated "Phase A–Phase B" in his briefcase. Phase A–Phase B was a flexible plan for de-escalating the war in South Vietnam gradually in such a manner that neither the United States nor the North Vietnamese would lose either face or military advantage.

Cooper had instructions to present this plan to Harold Wilson. The prime minister, in turn, would be authorized to relate it to Premier Kosygin during the coming week's talks. In representing the United States' views, Wilson would be able to use such phrases as "I am confident the President believes . . ." Kosygin, as far as is known, never questioned Wilson's authority to speak for the United States.

Phase A referred to an American cessation of the bombing of North Vietnam. On the surface, when such a cessation did come, it would appear to all the world as a unilateral decision, an acceptance finally of the North Vietnamese demand that bombing must stop unconditionally before talks could take place.

In fact, however, Phase A would only be put into effect by the United States after Washington and Hanoi had secretly

agreed on Phase B—an act of de-escalation of the ground war
by both sides. The United States would move first in Phase B
as well. It might, for instance, pull back American troops from
a position near the demilitarized zone along the 17th parallel.
The North Vietnamese would be expected to meet this with a
measurable reduction of infiltration of their troops into the
South. Or the first United States Phase B move might be a
reduction in troop reinforcement which would similarly be met
by a North Vietnamese cutback in infiltration. Thus, it would
appear as if North Vietnam were responding not to the halt in
bombing—which the United States had been publicly demanding
—but to a slowdown by the Americans in the ground war.
Other details of Phase A–Phase B were negotiable as well—
for example, the speeches and statements each side would make
to explain its moves.

Most important, the question of a time lag between imple-
mentation of the two phases would have to be worked out carefully between the two sides. If the war was quiescent and the
activity of enemy forces was low, the United States might be
willing to wait as much as three weeks or a month after undertaking a Phase A bombing halt before implementing an agreed-
upon Phase B withdrawal. If, however, enemy forces were un-
usually active and occupying menacing positions, the United
States would reduce the time lag acceptable to just a week or
a few days. It might even insist on a Phase B simultaneous with
Phase A.

The Phase A–Phase B scheme was no peace plan, as such.
It was more a plan to get the talks started and cool off the war
in the hope that once that was accomplished, serious negotiations involving the interests of the Saigon regime and the National Liberation Front, as well as the United States and North
Vietnam, would result.

The Phase A–Phase B plan was not created specifically for
the London talks between Wilson and Kosygin. It had been de-
vised before the Manila Conference of 1966 and had become a
kind of skeleton for American negotiating policy. The Manila
Conference Declaration and the American basis for the Marigold
ten points had elements of the plan in them. In a sense, when
Lyndon Johnson, Dean Rusk or William Bundy said, as they

sometimes did, that the United States could not stop its half of the war without knowing what the other side would do, they were inviting a response from North Vietnam about Phase B.

Accounts vary on just how much of a time lag between A and B Cooper had been authorized to present in London. There are indications, however, that the day he left Washington, when the President was in his "just-almost-any-step" mood, the United States was taking a liberal attitude toward the time lag. Officials apparently were willing to allow as much as three weeks between A and B.

Cooper was no stranger to London. Between 1955 and '57 he had served as a special representative of the Central Intelligence Agency in London and had developed contacts not only with the British Intelligence Services, M.I. 5 and M.I. 6, but with political figures. He specialized in getting to know the "outs" of that time, the leaders in the opposition Labor Party who would certainly return to power someday.

Between Friday, February 3, and Monday, February 6, Cooper briefed Wilson and Foreign Secretary George Brown on the latest variations of Phase A–Phase B. He told them of the Guthrie channel in Moscow and, one source said, he had been given permission to tell Wilson alone, if the occasion occurred, that the President might soon send a personal letter to Ho Chi Minh. The draft of the letter Cooper had seen conformed to the A-B plan he presented to Wilson. Cooper did not find it necessary to go into too much historical detail. He had made a briefing trip to London during January.

It has been said of Harold Wilson that he is so optimistic that if he had been master of the *Titanic* when that ship suffered its maiden-voyage disaster, he would have informed the passengers the ship had stopped to take on a supply of ice cubes. This characteristic of the British prime minister showed on February 6 when he drove out to London Airport North in his big black Rolls Royce limousine to greet Kosygin. "*Moi stari drug* [My old friend]," Wilson exclaimed, pushing his meager Russian to the limit in a buoyant effort to show off the promising possibilities for the upcoming meetings.

The two leaders went into conference together within four hours of Kosygin's arrival. They talked at 10 Downing Street privately at first (with only their interpreters present) and later with all of their advisers. They had a long list of subjects to cover, ranging from ways of improving trade between their two nations to the pressing questions of world-wide international relations. Vietnam, however, with the Tet truce scheduled to start in two days, dominated the first session and all those which followed.

During the first discussion Kosygin stressed the interview Trinh had given Wilfred Burchett. Trinh's proposal, he said, was a genuine signal that Hanoi wanted to talk and was a major concession. He reportedly even went further than Trinh in telling Wilson talks "would" follow a halt in the American bombing of North Vietnam, whereas Trinh had been conditional on this point. Kosygin, presumably speaking for Hanoi, said the talks would begin three to four weeks after the bombing stopped.

Wilson replied by stating that Americans wanted reciprocal military de-escalation by the North Vietnamese in a Phase A–Phase B context. Kosygin insisted the Trinh interview's gesture was enough to get talks started. Once they were under way, Kosygin said, everything else would fall into place.

That night the two met for an informal dinner at 10 Downing Street. During the evening Wilson took his visitor aside and told him his views would be transmitted to Washington.

Wilson and Kosygin were highly competent to discuss the Vietnam problem. Their governments, at the Geneva Conference of 1954, had provided the co-chairmen for the meetings that were supposedly settling the Indochina problem permanently. As the Vietnam war began escalating in 1964, many statesmen, including Wilson, were calling for a reconvening of the Geneva Conference, but the Soviet Union had always refused.

Wilson eagerly sought to renew the British role as Vietnam arbiter for at least three reasons. Credit as an international peace-maker would help the British take their minds off the politically dangerous economic problems at home. Further, even though Britain was giving up its military position in the world, it still yearned to make itself felt diplomatically in international affairs. Lastly, there was a large and vocal peace bloc in the British Isles and inside the Labor Party itself which had been pressuring Wilson to dissociate himself from the American Vietnam policy.

Until he arrived in London, Alexei Kosygin (and the rest of the Politburo) consistently maintained the hands-off attitude on negotiations. Thus, it was somewhat surprising when the dour Kosygin in London, for the first time, gave serious and prolonged attention to the matter of a negotiated settlement in Vietnam. Diplomats in London even thought they detected nuances now and then indicating he saw at least some reasonableness in the American position. They also detected a motive: Kosygin was visibly and audibly disturbed by the growing power of the Chinese Communists and seemed to recognize that when the time came, his country's interests would lie more in concert with the Western world than with the Chinese.

Even considering Kosygin's apparent good will, the Johnson Administration was by no means sanguine about the prospect of striking the kind of bargain it wanted with the North Vietnamese in London. It maintained the direct channel opened in Moscow. On the day Kosygin arrived in London, John Guthrie made his fifth call at the North Vietnamese Embassy in Moscow in twenty-six days. That kept the "negotiating process" to which Walt Rostow had referred over the weekend open on both fronts.

At 7 A.M. Wednesday, February 8, Vietnam time, the guns fell silent in South Vietnam and the United States suspended the bombing of North Vietnam to keep the Tet truce. The cease-fire had been scheduled for four days; fighting was due to resume at 7 A.M. Sunday in Vietnam. The festival cease-fire was the signal for many world figures to begin clamoring for steps that would lead to a permanent halt in the fighting. But in London, a quirk in scheduling did not allow for any Wilson-Kosygin talks on the first day of Tet. Instead, the day was given to ceremony, sightseeing and speechmaking by the visiting premier. Kosygin appeared at Guildhall for a luncheon given by the Lord Mayor of London, and in a speech the Russian attacked the United States for creating the Vietnam problem. "Today the major factors in international tension are the Vietnamese events," he said, "and it is the American aggression that is the real, and in effect, the only cause for war in Vietnam." He said the Soviet Union and the United Kingdom could play a role in bringing about a settlement based on the Geneva accords of 1954, but only after the United States unconditionally terminated the bombing of North Vietnam and all other acts of aggression. This cessation, he said, was essential for talks. The public speech was a good indication of the hard bargaining going on in private.

But the United States was dissatisfied. Wilson conveyed the wish of the Johnson Administration for more of a response from Hanoi than proposals in newspaper articles.

As the week progressed, Washington officials grew more disturbed by supply movements in the southern part of North Vietnam which indicated the North Vietnamese were making good use of the truce to refurbish their military machine. Three times the United States asked Wilson to call this to Kosygin's attention as a situation that would impede efforts to begin talks. The third time Cooper gave Wilson a detailed description of just what American reconnaissance had discovered about North Vietnamese supply movements. He reportedly urged Wilson to "ask the Russians if there was anything they could do to put a damper on the flow."

On Thursday, Wilson suddenly changed the location of the talks for the day from Downing Street to Kosygin's suite at Claridge's Hotel, where, he said, the principals could be less formal. The switch also heightened interest in their discussions. That afternoon Kosygin went before newsmen for an internationally televised press conference. It was broadcast live in the United States via satellite, and one of the home viewers was Lyndon B. Johnson. The President watched as Kosygin, a mournful look on his face, drew the world's attention once again to the Trinh proposal as the best prospect for peace talks. "That proposal was highly constructive and we think the United States should take advantage of it," the Soviet leader said, adding that it offered "a way out" of the negotiations impasse.

Within a couple of hours Mr. Johnson reacted through his press secretary, George Christian, who said: "Mr. Kosygin commented on the military action the United States should take but made no mention of the military action the other side should take."

The more Kosygin reiterated the Trinh interview as the way to talks, the stiffer the United States grew in its demand that North Vietnam show some reciprocal military de-escalation in return for the bombing pause. Wilson, however, kept insisting to Kosygin that the details of the de-escalation, through the Phase A–Phase B scheme, were negotiable enough to please the North Vietnamese.

Friday morning, February 10, Kosygin, for the first time since he arrived, asked Wilson to put the details of the Phase A–Phase B plan (although Kosygin, of course, did not know it by that name) in writing. The Russian wanted to send the message to his colleagues in Moscow that day.[1]

Kosygin's request came during a meeting that began at 10 Downing Street at 10:30 A.M. and, including an informal luncheon, lasted until almost 3:30 P.M. Kosygin then returned to his hotel to grant an interview to the *Times* of London (in which he again condemned the American Vietnam policy). Wilson and Cooper drafted a page-and-a-half memorandum detailing the Phase A–Phase B proposal the United States thought would meet the demands of the Trinh interview while at the

---

[1] Throughout the week Kosygin never explicitly said he was acting as an agent for the North Vietnamese, although it was generally assumed that the Russians had received the authority to do some bargaining for the Hanoi leaders. President Johnson, by several accounts, was afraid Wilson might go too far in compromising the United States' position. The President was nervous about the publicity the London talks were getting and the resulting pressure it could put on him to extend the bombing pause. In the same manner, there were suggestions that Brezhnev and Ho Chi Minh were anxious that Kosygin, a strong advocate of peaceful coexistence, might go too far in trading away Hanoi's strongly held positions.

same time taking into account the worries in Washington over the North Vietnam supply build-up.

Cooper and Wilson worked with the full knowledge that theirs was not the only channel through which the United States was dealing with the North Vietnamese at the time. They knew, in fact, that only two days before, Guthrie had paid his sixth visit to the Bolshaya Pirogovskaya address in Moscow and that this time he had delivered the previously contemplated personal letter from Mr. Johnson to Ho. The message the two men in London drafted for Kosygin conformed fully, they thought, to the ideas the President had expressed in his letter to Ho.

They nonetheless sent the text via cable to Washington. It must have been somewhere around 4:30 P.M. London time (11:30 A.M. in Washington) when the coded cable left Downing Street and began arriving simultaneously at the White House Situation Room and the State Department Operations Center.

President Johnson's schedule is never only what the publicly announced calendar shows. He has off-the-record appointments each day. Very often it is the off-the-record engagements that are most interesting. The public calendar for the President and Dean Rusk on February 10 showed both men busy with matters of peripheral importance. Just as the Wilson-Kosygin luncheon was ending in London, for example, Rusk was meeting with Hassan II, King of Morocco, Prince of the Faithful, who was on a state visit to Washington. At 1 P.M., Rusk, along with Averell Harriman and Robert Komer, the Vietnam expert on Walt Rostow's staff at the White House, went to the Moroccan Embassy for a luncheon in honor of the king. Rusk signed a cultural exchange agreement with Morocco and the Americans remained at lunch until 3 P.M.

President Johnson's morning schedule was occupied with domestic matters. He met with Comptroller General Elmer Staats; then with Budget Director Charles Schultze and Special Assistant Joseph Califano, and finally with John Macy, chairman of the Civil Service Commission. At 5:30 he met with Peace Corps Director Jack Hood Vaughn and in the evening he had an unannounced meeting with King Hassan.

Sometime during that schedule, probably in the late after-noon following the return of Rusk from the Moroccan Embassy, the President turned his attention to the cable from Harold Wilson. Rusk and Rostow—perhaps others as well—were sum-moned to the Situation Room in the basement of the White House. There was alarm. The Wilson message simply would not do.

In London, Cooper, confident there would be no problems, took the night off. Harold Wilson stuffed an envelope contain-ing the message into the breast pocket of his jacket. He left 10 Downing Street, climbed into his Rolls Royce and went to the Soviet Embassy to spend ninety minutes at a reception the Soviet ambassador was giving to honor Kosygin. Wilson ar-rived at 5:30 P.M. Some 250 guests were gathering, including Philip M. Kaiser, the deputy chief of the United States Embassy in London. Kaiser, who had been assisting Cooper in the liaison work during the week, was the only American spotted by Soviet diplomats that evening.

Sometime during the party Wilson and Kosygin went into an anteroom, where Kosygin asked if the document was ready. The British prime minister apparently felt it was all right to turn it over. If anything was wrong, he thought, he would have heard from Washington by then. He had received no such word. He took the memorandum out of his pocket and gave it to Kosygin.

Wilson left the Soviet Embassy at 7 P.M. and went back to Downing Street to spend a quiet evening. Kosygin must have turned the message over to communications people for trans-mission to Moscow while he dined with fifty guests at the em-bassy. At 10:15 P.M. his schedule called for his departure from the embassy for the ten- to twenty-minute ride to the Euston Railroad Station, where a special train waited to take him to Scotland. Saturday, the last day of the Tet truce, he would visit an atomic energy power station and take in a soccer game in fabled Kilmarnock, the small textile- and whiskey-producing town where Robert Burns' poems were first published in the eighteenth century.

About the time the Russian set out from the embassy, transatlantic chaos set in. In the Situation Room at the White House, Walt Rostow clung to a phone while a White House operator called around London, trying to find Cooper. Meanwhile, the men in the room were drafting a new paragraph to substitute for the unacceptable section in the Wilson message to Kosygin. The problem was that Wilson had, in presenting a Phase A–Phase B proposal, allowed too much time lag between the two phases. One source said he had allowed about three weeks between the bombing halt and the Phase B de-escalation. Another said the lag was only "several days." Either way, the President found it unsatisfactory and wanted it changed—immediately. If possible he wanted the message changed before it left London for Moscow; if not, then before it went from Moscow to Hanoi, and if not that, at least before the North Vietnamese began taking it too seriously.

Finally Cooper was found and Rostow ordered him to the American Embassy, where he could talk to the Situation Room on a secure phone—one on which his voice signal would be electronically scrambled for the trip through the undersea cable to avoid dangers of wire-tapping. By the time Cooper arrived at the embassy, Rostow told him to forget conversation and to rush off to 10 Downing Street instead. Wilson was apparently already in direct contact with the Situation Room. The White House was, in fact, dictating the substitute paragraph to Wilson.

It was now approaching 11 P.M. in London (6 P.M. in Washington). There were only minutes to spare before Kosygin's train was due to leave for Scotland.

The substitute paragraph was typed on Downing Street stationery and entrusted to one of Wilson's aides. He was ordered to give the note to Kosygin personally. Off went the aide into the London evening, his car racing toward the Euston Station. He dashed through the doorway of the building—it looks more like a subway station than a proper railway depot—down the stairs, through the crowds and finally, out of breath, to Platform Number 1. He barely made it.

If Kosygin was startled or annoyed when the aide to the Queen's prime minister explained, there is no record of it. But at Downing Street "the British were embarrassed." Wilson had dealt with Kosygin in good faith. Now the prime minister found himself in a predicament. Wilson was being forced to admit, in effect, that he had misrepresented the American position to Kosygin.

The British were not alone in their embarrassment. Americans were shamed as well. "Everybody who knew was embarrassed. It shouldn't have happened," a source said.

How had Wilson taken it?

"He took it like a man," a source answered, acknowledging there are many ways a man can react but refusing to amplify.

CHAPTER THIRTEEN

Two Letters to Ho Chi Minh

For months Harold Wilson concealed the embarrassment Lyndon Johnson had caused him. Then, in the fall of 1967 in New York, Foreign Secretary George Brown momentarily dropped his guard.

Brown had gone to attend the opening of the regular United Nations General Assembly session. At the Assembly itself, he had been one of the few traditional American allies to speak up wholeheartedly in favor of United States policy in Vietnam. But on September 21 he was the guest of honor at an intimate, off-the-record luncheon given by the prestigious Council on Foreign Relations in its headquarters at Park Avenue and 68th Street. The luncheon group of some fifteen to twenty included Ambassador Arthur Goldberg. It was a relaxed affair. Brown had a few drinks. The talk turned to Vietnam and then to the Wilson-Kosygin meetings of the previous February. Suddenly Brown was saying that the problem in London that week had been a switch in the United States' position. (One of the men in the group thought Brown used the term "a hardening" rather than "a switch.") The foreign secretary caught himself. He shouldn't have said that, he remarked. He asked them please not to repeat it.

Brown's slip was an indication that the British held the Americans responsible for the confusion that resulted in the switched messages. Wilson had endured a heavy blow. Originally he suffered his hurt not realizing that American officials, earlier in that February week, had executed a change in attitude on what they planned to say in a far more important communication to Ho Chi Minh than Wilson's.

In the last few days before the Tet truce of February 8–11, 1967, the pressures at work on Lyndon Johnson over how to settle the Vietnam war bore down ferociously and from many directions. From antiwar critics such as Harry S. Ashmore, from political dissidents in his own Democratic Party led by Senator Robert F. Kennedy, from individuals in the national security bureaucracy who thought the time was ripe for talks, and from foreign statesmen such as Kosygin and U Thant.

Counterpressure, urging continued military action as the key to an honorable peace, if not out and out victory, came not only from generals and admirals but also from the government of Premier Nguyen Cao Ky and from powerful civilian advisers on national security affairs. In addition, the President had to recognize the growing frustration of millions of Americans who could not understand how their country—the most powerful in the world—had bogged down in fighting such a small enemy. Whatever inconsistency occurred in the Administration's policy —and it was plentiful—appeared designed to appease all these countervailing forces at once.

As Ashmore put it in another context, "the nerve that activates the consensus reflex" in Mr. Johnson had been "pinked." The President was riding all the conflicting currents at once.

The treatment of Ashmore and William Baggs after they returned from Hanoi in mid-January represented one effort by the President during that period to placate critics of his military policy. On January 16, Ashmore and Baggs reported to the State Department—through Undersecretary Nicholas Katzenbach and others—that Ho was in a conciliatory mood.[1] They said they thought he would consider mutual de-escalation and that he had invited continued contact either with them or with American officials through a direct channel in Phnom Penh. When Senator Fulbright, perhaps the most important antiwar critic in the country and a friend of both men, heard they had not been invited to discuss their findings with the President, he thought that a mistake. He raised the matter with Mr. Johnson at a White House social affair. The President said he did not wish to risk the speculation such a meeting might evoke if it became known. But he did ask the State Department to call Baggs and Ashmore in once more and suggested that Fulbright be present at the meeting.

Ashmore, Baggs and Fulbright attended a meeting on Saturday, February 4, at the State Department with Katzenbach, Averell Harriman, William Bundy and William Jordan, the Vietnam expert on the National Security Council, who was representing the White House. To Baggs and Ashmore it appeared that the President had convened the meeting to prevent Fulbright from "going around Washington saying the President wasn't responding to a possible opening from Hanoi."

The officials proposed a draft of a letter Ashmore would send to Ho Chi Minh. He and Baggs dismissed it as "pretty bad . . . State Department language . . . too stiff." The two travelers rewrote the letter and later went over their draft word-by-word with Bundy. The following morning Baggs and Ashmore waited an hour at the State Department while Bundy and

---

[1] Ashmore and Baggs did not go to Hanoi as representatives of the United States government but they did go with the State Department's consent and help. Before they left, they were briefed extensively, by Katzenbach and others, on the Administration's positions concerning peace negotiations. The Department urged them to keep their trip secret as long as possible, the two reported, and even had their passports validated in Hong Kong rather than in Washington in the hope of maintaining secrecy. They did do one diplomatic errand for the Department. At the request of Leonard Unger, then William Bundy's deputy, they asked Ho Chi Minh and other North Vietnamese leaders to allow representatives of the International Red Cross into Hanoi. Unger's idea—one shared by other American officials including Harriman, Cooper and McGeorge Bundy—was that the IRC could open negotiations about war prisoner exchanges which might lead later to more general negotiations.

others privately considered the rewritten version. Finally Bundy met with the two men and they all agreed to minor changes. A State Department secretary typed it on a letterhead from Ashmore's Center for the Study of Democratic Institutions. The letter was delivered to Ashmore at Fulbright's house, where he and Baggs were eating Sunday lunch. Ashmore signed it and mailed it to the North Vietnamese mission in Phnom Penh for forwarding to Ho.

The Ashmore letter, which the President had played a key part in arranging, was as conciliatory as the President's "just-almost-any-step" remark in his press conference three days before. The key passages in the letter were these:

> In our several discussions with senior officials of the State Department . . . they emphasized that the U. S. remains prepared for secret discussions at any time, without conditions, and that such discussions might cover the whole range of topics relevant to a peaceful settlement. They reiterated that the Geneva accords might be the framework for a peaceful solution.
>
> "They expressed particular interest in your suggestions to us that private talks could begin provided the U. S. stopped bombing your country, and ceased introducing additional U. S. troops in Vietnam. They expressed the opinion that some reciprocal restraint to indicate that neither side intended to use the occasion of talks for military advantage would provide tangible evidence of good faith of all parties in the prospects for a negotiated settlement. . . .

The letter—in asking "some reciprocal restraint"—sought some mutual de-escalation as did the President in his press conference. But like the press conference, the letter left the amount deliberately vague, indicating that something less than a complete halt in the North Vietnamese effort would be acceptable for a cessation in the American bombing.

The day after Ashmore mailed his letter, the President, reacting to what he considered a straightforward political challenge from Senator Robert F. Kennedy, indicated he was far from certain he would accept "just almost any step" or "some reciprocal restraint" from Hanoi in exchange for a bombing halt.

Kennedy had arrived home from his ten-day tour of Europe —some newspapers called it a "mission"—Saturday, February 4, the day Ashmore and Baggs were drafting their letter at the State Department. During his travels the senator had met not only with Manac'h and de Gaulle but with Pope Paul, Italian Foreign Minister Amintore Fanfani and other statesmen. After he cleared customs at New York's John F. Kennedy International Airport, he immediately encountered a crowd of newsmen who wanted to know whether he thought his talks "had upset the delicate balance of international relations."

Mounting a chair at the terminal, he denied any such implication, saying: "All I was interested in was in doing all I can toward a peaceful solution in Southeast Asia. . . . I think we are all interested in learning the facts." The situation in Vietnam, he said, was "important for all of us." Then he reiterated the belief he had expressed throughout Europe that the next few weeks would be critical in the search for peace.

The next evening the first copies of a new issue of *Newsweek* magazine arrived in the offices of New York newspapers and wire services with a report that Kennedy, during his stop in Paris, had received a "peace feeler" from Hanoi. The editors of the *New York Times* saw enough significance in the *Newsweek* report to feature a story on it as the most important in their Monday morning edition. The second paragraph of the *Times'* story said: "A spokesman for New York's Democratic senator said yesterday that Mr. Kennedy would have no comment on the report until he had had a chance to confer 'with the Executive Branch of the government.' "

The White House immediately assumed Kennedy had leaked the story to embarrass the President politically. Kennedy knew the President and his aides would jump to this conclusion. Newsmen saw a good story combining all the interest of the well-known Robert Kennedy–Lyndon Johnson feud with that of the Vietnam war. The first thing Monday morning, February 6, they were clamoring for more details at Kennedy's office on Capitol Hill and at the White House. Kennedy decided he should meet with the President to explain the situation if Mr. Johnson desired it. He called Marvin Watson, then the President's appointments secretary. Watson said he thought a meeting would be helpful and would let the senator know. Shortly thereafter, Kennedy received a call from Katzenbach, an old friend and former deputy to Kennedy when he had been attorney general during his brother's Administration. Kennedy got the impression the President had detailed Katzenbach to talk to him and that the President did not want to see him. The senator and the undersecretary met for lunch in Kennedy's office. Kennedy explained he had not been the source of the leak to *Newsweek*. While they were talking, Watson called to say the President would see them both at 4 P.M.

As Kennedy entered the oval office of the President, he shook Mr. Johnson's hand, but after that the two men were something less than civil toward each other. The President, obviously angry, began by bringing up the *Newsweek* leak. At that point neither man knew how the story had gotten into the magazine. Kennedy denied any part in the publication. The President did not believe him. Kennedy suggested the leak had come "from your State Department."

The remark enraged the President. "It's not my State Department," he retorted. "It's your State Department."

That must have shaken Katzenbach, who was sitting there as servant to one man and close friend of the other. Katzenbach was only one former Kennedy appointee in the State Department. The senator, as confidant to his late brother during the New Frontier years, had been given the authority to place many men in the national security bureaucracy. Now he maintained channels of intelligence into the Johnson Administration far more sensitive than those ever enjoyed by a junior senator. Mr. Johnson was not unmindful of this.

Kennedy began describing the findings of his trip. He told the President of the universal opinion among European leaders that only an American bombing halt could lead to negotiations. He urged a test of Hanoi's position by extending the four-day bombing pause that had already been announced for Tet. He said such a move would improve America's position in the world community by shifting any onus for avoiding talks to the North Vietnamese.

When Kennedy finished, the President said, according to one version: "There's not a chance in the world I'll do that."

The meeting grew more heated. At one point the President warned Kennedy he was jeopardizing his political future with his advocacy of a bombing halt and negotiations. The Chief Executive defended his Vietnam policies, asserting that the war was going very well and that further significant progress was just ahead.

"If you keep talking like this, you won't have a political future within six months," the President told the senator. In one account he followed this up by saying, "In six months all you doves will be destroyed." According to another account, the President did not use the word "doves" but some other term to describe those in favor of negotiations and said "finished" rather than "destroyed."

"I don't have to sit here and take that," the senator responded.

As the forty-five-minute meeting drew to a close, the President urged Kennedy to leave through the west lobby and tell reporters waiting there the United States had never received any genuine peace feelers. Kennedy demurred, saying he had not seen any government cables. The President insisted. "We never received any peace feelers at all," he said. Then, turning to Katzenbach and Walt Rostow, the only other witness at the meeting, he asked, "Isn't that right?"

Both men said yes.

Finally Kennedy compromised and made this statement to reporters as he left the White House: "I never received the impression that I was any recipient of peace feelers. . . . I did not bring home any feelers."

It was all semantic, of course. John Dean had cabled home Mai Van Bo's message to Manac'h.[2]

After the senator left the White House, a reporter spotted Walt Rostow and asked him about the meeting.

---

[2] Though neither the President nor the senator realized it during their confrontation, John Dean's two-page cable had been leaked to *Newsweek*'s diplomatic correspondent, Edward Weintal, by a State Department official before Kennedy had arrived home. The official had no political motives.

"It was rough," Rostow said. "It was very rough."

Kennedy went back to his office with as clear a picture of the President's real attitude toward the war at that time as anyone could have. Were a bombing halt and negotiations on the President's mind? The confrontation showed him confident that continued military pressure on the enemy would provide the answers to the Vietnam problem. It showed him determined that the North Vietnamese would have to offer more than talks before he would grant them surcease from bombing.

"Well, that wasn't a very pleasant meeting," Kennedy told an aide when he returned to Capitol Hill.

The President's attitude on a bombing halt was hardly conducive to a successful attempt by the professional diplomats to attain immediate negotiations. In January, Administration officials had conceived of the idea of sending a letter from President Johnson to Ho Chi Minh. It seems likely that this was intended as a climax to the dealings John Guthrie was having in Moscow with Le Trang. By February 2 the diplomats had drafted a conciliatory letter—one containing a Phase A–Phase B proposal—for the President's signature. That letter was in Moscow, presumably ready for delivery to the North Vietnamese, by February 6, according to the State Department log of telegrams between Washington and foreign missions. John Guthrie visited Le Trang on February 6. He did not, however, deliver the letter. Since his instructions are unknown, it is impossible to say why.

February 6, it should be remembered, was the day after Ashmore mailed his letter to Ho. It was the day Alexei Kosygin arrived in London, saying the North Vietnamese sincerely wanted to talk. It was also the day of the explosive showdown between LBJ and RFK.

The following day Wilfred Burchett wrote an article for the Associated Press re-emphasizing Hanoi's desire for talks— but only after the unconditional bombing cessation. He said North Vietnam would offer nothing in return for the cessation except that "if the Americans cease sending their planes, we cease firing at them, shooting them down, cease killing or capturing their pilots."

Burchett's article became known in the last hours before the four-day Tet truce was to go into effect at 6 P.M. Tuesday evening, February 7, Washington time. Already the President, faced with the need to make a decision, had abandoned his "just-almost-any-step" attitude toward reciprocity and his reliance on a Phase A–Phase B scheme to get negotiations started. Just when the decision was made is not known.

As one bureaucrat put it: "The President of the United States does not idly send a letter to Ho Chi Minh. This is something that takes a lot of brewing and stewing." Drafts are written and rewritten. They can be changed at any moment up to the time of delivery. That the President had not been committed to an all-out campaign for immediate negotiations was indicated in the meeting with Kennedy. That he was less than certain about the propriety of a conciliatory course toward Ho was indicated by the fact that the letter in Moscow was not delivered on February 6. Apparently it was not until the evening of February 7, or the early morning of February 8 in Washington, that the President and his advisers finally decided what to say to Ho. They scrapped the Phase A–Phase B plan in the letter already waiting in Moscow and substituted a much more demanding proposal.

"What resulted could have been taken as an ultimatum," said one official who was in a position to compare the earlier letter with the delivered version. "It was drafted poorly."

The revised letter was moderate in tone, as indicated by this passage:

> If we fail to find a just and peaceful solution, history will judge us harshly.
>
> Therefore, I believe that we both have a heavy obligation to seek earnestly the path to peace. It is in response to that obligation that I am writing directly to you.

It acknowledged an offer from the North Vietnamese to talk in these words:

In the past two weeks, I have noted public statements by representatives of your government suggesting that you would be prepared to enter into direct bilateral talks with representatives of the U. S. government, provided that we ceased "unconditionally" and permanently our bombing operations against your country and all military action against it. In the last day, serious and responsible parties have assured us directly that this is in fact your proposal.

And then it presented the President's strong demand this way:

I am prepared to order a cessation of bombing against your country and the stopping of further augmentation of U. S. forces in South Vietnam as soon as I am assured that infiltration into South Vietnam by land and by sea has stopped.

The letter was hardly a "just-almost-any-step" document. It turned the Phase A–Phase B plan around completely and demanded that the North Vietnamese act first to stop all infiltration *before* the United States would cease the bombing. Early in the morning of February 8, John Guthrie delivered the letter to Le Trang in Moscow. The letter was dated the same day. The delivery came almost certainly after the Tet truce had begun, which was at 2 A.M. Moscow time.[3]

---

[3] When the President's letter was made public more than a month later, State Department officials told newsmen the letter Guthrie delivered on February 8 was written on February 2. Tom Lambert of the *Los Angeles Times* was told by a source who checked the Department's log that the February 2 draft was transmitted to Moscow by February 6. In first claiming that the letter delivered by Guthrie was drafted on February 2, officials overlooked evidence in the letter itself (such as the President's reference to having received assurances "in the last day") that it was at least revised on February 7 or February 8. Months later William Bundy, at a press conference, tried to lead reporters to think the President's letter had been written on February 8, although he would not say so unequivocally. He said that if State Department officials had previously said the letter was written on February 2, they had erred. Bundy's remarks gave credence to an otherwise unconfirmed later report that the February 2 draft was revised and hardened by the President and some advisers in the dark hours of early February 8 at the White House. The President was said to have been in a state of high excitement over the publicity

About the time Guthrie was delivering the President's letter, Pope Paul sent Tet messages to Mr. Johnson and Ho. The letter to the President said:

> Our heartfelt appeals for the return of peace in Southeast Asia have always found a favorable reaction on your part, Mr. President, and that of your countrymen. . . .
>
> We know quite well the obstacles to achieving such a goal, but have no doubt in your dedication, Mr. President, to a constant search for peace. Therefore we ask you to increase even more your noble effort in these days of truce for this great cause. . . .

President Johnson responded almost immediately, telling the Pope:

> We are prepared to talk at any time and place, in any forum, with the object of bringing peace to Vietnam.
>
> However, I know you would not expect us to reduce military action unless the other side is willing to do likewise. We are prepared to discuss the balanced reduction in military activity, the cessation of hostilities or any practical arrangements which could lead to these results.

The next day, February 9, it was left to Dean Rusk to explain that "any practical arrangements" leading to a balanced reduction in military activity did not mean "just almost any step." In an unusual move, the White House announced that Rusk would hold a press conference, thereby emphasizing the importance of what he would say.

In his opening statement, Rusk said:

". . . For some time now there has been evident a systematic campaign by the Communist side to bring about an unconditional and permanent cessation of the bombing of North Vietnam, without any corresponding military action on their side, in exchange for the possibility of talks—talks which are thus far formless and without content.

"We cannot accept a situation in which men and arms move,

---

being given the Wilson-Kosygin talks in London and was worried that Wilson might promise the North Vietnamese, through Kosygin, more than the United States was willing to offer.

without interruption by us, to cross the 17th parallel and attack allied armed forces and Vietnamese civilians in the South. We must know the military consequences of such a military action on our part. They must not expect us to stop military action by bombing when they continue their military action by invasion. No one has been able or willing to give us any information on this subject. . . .

"Let me say quietly and sincerely to all capitals on the other side: Let good sense take charge for all of us in this situation. Recognize the necessity for elementary reciprocity. . . ."

Rusk did not bother to explain that the press conference term "elementary reciprocity" referred to the demand in the President's still-secret letter for complete cessation of all North Vietnamese infiltration in advance of the bombing cessation.

The day after Rusk's press conference and the day before the Tet truce was due to expire, U Thant, at the United Nations, made a renewed appeal for an indefinite extension of the cease-fire and an end to the American bombing of North Vietnam. The secretary general said: ". . . An unconditional end to the bombing of North Vietnam could, I am convinced, bring about a favorable climate for peaceful talks between the parties."

Rusk had been deliberately imprecise on "elementary reciprocity" to maintain negotiating leeway. Thus, it was not only the American people who were unable to judge the true attitude of the government, neither could Harold Wilson, the United States' spokesman in the London meetings. Wilson had not been given a text of the President's letter to Ho. He had been given only a summary which made it appear as if the United States was still seeking a Phase A–Phase B solution to the impasse on talks. That lack of information concerning the hardening in the American position led him and Cooper to draw up the memorandum Kosygin requested on February 10, the day after Rusk's press conference. The reason the President was so insistent on having Wilson change the message immediately related to the maintenance of the United States' credibility in the Kremlin's estimation. Kosygin would certainly find out about the contents of the letter to Ho, if he did not know them already. When he did, the comparison with what he had been told in London would make him assume the United States was speaking with two voices—softly to him and toughly to Ho. Ho would receive the President's letter the same day Kosygin received the memo from Wilson. Under these circumstances it was, for the President, far more necessary to risk embarrassment of Wilson than to mislead Kosygin or to confuse Ho.

Now in London, there was little left but to work against time in the hope that North Vietnam or the United States would suddenly alter an uncompromising position and allow talks to begin. Wilson and Kosygin could not get together on the Vietnam problem Saturday, February 11. Kosygin was touring Scotland. Wilson went to a wedding.

In Washington that Saturday, the last twelve hours before the Tet truce was to expire were busy. Reconnaissance photographs from planes overflying North Vietnam showed the resupply activity continuing, though at a slackening rate. The enemy appeared to have anticipated a resumption of bombing. The military wanted to resume the strikes immediately. Political considerations prevailed, however, and it was decided to maintain the pause in the air war over North Vietnam until Kosygin left London. Wilson had pleaded that to do otherwise would cause him political embarrassment. The fact that the President's letter to Ho had not yet drawn a reply did not seem to enter into the decision. The nature of the reply seemed anticipated.

About 11 P.M. on Saturday, those at 10 Downing Street watched Harold Wilson's usual optimism drain away—"There was a clear feeling that we were running out of sea."

Sunday morning Kosygin, back in London, went to High Gate Cemetery to lay a wreath at the grave of Karl Marx. Then he addressed a Conservative Party luncheon at the Carlton Club. Finally, at 3:20 P.M., he joined Wilson at 10 Downing Street for the forty-minute ride to Chequers, the 647-year-old estate that is the country residence of British prime ministers. The two were together there for seven hours. Kosygin returned to his hotel at midnight. Wilson arrived at 10 Downing Street at 12:30 A.M. Observers said they thought Wilson spoke to President Johnson at that hour.

Then, a half hour after arriving home, Wilson, accompanied by George Brown and other aides, rushed out of 10 Downing Street and over to Claridge's to see Kosygin again. The middle-of-the-night mission suggested that just one more attempt was being made to keep the lid on the war, perhaps by Wilson presenting a modification of the embarrassing Friday night message. There were also indications that Wilson used these last fifty minutes of talks to inform the Russian that the bombing of North Vietnam would be resumed later in the day. Wilson and Brown left the hotel suite at 2 A.M. Kosygin left London at 11:15 A.M. for the flight back to Moscow. At 4:30 P.M. Wilson met reporters and said:

"We believe the road to a solution is open. Even if we are disappointed on this occasion, there is no reason why—at the appropriate moment—the road should not be opened again."

Only a half-hour after Wilson's remarks and shortly after Kosygin landed in Moscow, the Tet bombing pause ended as two Air Force F-4C Phantoms—each of which can carry up to six tons of bombs—struck a highway bridge at Vinhtuy, forty miles north of the demilitarized zone. They struck at night, in bad weather. A military spokesman in Saigon said it was impossible to assess the success of the raid.

Four hours later the White House issued the following statement by President Johnson:

> It had been our hope that the truce periods connected with Christmas, New Year's and Tet might lead to some abatement of hostilities and to moves toward peace. Unfortunately, the only response we have had from the Hanoi government was to use the periods for major resupply efforts of their troops in South Vietnam.[4]

---

[4] Though the President spoke of a major resupply effort of North Vietnamese troops in *South* Vietnam, the Administration furnished only tenuous evidence of that. On March 17 the Pentagon held a

Despite our efforts and those of third parties no other response has yet come from Hanoi. Under these circumstances, in fairness to our own troops and those of our allies, we had no alternative but to resume full-scale hostilities after the cease-fire period. But the door is open and will remain open, and we are prepared at any time to go more than halfway to meet any equitable overture from the other side.

Just before the bombing was resumed, Ho Chi Minh's reply to the Pope was published. North Vietnam's terms also seemed to have hardened.

"The U. S. imperialists," Ho said, "must put an end to their aggression in Vietnam, withdraw from South Vietnam all American and satellite troops, recognize the South Vietnam National Front for Liberation and let the Vietnamese people settle themselves their own affairs. Only in such conditions can real peace be restored in Vietnam."

The day following the resumption of bombing, Harold Wilson, first in Parliament and later on television, tried to explain why nothing had come of his Vietnam talks with Kosygin the previous week. An elaborate secret plan existed, he said, that could bring peace to Vietnam in a day. "It requires a very, very small movement to activate all the complicated machinery that could bring peace," he said in Parliament. He placed the

---

briefing to present "fairly extensive and extremely reliable information on the nature and magnitude of North Vietnamese efforts to take full advantage of the [Tet] bombing pause." The briefing officer showed a series of photographs of trucks, trains, ships and barges on the move in North Vietnam and the Gulf of Tonkin, which, he said, delivered a record 23,000 tons of supplies during the pause. Some of the trucks appeared headed for the start of the Ho Chi Minh Trail in the Annamite Mountains straddling the border with Laos. But the briefing officer stressed that much of the resupply effort was *not* aimed at improving capabilities in South Vietnam. At one point he said: "In addition to the movement of military supplies, some of this activity was believed to be associated with the redistribution of food and other nonmilitary products required by various segments of the economy, including the military forces stationed in that general area [the southern part] of North Vietnam." At another point he said: "It must be emphasized that this was not all bound for South Vietnam."

blame for failure squarely on the North Vietnamese. He said he and Kosygin had awaited only a "gesture" from the North Vietnamese, one simple act of trust which could have begun negotiations. Wilson's overstatement—and the implication that the "plan" (obviously Phase A–Phase B) had been his and not Washington's—resulted in little but derision from left-wing members of his own Labor Party. From their back benches, they stridently demanded to know where he had obtained information on the southward movement of North Vietnamese supplies. They were implying that if the Americans provided the intelligence, it could not be believed. Later, a hundred leftist members of the Labor Party signed a petition calling on Her Majesty's government to dissociate itself from the American resumption of bombing. They said the renewal of the raids would undermine Thant's proposal of February 10 for a bombing halt leading to negotiations.

After Wilson's epilogue, a British reporter encountered Nguyen Van Sao, a North Vietnamese serving as Ho Chi Minh's nonaccredited representative in London. The reporter asked Sao how he thought the Wilson-Kosygin talks had gone.

Sao replied: *"Un vrai rigolo."*

It was a futile and puzzling exercise. It might have been a tragicomedy. It was not, however, by any standard "a real comedy."

CHAPTER FOURTEEN

The Man in the White Dinner Jacket

Even within the Johnson Administration there were those who felt the President had resumed the bombing precipitately after the Tet bombing pause of 1967. But advocates of a prolonged pause could win no support. One official put it this way: "The feeling [in Washington] was so against a prolongation of the pause that we were lucky to squeeze it out until Kosygin got home."

Critics within the Administration argued that Ho Chi Minh was not allowed enough time to respond privately to the President's tough February 8 letter. Since Ho did not receive the document until February 10, he was allowed only three days to discuss the President's terms with his advisers and decide how to respond. The Administration maintained that the public statements of the North Vietnamese were enough to justify a resumption of the bombing. They pointed in particular to the harshness of Ho's February 13 reply to the Pope.

But the Administration's reasoning was challenged by one veteran official this way: "It is a fact that Ho has his problems —differences of opinion in his government, keeping the Chinese happy, not appearing to do anything that would undermine the morale of those fighting in the South—and perhaps he had to take the hard line publicly to avoid a charge of sellout. . . . After all, we often follow a double track ourselves, making public statements at variance with our private soundings. So why wasn't this sort of situation possible with Ho? We could have paused a few days longer to be sure of his response."

This also was a widely held private view in the British government, which had invested so much time and effort the previous week in trying to get talks started.

Even many American officials who were skeptical of a favorable response from Hanoi felt that the United States would have created a propaganda advantage by extending the pause in 1967 as it had done for thirty-seven days during the winter holidays of 1965–1966.

One view was this: "I don't feel a bombing pause extension after Kosygin left would have produced anything. But I wish we had called somebody's bluff—U Thant's—by taking a chance and halting the bombing while reserving the right to resume if nothing happened after a reasonable time. We could have shifted the burden a little to the other side and our standing in the world would have improved somewhat."

But the President chose not to wait. The bombing of North Vietnam had already resumed when John Guthrie made his last trip to the North Vietnamese Embassy on February 15 and received, from Trang, Ho Chi Minh's reply to Mr. Johnson's letter. It was obvious that Ho had no hope of winning a "definitive and unconditional cessation" of the bombing in return for an offer of talks.

He wrote a vitriolic reply addressed "To His Excellency, Mr. Lyndon B. Johnson, President, United States of America," saying in part:

> The U. S. government has committed war crimes, crimes against peace and against mankind. In South Vietnam half a million U. S. and satellite troops have resorted to the most inhuman weapons and the most barbarous methods of warfare, such as napalm, toxic chemicals and gases, to massacre our compatriots, destroy crops and raze villages to the ground. In North Vietnam, thousands of U. S. aircraft have dropped hundreds of thousands of tons of bombs, destroying towns, villages, factories, schools. In your message, you

apparently deplored the sufferings and destruction in Vietnam. May I ask you: Who has perpetrated these monstrous crimes? It is the U. S. and satellite troops. The U. S. government is entirely responsible for the extremely serious situation in Vietnam.

He then went on to state what he saw as the necessary steps for the "restoration of peace" (as distinguished from the achievement of "talks"). These four steps were the cessation of bombing and all other acts of war against North Vietnam, the withdrawal of all U. S. "and satellite troops" from South Vietnam, recognition of the NLF and the settlement of their own affairs by the Vietnamese people. He again reiterated that talks could only result from the cessation of bombing but never without such a step first by the United States.

"The Vietnamese people will never submit to force; they will never accept talks under the threat of bombs," he told the President.

The next day *Nhan Dan,* without revealing the still-secret Johnson letter or Ho's answer, charged that when the North Vietnamese had offered to talk, the Johnson Administration "immediately changed its language."

At the State Department, Carl Bartch, a deputy to Robert McCloskey, ridiculed the North Vietnamese comment. It was, he said, "just another plot to get us to unilaterally stop the bombing without getting anything from them in return."

For many months the Administration kept one important by-product of the Lyndon Johnson–Ho Chi Minh correspondence secret. That was the cessation of direct negotiations between the two countries. When Trang handed Ho's letter to Guthrie, he told him there would be no more direct contact until the United States unconditionally halted the bombing.

"They slammed the door and threw down the receiver," an American official explained almost a year later. "When Ho's reply was delivered we were told this ends it."

It was the North Vietnamese who finally made the Lyndon Johnson–Ho Chi Minh correspondence public. They released the exchange of letters on March 21, 1967, while the President,

Rusk and Rostow were high in the skies over the Pacific Ocean, returning to the United States from a war council they had just conducted on Guam. In addition to their deliberations on the progress of the fighting with General Westmoreland and Ambassador Lodge, the American officials had conferred with the South Vietnamese leaders Nguyen Cao Ky and Nguyen Van Thieu. They had brought to the President a ratified copy of the new South Vietnamese constitution, which promised a return to civilian rule. The United States was beginning to place great emphasis on this constitution as an important part of what was called the "nation building" process.

Between Honolulu and the West Coast the White House telephone aboard the President's plane rang. Undersecretary of State Katzenbach was calling for Rusk. The exhausted Secretary of State was awakened to learn of the release of the letters. Katzenbach said Washington should confirm the text of the President's letter. Rusk agreed.

Hanoi said it published the correspondence to show the "stubbornness and perfidy of the U. S. rulers." The Johnson Administration stressed the tone of the two letters, saying Mr. Johnson's sounded far more reasonable than Ho's. In addition, they pointed out, the President was offering not only a cessation in bombing but had gone a step further in offering to halt the reinforcement of American troops in South Vietnam in return for talks. For weeks afterward the President, in private conversations, expressed surprise that Ho Chi Minh should have released the correspondence, which made the United States appear so conciliatory in comparison to the North Vietnamese. Other officials followed the same reasoning. They ignored the demands the President had made on Ho in the letter.[1]

---

[1] The Johnson Administration has maintained on several occasions that it cannot talk about Vietnam diplomacy because Hanoi demands secrecy and this country must show Hanoi it can be trusted to keep a secret. Yet it was the North Vietnamese who released the letters. The reaction in Washington to the release was some indication that the desire for secrecy was at least as much on the United States' side as on Hanoi's. So was a paragraph in the President's letter which read: "Let me frankly state that I see . . . great difficulties for this proposal [the Trinh interview proposal]. In view of your public position, such action on our part would inevitably produce world-wide speculation that discussions were under way and would impair the

About the time Ho's letter was delivered, Harry Ashmore received a cablegram at his Santa Barbara office. It was the first indication that his efforts at conciliation had become irrelevant. He and Baggs had offered to go back to Hanoi if it was thought desirable to keep their channel open. The cable told Ashmore such a trip would be pointless.

By coincidence, some American reporters met South Vietnam's Premier Nguyen Cao Ky at a diplomatic reception on February 15. Ky was natty in a white dinner jacket, and was relaxing with a Scotch in one hand and a cigarette in the other. A reporter engaged him in conversation about all the recent peace talk. "What is there to negotiate?" the reporter asked.

Ky was outspoken. "That is the point," he said. "Everybody talks about negotiations. So to be in fashion, I have to talk about negotiations. . . . I think we must intensify the military [side of the war] to the point where the Communists realize they cannot win."

There were those in high office in Washington who agreed.

---

secrecy and privacy of those discussions." The Administration meant this letter to remain an archival secret for many years. Hanoi's release of the Johnson letter also incidentally led to the disclosure of the existence of the Guthrie-Le Trang channel. The President had alluded in his letter to the direct contacts in Moscow between the United States and North Vietnam.

CHAPTER FIFTEEN

Summer Channel, Spring Talks

At 9 P.M. on Sunday, March 31, 1968, all three major television networks in the United States interrupted their regular prime-time entertainment to allow Lyndon Baines Johnson to deliver a modern-day fireside chat from the oval office of the White House. The speech was to be another in his series of major declarations on Vietnam policy. Like previous ones, it was based on an intensive review of the Vietnam war by the President and his key advisers. Many expected that the speech would deal with the need to escalate the war by sending more troops to South Vietnam and perhaps stepping up air attacks on North Vietnam.

In forty-one minutes that night the President produced more drama than Madison Avenue and Hollywood could produce in years of prime-time extravaganzas.

Instead of announcing further escalation of the war, he stated there would be a de-escalation, limiting the bombing of North Vietnam to an area north of the demilitarized zone. (The area was poorly defined, but he said the bombers would be banned over territory in which ninety percent of the North Vietnamese population lived.)

And if that sudden turn-around in the policy that had

brought three years of steady escalation in the level of violence was not enough, the President, at the end of the speech, added some personal and political drama. He said he would not be a candidate to succeed himself in the 1968 presidential election.

Lost in all the excitement over the announcements was a single sentence in the speech in which the President mentioned a previous offer to Hanoi to begin negotiations.

"Tonight," Mr. Johnson said, "I renew the offer I made last August."

There was a long, untold story behind that sentence. It involved a Harvard professor, two unheralded Frenchmen, a trip to Hanoi, clandestine meetings in France, talks in a Polish seaside resort and a secret message from the White House to the Presidential Palace in Hanoi.

The Frenchmen were Professor Herbert Marcovich, a forty-seven-year-old microbiologist at the University of Paris, and Raymond Aubrac, a fifty-three-year-old director of the Food and Agricultural Organization, one of the specialized agencies in the United Nations family. Both men had a strong interest in improving East-West relations. Marcovich's interest led him into joining the Pugwash Conferences, those meetings of scientists from all over the world organized during the height of the Cold War by Cyrus Eaton, the Cleveland industrialist who believed passionately in peaceful coexistence. Over the years Marcovich became a member of the "continuing committee" of the Pugwash Conferences, the body that governed the organization.

In 1946 Raymond Aubrac, then a rising young member of the post-World War II French government, befriended Ho Chi Minh. While the Vietnamese leader was in Paris negotiating the independence of his country from France, he stayed at Aubrac's suburban Paris villa, and the two men soon became good friends. Ho took his meals with the Aubrac family. Aubrac, who had distinguished himself as the provisional ruler of the Marseilles region after the Allied liberation in 1944 and had freed Vietnamese laborers from inhuman treatment in concentration camps, introduced Ho to the rising young generation of French government leaders. The talks between Ho, Aubrac and Aubrac's friends around the dinner table at the villa were stimulating. The friendship grew so close that when Mrs. Aubrac, during that period, gave birth to a daughter, Elizabeth, Ho Chi Minh, bearing flowers and toys, was one of the visitors to her hospital bedside. He became known, in fact, as Elizabeth's godfather.

It was on this relationship that the United States, in 1967, hoped to capitalize. The summer of 1967 was a period in which the Johnson Administration was finding great difficulty getting word into Hanoi through trustworthy channels.

The availability of Aubrac and Marcovich coincided with a belated realization in Washington that the Johnson Administration might have misread the military and diplomatic situation the previous February. At that time President Johnson had suddenly toughened his terms for negotiating with Ho Chi Minh and embarrassed British Prime Minister Harold Wilson by compelling him to revise a relatively lenient proposal he had just given Soviet Premier Alexei Kosygin. Would a more moderate proposal from the President have made any difference? Some American officials thought so. "We began to think Hanoi really wanted to talk in February," one official said.

Thus began a new phase in Vietnam diplomacy.

Dean Rusk had often said contact with Hanoi was no problem. But in fact it was. In January, 1968, an important State Department official was asked about direct American–North Vietnam contacts on negotiations and revealed there had been none in almost a year.[1] "They've insisted on not having direct contacts since last February," he said. "We've tried many times. . . . They've made clear that until the bombing stops unconditionally, there will be no more direct contact of the kind undertaken by Guthrie." (He was referring to the meetings between John Guthrie and Le Trang in Moscow during January and February, 1967.)

Out of necessity, then, rather than choice, the United States sought out nonprofessional intermediaries or third-government diplomats to carry its messages to the enemy. Dealing through

---

[1] Not until April 3, in response to the President's March 31 de-escalation proposal, were direct contacts on negotiations resumed, according to high officials.

intermediaries is a delicate business. The professionals resort to the use of amateur volunteers only reluctantly.

As one former official put it: "The trouble with the so-called volunteers is 1) they're lousy reporters who put more emphasis on how something is being said rather than what is being said; 2) they don't know the context in which discussions are going on, and 3) they just want a Nobel Peace Prize. They just talk too much about what is going on. . . . You learn to pay a helluva lot more attention to what's going on through the professionals than volunteers." Nevertheless, he continued, "the North Vietnamese have shown a desire at times to deal through volunteers rather than professionals." [2]

There is a suggestion that the original idea for the Aubrac-Marcovich mission belonged to the two Frenchmen themselves and not to any American official. Whether or not this is true soon became immaterial. They were not crosses to bear in the State Department's estimation. They were, rather, encouraged and pushed along. The man who ran their operation was a mystery figure in the national security apparatus—Professor Henry Alfred Kissinger, the forty-four-year-old director of Harvard's Defense Studies Program. Kissinger had been a consultant of one kind or another for the Defense and State Departments

---

[2] In Prague in the fall of 1966, Senator Joseph Clark almost made himself an intermediary when, over the objections of Ambassador Jacob Beam, he sought an appointment at the North Vietnamese Embassy. The North Vietnamese turned him down. Clark's attempt was an example of the fact that not all intermediaries are specially selected for their roles by one government or the other. Sometimes they intrude themselves into the situation.

Though reluctant to use intermediaries, other officials recognize that sometimes this is advantageous. "They can move around easily without arousing suspicion," one official said, "and they can say things that are deniable later on if problems arise."

The most important intermediary in the two-decade history of the Indochina war was self-appointed. He was Svante Löfgren, who, as Paris correspondent for Stockholm's *Expressen*, cabled Ho Chi Minh on November 5, 1953, asking if the Vietnamese leader thought the time was ripe for an armistice. Ho's reply was: "if, having learned the lesson of these years of war, the French government wishes to have an armistice and settle the question by negotiations, the people and government of the Democratic Republic of Vietnam are ready to examine the French proposals." The French government at first shrugged off the statement as meaningless. But later Paris reconsidered and the Geneva Conference of 1954 resulted.

for the past seventeen years. He was an expert on nuclear strategy and foreign policy and had, from time to time, advised Governor Nelson A. Rockefeller, among others. It had hardly been noticed, but since 1965 Kissinger had been intimately involved in the Vietnam war, advising on internal political matters in South Vietnam and the American effort to pacify the countryside. He was also secretly involved in the peace search, meeting frequently with Averell Harriman and others not only to give advice but to carry out operations.

Kissinger and Marcovich had met during the Pugwash meetings and became well acquainted at the September, 1966, conference in Sopot, Poland, a Baltic resort. They talked about Vietnam. It was here, most likely, that Kissinger learned of the connections Marcovich's friend Aubrac had with Ho Chi Minh. He probably learned also that Aubrac was a man who was deeply troubled by the Vietnam war.

An engineer and administrator trained at Harvard and Massachusetts Institute of Technology, Aubrac had drifted over the years from the exciting life of a wartime Maquis leader through various governmental roles in the reconstruction of France into work designing an irrigation system for Morocco. But by 1967 he was a mere cog in the United Nations machinery and his main concern had become the installation of an information retrieval system for the FAO headquarters in Rome. He thought about computers by day and the Vietnam war by night. Often his thoughts turned into nightmares about the enlargement of the war and the involvement of more countries. If his old, interrupted friendship—Ho and Aubrac lost touch when France and the Viet Minh went to war—could help in bringing about a settlement, he was available.

Arrangements were made. Kissinger briefed the two men on the American position. He gave them details on just what the United States would like said to Ho Chi Minh. There were instructions on what to look for in replies. Then, in July, Aubrac went to see his chief at the FAO. He was taking a short leave of absence, he said. He was going to Hanoi for personal reasons. He said he felt obligated to tell his superior since North Vietnam did not belong to the FAO or any other UN agency, but he

would prefer that the news of his trip go no further. Aubrac's
chief respected his confidence.

Aubrac and Marcovich attracted no public notice as they
flew from Western Europe to Phnom Penh, the capital of Cambodia, and then, on Friday, July 21, 1967, aboard the ICC
Stratoliner to Hanoi. They arrived in the North Vietnamese
capital as run-of-the-mill visitors, two of many Hanoi's leaders
have permitted in the city during the past three years. Little
in their backgrounds indicated they were semi-official emissaries
of the United States government about to become deeply involved in the secret search for peace in Vietnam.

The two Frenchmen spent four days in Hanoi—the shortest
possible period between flights. Marcovich, a former doctor in
the French army, visited Hanoi's Pasteur Institute and came
away impressed with the manner in which the Vietnamese were
making a little go a long way in medical care for the war
wounded. For example, he noted how they had developed a
technique for spreading a simple, curative bacillus on wounds
to prevent infection. The rest of Marcovich's itinerary was not
unlike that of other visiting journalists, businessmen, labor
leaders, scientists, scholars and anti-war critics who have visited
Vietnam.

Aubrac's dealings were less conventional. He went to the
Presidential Palace for a talk with his old house guest, delivered
the American viewpoints and received Ho Chi Minh's replies.

On July 25 the two Frenchmen went out to Gialam Airport,
a MiG base as well as commercial field that had been spared
American bombing so that missions like theirs would not be
impeded, and caught the ICC flight out to begin their trip home.

In August the peripatetic Professor Kissinger went to France
to debrief Marcovich. Kissinger's report was hopeful according
to one official, who said:

"Aubrac and Marcovich brought back something that
sounded interesting. It was worth following up."

The State Department decided it would like the two to return to Hanoi with a further proposal. Aubrac and Marcovich

were willing to go and applied for visas from North Vietnam. This time, however, Hanoi refused the permission. The suggestion apparently was made that if it was simply a matter of delivering a message, it could be done through Mai Van Bo, the North Vietnamese representative in Paris. Aubrac once again left his office in Rome and went to Paris. There he met with Kissinger and Marcovich. Kissinger gave the two men a written message, dated August 25, from the United States government addressed to the government of North Vietnam. On that date Aubrac and Marcovich took the message to a prearranged meeting with Bo. The message was a version of what has since come to be known as the "San Antonio Formula," which stated that the United States would stop the bombing, under the assumption that North Vietnam would reduce its infiltration in the South. The only condition for the bombing halt would be assurance that it would lead "promptly" to "productive discussions." According to one source, the message specifically allowed the North Vietnamese to continue with what was called "normal" infiltration in the South. It was assumed that Bo cabled the message immediately to Hanoi and that it arrived in the Presidential Palace on August 26.

All of this was happening without apparent relationship to other phases of Vietnam policy. In August, President Johnson, under pressure from military commanders and the Preparedness Subcommittee of the Senate Armed Services Committee, approved air strikes against some fifty targets that had been previously kept off limits by the Tuesday lunch group. Between August 19 and August 24, the day before the Paris meeting, United States planes bombed the Hanoi area five times and hit, according to an Agence France-Presse report, a hospital. One of the targets was a power station only one mile from the center of the city.

Sometime after Bo, Aubrac and Marcovich met, the United States declared another moratorium on any targets within the ten-nautical-mile radius of Hanoi's center. An official later said there was a relationship between that restraint and the message Aubrac and Marcovich delivered in Paris. The restraint, however, also could have been related to the September 3 elections in South Vietnam in which Nguyen Van Thieu and Nguyen Cao Ky were elected president and vice-president by a disappointing 34.8 percent plurality. President-elect Thieu had promised new peace overtures to Hanoi during his campaign.

The Johnson Administration seemed to feel a constitutionally mandated civilian government would give the allies a strengthened bargaining position, but there was virtually no possibility at all that Ho would ever meet Thieu. The North Vietnamese and the National Liberation Front considered the Saigon government nothing more than a puppet regime placed in power by the United States. The enemy granted the Thieu-Ky regime the same recognition the regime granted the NLF: none.

In mid-September, as the United Nations General Assembly gathered for its annual session, new pressure for a bombing halt developed. U Thant called on the United States to risk a pause and so did Corneliu Manescu, the Rumanian foreign minister who had been agreed upon for election as Assembly president.

The American reaction was to reveal part of the message Aubrac and Marcovich had already given the North Vietnamese. On September 21 Ambassador Arthur Goldberg, in an opening-day General Assembly speech, said: "The United States would be glad to consider and discuss any proposal that would lead promptly to productive discussions that might bring about peace to the area."

The speech had been written jointly by the U.S. Mission to the United Nations, the State Department and the White House. Newsmen were told the Johnson Administration considered it significant. In it, Goldberg asked the oft-repeated questions concerning just what North Vietnam or its allies would do if the United States stopped the bombing.[3]

---

[3] The speech did little to still the criticism of the United States at the UN. During the ensuing debate forty-five countries, mostly Communist, neutral or underdeveloped but including five North Atlantic Treaty Organization members (Canada, Denmark, France, The Netherlands and Norway), called for a bombing halt. Only four countries expressed unreserved support for the American position. They were Australia, New Zealand and Thailand—all of which had troops fighting with the allies in South Vietnam—and Nationalist China, which would have

In San Antonio, on September 29, President Johnson made Goldberg's disclosure even more specific as he substituted a proposal for the ambassador's questions. Speaking to the National Legislative Conference, the President said:

"Our desire to negotiate peace . . . has been made very, very clear to Hanoi, directly and many times through third parties.

"As we have told Hanoi time and time and time again, the heart of the matter is really this: The United States is willing to stop all aerial and naval bombardment of North Vietnam when this will lead promptly to productive discussions.[4] We, of course, assume that while discussions proceed, North Vietnam would not take advantage of the bombing cessation or limitation."

To emphasize the sincerity of his offer, Mr. Johnson said: "Why not negotiate now? so many ask me.

"The answer is that we and our South Vietnamese allies are wholly prepared to negotiate tonight. I am ready to talk with Ho Chi Minh and other chiefs of state concerned tomorrow. I am ready to have Secretary Rusk meet with their foreign minister tomorrow.

"I am ready to send a trusted representative of America to any spot on this earth to talk in public or private with a spokesman of Hanoi. . . ."

The San Antonio Formula represented a marked departure from the harsh proposal the President had made in his Tet letter to Ho Chi Minh the previous February. Then he had demanded the North Vietnamese cease all infiltration before a bombing pause. Now he was saying they could continue to infiltrate even after the pause, although he still left it up to the United States to judge just what constituted taking advantage

---

gladly sent troops if the South Vietnamese had permitted it. Another forty-eight countries took no stand on the bombing.

[4] An Administration official was asked several months later if the demand for productive discussions—carrying with it the implication that the Administration could arbitrarily decide what would make them productive—was not too strong. He explained that the phrase had been carelessly drafted by a speech writer caught up in using the alliteration of "prompt and productive." He said "serious"—a word the President would substitute in his 1968 State of the Union message—would have been better usage than "productive."

of any pause. The proposal was the most conciliatory Washington had made.

But articles in *Nhan Dan,* the North Vietnamese Communist Party newspaper, rejected the proposal as a "faked desire for peace" and "sheer deception" on October 3 and again on October 19. On October 20 Wilfred Burchett, in an article for the Associated Press, based on conversations with North Vietnamese Premier Pham Van Dong, Foreign Minister Nguyen Duy Trinh and others, said Hanoi would not negotiate the terms of a bombing halt. "There is no possibility of talks or even contacts between North Vietnam and the United States," he wrote. "Hanoi is in no mood for concessions or bargaining. There is an absolute refusal to offer anything—except talks— for a cessation of the bombardment. The word stressed is 'talks,' not 'negotiations.' " [5]

Burchett quoted Trinh as saying that "his statement to this correspondent last January 28—that talks could start if the bombing halted—was still valid. He said there could be 'meaningful' talks. Whether they would be 'fruitful' or 'productive' depends on the United States, he added." Clearly, Hanoi viewed modifiers as something more important than a speech writer's literary device.

Burchett also indicated what *Nhan Dan* meant by its "sheer deception" remark when he wrote:

> One difficulty that foreign diplomats have in persuading Hanoi to make any new peace gesture is what one of the leaders referred to as a "credibility gap" between what President Johnson says and does. Because of experiences in certain earlier private and secret moves—which no leader with whom this correspondent talked would precisely specify —there has been deep skepticism about any public statements or private feelers coming from Washington through diplomatic and other channels. . . . I know of no leader who believes that President Johnson is sincere in stating that

---

[5] Burchett's distinction between talks and negotiations was an aside making clear that any discussions between North Vietnam and the United States would only be preliminary. It implied strongly that any real peace negotiations would have to include the NLF at the bargaining table.

he really wants to end the war on terms that would leave the Vietnamese free to settle their own affairs or that he does not intend to keep a permanent United States military presence in South Vietnam.

Despite the distrust indicated in Burchett's article, the Johnson Administration continued attempts to start a dialogue. On November 27 Averell Harriman, on another long trip, stopped in Bucharest to confer with Rumanian officials who had recently returned from Hanoi.

Then Foreign Minister Trinh made a statement in Hanoi indicating his government had reconsidered some verb tenses. In the famous January 28, 1967, interview with Burchett, Trinh had said talks "could" result from a bombing halt. On December 29, 1967, speaking at a reception for a Mongolian delegation, Trinh said talks "will" result from a bombing pause. On New Year's Day, Hanoi Radio broadcast the statement this way:

> The U.S. government has unceasingly claimed that it wants to talk with Hanoi but has received no response. If the U.S. government truly wants to talk, it must, as was made clear in our statement on 28 January 1967, first of all stop unconditionally the bombing and all other acts of war against [North Vietnam]. After the United States has ended unconditionally the bombing and all other acts of war, [North Vietnam] will hold talks with the United States on questions concerned.

The State Department readily acknowledged that Trinh's statement was a "new formulation," to quote Dean Rusk, but stress was put on the unanswered questions: How soon after the bombing halt would talks begin? Would Hanoi stall at the conference table while it took military advantage of the bombing cessation? What would Hanoi agree to talk about?

Officials also noted that Trinh's one-word change in policy on peace talks was prefaced by a renewed demand for determination of South Vietnam's future in accordance with the political program of the National Liberation Front. Washington and Saigon officials had long insisted that this condition was unacceptable. Their stress on the complications in Trinh's statement was an augury that all of the diplomatic probing going on to get at its hidden meaning—if any—would be unproductive.

Part of that probing again involved an intermediary. This time it was a high-ranking Rumanian official. The State Department empowered him to present, once again, the message Aubrac and Marcovich had given to Bo in Paris the previous August. In January, 1968, this Rumanian took the message to Hanoi. Why was it repeated? "Because the Rumanians didn't know what happened in August. They thought they had something new and would therefore try to do a selling job in Hanoi," one American official said.[6]

The salesmanship did not work. Hanoi continued to insist on the unconditional bombing halt. Even to ask what would happen militarily if the planes stopped flying was, by North Vietnamese reckoning, to impose a precondition to the halt.

On January 17, 1968, President Johnson delivered his fourth State of the Union message in which the Vietnam war figured prominently and ominously. But he eased the American stand on negotiations from that presented in San Antonio with the substitution of a call for "serious" rather than "productive" negotiations. When he told his election-year audience the North Vietnamese "must not take advantage of our restraint," newsmen mistakenly saw this as a hardening of the San Antonio formula. No hardening was intended, as Secretary Rusk said the next day.

In fact, the Johnson Administration's position was more reasonable than it had ever been, as Defense Secretary-designate Clark M. Clifford revealed on January 25 when he appeared before the Senate Armed Services Committee for his confirmation hearing. Clifford answered some questions on negotiations by the conservative, hawkish South Carolina Republican, Senator Strom Thurmond, and this exchange resulted:

Thurmond: When you spoke of negotiating, in that case

---

[6] It may be, however, that the January message contained even further concessions by the United States than the terms of the message delivered in August.

you would be willing to have a cessation of bombing. I presume that would contemplate that they would stop their military activities too, if we would be expected to have a cessation of bombing.

Clifford: No, that is not what I said. I do not expect them to stop their military activities. I would expect to follow the language of the President when he said that if they would agree to start negotiations promptly and not take advantage of the pause in the bombing.

Thurmond: What do you mean by taking advantage if they continue in their military activities?

Clifford: Their military activity will continue in South Vietnam, I assume, until there is a cease-fire agreed upon. I assume that they will continue to transport the *normal* [italics by authors] amount of goods, munitions, men to South Vietnam. I assume that we will continue to maintain our forces and support our forces during that period. So what I am suggesting is, in the language of the President, that he would insist that they not take advantage of the suspension of the bombing.

Thurmond: How would you keep them from taking advantage . . . ?

Clifford: There is no way to keep them from taking advantage. If they state that they are going to refrain from taking advantage, and then refuse to do so, then they have not met their agreement, and the conditions for negotiations have failed.

Thurmond: And then, if they did violate that, you would favor, then, resuming bombing, I would presume.

Clifford: I would assume we would have no alternative. . . .

Undoubtedly, it would be difficult for both sides to agree on what constituted "normal" infiltration. Nonetheless, Clifford's testimony was a quantum leap in precision from Dean Rusk's standard rumination about the United States refusing to stop its half of the war while the Communists continued their half. Officials immediately made it known that Clifford's formulation had previously been transmitted privately to Hanoi. Without saying so, they were referring to the Aubrac-Marcovich and Rumanian contacts.

The State Department, three days after the testimony, formally endorsed Clifford's explanation. The pressure from some critics of President Johnson eased temporarily as a result of the major concessions in Clifford's careful answers to Thurmond.[7]

The American public had hardly digested this new chapter in Vietnam diplomacy when the Viet Cong and North Vietnam marked the start of the 1968 Tet holiday by launching attacks on about half of South Vietnam's provincial capitals, including Saigon and Hue. The scope, intensity and coordination of the assaults, combined with the build-up around the Marine base at Khesanh, stunned the Administration. The prospect of peace talks receded. Officials said Hanoi had decided on a daring attempt to improve its bargaining position with military pressure. Rusk's acid reaction to the offensive, given in a "Meet the Press" interview on February 4, was typical:

". . . They've known from earlier years that we've been interested in converting something like a Tet cease-fire into a more productive dialogue, into some opportunity to move toward peace.

"Now in the face of all these elements they participated in laying on this major offensive. Now I think it would be foolish not to draw a political conclusion from this that they are not seriously interested at the present time in talking about peaceful settlement or in exploring the problems connected with the San Antonio Formula."

Rusk disclosed that during the weeks of diplomatic probing of Trinh's "will talk" statement, American bombing of North Vietnam had been limited, "particularly in the immediate vicinity of Hanoi and Haiphong," to avoid "difficult incidents." He stressed that "Hanoi knows this."

Observing that Washington's peace proposals "remain there on the table for anyone who is interested," Rusk said of Hanoi:

---

[7] Some of Washington's most experienced newsmen were skeptical about the concessions Clifford had made in his testimony. A week before, at a "background" session, they had heard a Tuesday lunch group member say that no resupply of North Vietnamese troops could be considered proper by the United States after a bombing halt. He also indicated the San Antonio Formula would not permit continued infiltration from North Vietnam.

"They know where we live and we will be glad to hear from them sometime, at their convenience. . . ."

On the day of Rusk's television interview, two North Vietnamese diplomats quietly arrived in Rome for talks with Italian Foreign Minister Amintore Fanfani and Giovanni D'Orlandi, who had returned, in poor health, to Rome after the Marigold initiative to become inspector general of the Foreign Ministry. The North Vietnamese emissaries left town two days after they arrived.

On February 14 the Italian Foreign Ministry disclosed the meetings, saying Hanoi's representatives had asked to meet Fanfani "for talks about the Vietnam conflict and about possible hypotheses of a start of negotiations to settle it." The Italians said they had "speedily informed" Washington about the talks, which, other sources reported, covered a broad approach to negotiations patterned after the old Marigold "ten points."

The timing of such an overture in the midst of the Tet offensive was taken by Washington officials as additional confirmation of their belief that Hanoi had embarked upon a fight-and-talk strategy: whipsawing the President with almost simultaneous military punishment and diplomatic allurement in an effort to force concessions. It was a strategy Lyndon Johnson himself had employed against Hanoi. Indeed, one could almost imagine North Vietnamese leaders saying, as Johnson Administration officials had of Hanoi after the failure of Marigold, "If Washington really wants to talk, one little attack more or less isn't going to stop them from accepting our offer."

Fearful that the war was on the brink of still another escalation, U Thant once more set off on a mission to keep the diplomatic channels open. During a visit to New Delhi, Thant met on February 8 with Nguyen Hoa, North Vietnam's consul general in the Indian capital. Thant put some questions to Hoa, who promised to transmit them to Hanoi. While Hanoi considered the secretary general's questions, Thant continued around the world, stopping in Moscow to talk to Soviet leaders and in London to meet with the British leaders. Then he went to Paris to talk to Mai Van Bo and receive Hanoi's answers. If he learned anything new, he did not reveal it. He came back to the

United States more convinced than ever that the Johnson Administration must stop the bombing before anything else could happen. He reported to the President, but few thought anything would come of it.

The Johnson Administration was at the moment preoccupied with critical conditions in South Vietnam after the Tet offensive. There was concern that the Thieu-Ky government on which the Administration had banked so heavily might not measure up to urgent new challenges. There was concern about the standstill in the all-important pacification program. There was unease about the military situation.

It was a time, too, for what came to be known as an "A to Z" Vietnam policy review in which the prospects for negotiations were but one file to be studied among many—including those for new troop requests, command changes, financial considerations, other foreign relations and the political situation at home.

As part of the review, Clark Clifford, now established in the Defense Department, went over the detailed records of the strategic bombing of the northern part of North Vietnam. "Clifford, the big hawk when he was an unofficial adviser to the President, studied the records and came to the same conclusion McNamara had," one official said. "He discovered that the bombing did not help that much. He recommended a cutback to the President. The President believed him even though he never believed McNamara on this."

At the State Department, experts debated just what type of gesture the United States should make. When Clifford proposed a restriction in bombing, Undersecretary of State Katzenbach opposed it. He wanted a complete halt in bombing to take effect later in the spring after the threat to the Marine base at Khesanh was eliminated. He was fearful that a limited bombing cutback would not work. In short, Katzenbach's associates said he argued that the President had just one opportunity to make a major peace gesture and if the Clifford idea failed the President could not easily try something else. (Katzenbach later expressed delight when North Vietnam's positive response proved him wrong.) In the White House, Walt Rostow opposed the limited bombing halt, but for a different reason. He was against easing the pressure on North Vietnam. He stood stolidly for continued bombing, as did military commanders.

Where did Dean Rusk stand? The indication was that he supported the Clifford proposal, but few outside the Tuesday lunch group were certain. "Would old stone face ever tell you where he stands?" one official commented. "Would Rusk put an opinion in writing? Would he commit his emotions to paper?"

The President weighed the conflicting advice, then adopted Clifford's reasoning. He decided on a limited cutback in bombing, first to an area of North Vietnam south of the 20th parallel and later south of the 19th parallel. All of the heavily populated areas were in the bomb-free zone.

The A to Z review led to the March 31 announcement of the de-escalation and the withdrawal of the President from politics as a possible candidate. Mr. Johnson's decisions did not flow only from fresh doubts about bombing in the North and the disruption in the South caused by the Tet offensive. The President also placed emphasis in his speech on the division within the United States created by the Vietnam war. Later he made reference to what he considered his own failure to communicate with the American people. This was dramatized by the suddenly announced candidacy of Senator Robert F. Kennedy for the Democratic presidential nomination, coming as it did after Senator Eugene J. McCarthy won a dramatic victory with his peace campaign in the New Hampshire primary. Other factors certainly related to the standing of the United States in the world. As examples: North Korea's seizure on January 23 of the spy-ship *Pueblo* without an effective American response challenged and humiliated the Johnson Administration. Then the heavy drain on America's international balance of payments and the huge budget deficits associated with war financing left the nation vulnerable to the sustained attack in the spring on the dollar and the continuing gold crisis. All this was considered by the President before he made the March 31 offer, culminating the new diplomatic phase that began the previous summer.

Instead of falling back on its demand for a complete halt in the bombing before direct contacts could be resumed, North

Vietnam, three days after the President spoke, agreed to a preliminary meeting to talk about the cessation of the bombing and all other acts of war against the North. After this, Hanoi said, negotiations could be held.

Many suspected that the President made his gesture of a bombing limitation after receiving an indication that the North Vietnamese would react positively. There had certainly been opportunities to obtain such information—through intermediaries and at least one direct contact.

In addition to U Thant and the Italians, the Swedish government and the Swiss government—both old-line neutral nations—became active in making contacts with the North Vietnamese. Also, Ambassador Llewellyn E. Thompson had begun paying numerous calls on Soviet Premier Kosygin and other Russian officials before being called home for consultations just prior to the President's March 31 speech.[8]

The direct contact was made with North Vietnam in Vientiane, Laos, in March when Robert A. Hurwitch, the deputy chief of the American mission, negotiated the release of three North Vietnamese sailors held in South Vietnam. The sailors were freed in return for the release by Hanoi in February of three American pilots as a gesture to the American peace movement.

Hurwitch, who was deeply involved in ransoming the Bay of Pigs prisoners from Cuba in 1962, reportedly only talked about the prisoner exchange. Nevertheless, the North Vietnamese understood perfectly well that the United States had been hoping for years to begin discussions on prisoners of war

---

[8] Thompson, along with Peace Ambassador Harriman, was originally named by the President as an American negotiator waiting to meet with the North Vietnamese. His name was quietly removed in the succeeding days and Cyrus Vance, former Deputy Secretary of Defense and an often-used troubleshooter, was substituted. Although a negotiator of great skill, Thompson may have been removed from the team at Soviet insistence because his presence might imply more Moscow involvement in the preliminary talks than the Russians were willing to admit. In any case, Harriman appeared to be a member of the team more for his prestige than for any other reason. During much of the pre-talk maneuvering he vacationed at his Hobe Sound, Fla., residence. On April 23, Ambassador Arthur Goldberg resigned amid reports that he was miffed at not having been selected for the negotiating team.

that could later expand into peace talks. In that sense, even if the first Vientiane contact was only about prisoners, the fact that such a meeting was held at all could have been taken as the kind of signal Mr. Johnson needed to set the negotiation train in motion on March 31. Indeed, the Vientiane channel became the private side of a curious public-private maneuvering leading to the first talks.

In his speech, President Johnson proposed Geneva as a negotiating site—or any other "suitable" place. He was no longer as willing to go to "any spot on earth" as he had been at the time of his San Antonio speech.

The first North Vietnamese suggestion of a site—almost immediately confirmed through official channels—was carried out of Hanoi by three Americans who were visiting there when the President made his speech. They were Harry Ashmore and William Baggs, who had been to Hanoi a year earlier, and CBS correspondent Charles Collingwood. All three, along with Mary McCarthy, author and severe war policy critic, were on the same ICC flight from Hanoi on April 5. Baggs, apparently without telling his companions, delivered the message to an American diplomat almost immediately. He left the plane in Vientiane, its first stop, and called on Ambassador William H. Sullivan.

Through Baggs—and through official channels a day later—North Vietnam countered with Phnom Penh, the capital of Cambodia, which was rejected by the United States. Neither Washington nor Saigon had diplomatic representation there. The United States proposed four neutral capitals in Asia—New Delhi, Rangoon, Vientiane, and Jakarta. North Vietnam in turn suggested Warsaw, where the United States had been so anxious to hold talks during the Marigold initiative. But now the Johnson Administration found Warsaw, too, unacceptable. The Administration said the "any spot on earth" pledge should not have been taken literally. There was concern in the Administration that the location of the preliminary talks might become the site for a full-scale peace conference. The United States had to be certain the city selected would be acceptable to its allies. South Vietnam and South Korea had no diplomatic missions in Poland and Cambodia. Thus, the North Vietnamese proposals were unacceptable to them. In addition, there was a problem of face on both sides. For either one to accept the proposal of the other would appear to be acceding to a demand. For this reason a third party might have to suggest a site both sides could accept gracefully.

Increasingly bitter recriminations accompanied the exchanges. The United States charged North Vietnam with seeking propaganda advantage in selecting the site for talks; North Vietnam accused the United States of going back on its word to meet anywhere, anytime. The Administration encountered criticism at home as well. The longer the impasse over choosing a site continued, the more Senator Fulbright and other Vietnam policy critics evidenced impatience with what they regarded as the Administration's inflexibility. The President's oft-repeated pledge to go anywhere on earth for peace talks proved an increasing embarrassment. Along with other officials, Vice President Humphrey—after announcing his candidacy to succeed the President—said Mr. Johnson had overspoken himself and sought to justify the hard bargaining over a site.

After proposing Geneva and the four Asian cities where both governments had representation, the United States escalated the propaganda war by publicly suggesting ten additional capitals in Asia and Europe although officials privately acknowledged they knew none would be acceptable to North Vietnam. This was precisely the objective—to have North Vietnam appear obdurate in rejecting the new sites. The North Vietnamese did not have an embassy in any of those ten countries. Some American officials were privately unhappy over the new offer. They felt the United States had made a logical proposal of Geneva and the four neutral Asian capitals, and that this sound position was diluted by the propaganda-motivated follow-up offer.

Through April, North Vietnam refused to budge from its insistence on Phnom Penh or Warsaw. In public, both sides conspicuously avoided official mention of Paris, leading to wide speculation that the French capital would be the compromise, face-saving site. Privately some American officials predicted the talks would be held in Paris. On April 18, French Foreign Minister Couve de Murville said Paris would be available if the combatants desired to meet there. And U Thant recommended the French capital. The United States Information

Agency quietly alerted some of its personnel to be prepared to cover a peace conference in Paris.

Meanwhile, what some described as the "niggling and haggling" contest over a site was centered in Vientiane, where American and North Vietnamese diplomats met to talk or exchange notes about a dozen times during April. The Vientiane contacts—involving Ambassador Sullivan and his deputy, Robert Hurwitch, and Nguyen Chan, deputy chief of North Vietnam's Embassy there—proceeded far more rapidly than the series of seven meetings during a 36-day period in Moscow in the winter of 1967.

The haggling even involved a suggestion by a third party for talks on the high seas. On November 11, 1967, in a variation of his anywhere, anytime theme, President Johnson had proposed peace talks aboard a neutral ship in neutral waters. Now Indonesia offered one of its ships for a conference, perhaps in the Gulf of Tonkin, in an effort to break the site impasse. On May 1 the White House accepted publicly. United States officials anticipated a quick, formal rejection by North Vietnam, but the Hanoi regime remained silent.

On May 2 the White House announced the President would hold a nationally-televised press conference in the East Room at 10 the following morning, the first such meeting with reporters since the previous November. Press Secretary George Christian said the President was responding to requests from newsmen for a press conference and had no special announcements in mind.

About 1 A.M., May 3, the White House Situation Room received a message from Ambassador Sullivan relaying a proposal from the North Vietnamese mission in Vientiane that talks begin in Paris on May 10 or shortly thereafter. Walt Rostow, awakened at his home by the Situation Room duty officer, in turn awakened the President. After Mr. Johnson checked the Situation Room for another reading on Sullivan's message, he had a lengthy telephone discussion with Dean Rusk, and also telephoned Arthur Goldberg. About 8 A.M., the President met with Rusk, Rostow, Vance, Clifford, Christian and former Undersecretary of State George Ball, who had been designated to succeed Goldberg at the United Nations. Mr.

Johnson discussed with them a proposed reply to Hanoi which he had already drafted. (The President later told associates he awoke at 6 A.M. and began drafting a message at 7.)

The first public hint of the impending dramatic breakthrough in the search for peace came in a Hanoi Radio broadcast about an hour before the scheduled start of Mr. Johnson's press conference. North Vietnam, referring to Couve de Murville's April 18 statement, said it regarded Paris as a suitable site and disclosed it had appointed Xuan Thuy, former foreign minister, to enter into formal talks in the French capital with American representatives. North Vietnam said the purpose of the talks in Paris would be "to determine with the U.S. side the unconditional cessation of the U.S. bombing raids and all other acts of war against the D.R.V., and then to hold talks on other problems of concern to the two sides."

On his way to the East Room for the press conference, the President approved a cable to the North Vietnamese accepting the proposal. A few moments later, Mr. Johnson announced to the world: ". . . I have sent a message informing Hanoi that the day of May the 10th and the site, Paris, are acceptable to the United States." Paris, which had played such an important role in secret Vietnam diplomacy, now was to be the stage for the first formal American–North Vietnamese talks since the United States supplanted France as the dominant Western power in Indochina.

Thus, despite all the acrimony, the push to the conference table appeared irreversible, just as, in previous years, the trend had pointed clearly toward increasingly intensive fighting even though both sides spoke of a desire for peace. Nevertheless, serious problems remained, as the President himself suggested at his news conference: "This is only the very first step and there are many, many hazards and difficulties ahead."

Indeed, the move toward talks opened up a set of problems for consideration that only a few officials were previously willing to think about. For example: Who would do the talking at a full-scale peace conference? What roles would the United States' allies—particularly the South Vietnamese government—have in the talks? What would be the role of the National Liberation Front? What kind of ultimate settlement would be tolerated by either side? What provision would be made for the reunification of Vietnam? Would South Vietnam be tied to any alliances with outside countries? What nations would guarantee Vietnam's future security? Would Communist China participate in the settlement? These were the kinds of problems that far overshadowed the relatively simple question of how to get talks started.

Those who study the record of Vietnam diplomacy could well ask a more important question: Can the United States in 1968 achieve a more satisfactory settlement in Vietnam than might have been obtainable a year before, or even earlier?

The record suggests that the Johnson Administration missed opportunities over the years to secure, if not peace, at least negotiations; if not negotiations, at least talks; and if not talks, at least a propaganda advantage over the enemy that would have improved the nation's standing in the world community and the President's credibility at home.

A period had been reached which might best be described by the last words of T. S. Eliot's "Little Gidding," the poem that so impressed Robert S. McNamara the night his wife read it to him:

> Quick now, here, now, always—
> A condition of complete simplicity
> (Costing not less than everything)
> And all shall be well and
> All manner of things shall be well
> When the tongues of flame are in-folded
> Into the crowned knot of fire
> And the fire and the rose are one.

Index

About the Authors

STUART H. LOORY, a native of Dover, N.J., was graduated from Cornell University and the Columbia Graduate School of Journalism, where he won a Pulitzer Traveling Scholarship. He joined the Newark *News* in 1955 and the New York *Herald Tribune* in 1959. He covered all the early manned space flights, the thalidomide disaster, the debate over the nuclear test ban treaty, Freedom Rides and the Sino-Indian War of 1962. In 1964 he became the *Herald Tribune*'s last Moscow correspondent and won an Overseas Press Club citation in 1966 for reports from Siberia. In 1967 he joined the *Los Angeles Times* as White House correspondent. He has written numerous magazine articles.

DAVID KRASLOW, a native of New York, was graduated from the University of Miami (Fla.) and was a Nieman Fellow at Harvard University. He joined the Miami *Herald* in 1948, reported sports and city and county government, winning two state awards, before moving to the Washington Bureau in 1956. He joined the *Los Angeles Times* in 1963. He has covered the White House, national politics, the Cuban Bay of Pigs and missile crisis stories and the Dominican Republic rebellion, and has specialized in investigative reporting. He is co-author (with Robert S. Boyd) of the novel *A Certain Evil* (Little, Brown, 1965). He was named Washington Bureau News Editor by the *Times* in 1966.